MARKETING AND MULTICULTURAL DIVERSITY

To our grandchildren

LEKHA
PRAVEEN
AVANTHI
HARISH
ARJUNA
MEENAKSHI
SAMEERA

who perpetuate our heritage

*I would like to acknowledge with sincere thanks
the help, support and guidance of my friend
Adel Al-Wugayan of Kuwait University
in bringing this project to a successful conclusion*

Marketing and Multicultural Diversity

Edited by

C.P. Rao
Kuwait University, Kuwait.

ASHGATE

Published by
Ashgate Publishing Limited
Gower House
Croft Road
Aldershot
Hampshire GU11 3HR
England

Ashgate Publishing Company
Suite 420
101 Cherry Street
Burlington, VT 05401-4405
USA

Reprinted 2006

Ashgate website: http://www.ashgate.com

British Library Cataloguing in Publication Data
Marketing and multicultural diversity. – (New perspectives
   in marketing)
   1. Marketing 2. Multiculturalism
   I. Rao, C. P.
   658.8' 02

Library of Congress Cataloging-in-Publication Data
Marketing and multicultural diversity / edited by C.P. Rao.
          p. cm. -- (New perspectives in marketing)
   Includes bibliographical references and index.
   ISBN 0–7546–4326–3
   1. Consumer behavior. 2. Market segmentation. 3. Marketing -- Social aspects.
I. Rao, C. P. II. Series.

HF5415.32.M37 2006
658.8' 02--dc22

2005026816

ISBN 0 7546 4326 3
ISBN 978 0 7546 4326 5

Printed and bound in Great Britain by MPG Books Ltd. Bodmin, Cornwall.

Contents

Part III: Majority Versus Minority Consumer Behaviors

Part IV: Ethnic Consumer Behaviors

Part V: Organizational Cultures and Relationships

Part VI: Global Consumer Diversity

About the Contributors

Joseph Aiyeku is Professor of Marketing and Chairperson of the Marketing Department at Salem State College. His research focuses on macro-marketing, marketing and entrepreneurship, marketing and development, and global marketing strategy. He has authored over forty articles and co-authored two books. He serves on the editorial boards of two journals and as an associate editor of another one. He was a guest editor of the Spring 1999 issue of the *Journal of International Marketing and Exporting*. He has served as consultant to numerous corporations and has advised government agencies in Africa, the Caribbean, and Latin America.

Patricia M. Anderson, Emeritus Professor of Marketing and former Chairperson of the Marketing and International Business Department at Quinnipiac University, has published in the areas of marketing and consumer behavior with respect to marketing communication and other environmental cues. Her research in international marketing has been published in various journals and books, including the *Journal of International Consumer Marketing Management, Journal of Consumer Marketing* and *Journal of Contemporary Business Issues*.

Alvin M. Chan obtained his Ph.D. from the Australian Graduate School of Management, University of New South Wales, Australia. He is currently on the faculty of the School of Marketing and International Business, University of Western Sidney, Australia. His research interests include cross-cultural consumer behavior and marketing for ethnic minorities.

Won-Joo Cho

Irvine Clarke III is currently Associate Professor of Marketing at the James Madison University. His research interests include international marketing and methodological issues in cross-cultural consumer behavior.

Colleen Collins-Dodd is a faculty member in the Faculty of Business Administration, Simon Fraser University, Burnaby, British Columbia. Her interests include research methodology and marketing strategy.

William K. Darley is Professor of Marketing at the University of Toledo. He received his Ph.D. from Indiana University. His research interests include consumer choice processes, consumer response to advertising and research methods. His work has appeared in the *Journal of Marketing, Journal of Business Research, Journal of Consumer Research, Journal of Consumer Affairs, Journal of the Academy of Marketing Sciences, Psychology and Marketing*, and elsewhere.

Ronald J. Ferguson

Mabel Fung received her MBA from Simon Fraser University and is principal of Mabel Fung Consulting Services. She has worked in Banking in Canada and Hong Kong.

J.B. Ha is currently on the faculty of the School of Business, Pyongtaek University, South Korea. He received his Ph.D. from Old Dominion University. His research interests are in the areas of buyer-seller relationships in international channels of distribution, relationship marketing in international settings and services marketing.

Xiaonhong He, Professor of International Business, teaches at the School of Business at Quinnipiac University where she Chairs the Marketing and International Business Department. Her research in international business has been published in various academic journals and books, including the *Journal of International Consumer Marketing, Journal of Marketing Management, Journal of Transnational Management Development, Journal of Consumer Marketing, Journal of Contemporary Business Issues, Multinational Business Review, Business and the Contemporary World Journal, Investment Research Journal, International Journal of Business, and Journal of International Accounting, Auditing and Taxation.*

Michael Hui is Associate Professor of Marketing at the Chinese University, Hong Kong. He received his Ph.D. in Marketing from the London Business School. His research interests include cross-cultural consumer behavior and services marketing.

Chankon Kis is Professor of Marketing at Saint-Mary's University, Halifax. He received his Ph.D. in Marketing from Indiana University. He has published numerous articles in refereed publications such as *Journal of Marketing Research.* His research interests include several aspects of consumer behavior, particularly ethnicity and family decision making as well as marketing research techniques and methods.

Mi-Ae Kwak is currently senior research manager at the Quality and Reliability Lab at DaeWood Electronics in Korea. She has directed more than 200 consumer research projects for global firms and is a MBA candidate at Sogang University, South Korea.

Michel Laroche is Professor of Marketing at Concordia University, Montreal. He is a Fellow of the Royal Society of Canada, American Psychological Association, Soceity of Marketing Advances and Academy of Marketing Science and the 2000 Concordia University Research Fellow. He received his Ph.D. from Columbia and D.Shc from Guelph. He has co-authored 27 books, including *Consumer Behavior: A Canadian Perspective*, numerous refereed articles and is currently serving as Managing Editor of the *Journal of Business Research.* He has received numerous awards for his accomplishments. His research interests include several aspects of consumer behavior, particularly ethnicity, persuasion, information processing and models of decision making.

Keun S. Lee is Associate Professor in the Department of Marketing and International Business at Hofstra University. He has a doctorate from the University of Kentucky. His extensive publications include articles in proceedings and journals including *Journal of Personal Selling and Sales Management, Journal of Global Marketing* and *Journal of the Academy of Marketing Science.*

Sonny Nwankwo is Senior Lecturer in Strategic Management and Marketing at Shefield Business School, Sheffield Hallam University, United Kingdom. Before entering the academic world he was a senior manager in the telecommunications industry. His most recent books are *Strategic Planning and Development: Developing Economies Perspectives*, and *Cross-Cultural Marketing.*

Alphonso Ogbuehi is currently Associate Professor of Marketing and International Business and Director of the International Business Center at the Ervan K. Haub School of Business, Saint Joseph University, Philadelphia. He holds a Ph.D. from the University of Memphis and is a founding member and Executive Secretary of the International Academy of African Business and Development (IAABD). His work has appeared in the *Journal of African Business, International Marketing Review, Journal of Global Marketing, Journal Marketing Theory and Practice, Journal of International Marketing and Exporting, Journal of Small Business Management, Journal of Euromarketing*, and *Journal of African Business.*

Mehdi Mourali is a Ph.D. student in Marketing at Concordia University, Canada. His research interests include several aspects of consumer behavior, services marketing and cross-cultural research.

Michele Paulin is Assistant Professor at Concordia University. Her research and teaching interests are in international business-to-business relationships, services management, and relationship marketing. She has presented papers at various U.S., European and other international Conferences. Her research has been published in the *European Journal of Marketing, The International Journal of Services Industry Management, International Journal of Bank Marketing*, and *Managing Service Quality.* She has won awards for excellence in research from the University of Quebec in Montreal and has experience in several managerial positions.

Marielle Payard

Frank Pons

C.P. Rao is Professor of Marketing and Director of the Case Research and Teaching Unit, College of Business Administration, Kuwait University. Past academic positions include William B. Spong Chair at Old Dominion University, and Wal-Mart Lecturer in Strategic Marketing and University Professor, University of Arkansas at Fayetteville. He has published extensively in the areas of marketing and international business. His current research interests include importer-exporter interaction processes, marketing ethics, and cross-cultural industrial buyer behavior.

Bina Raval is faculty member in the Department of Psychology at Towson University, and a licensed psychologist.

Dinker Raval is professor of Business Administration at Morgan State University where he has served as Acting Chair of Business Administration Department and as Chair of the University Council. His research interests include marketing, cross-cultural marketing, and international business.

Victoria A. Seitz is Professor of Marketing at California State University-SanBernadino. She has a Ph.D. from Oklahoma State University and is the author of *Your Executive Image* and *Power Dressing*.

Carol F. Suprenant is Associate Professor of Marketing at the University of Rhode Island and Director of the Research Center in Business and Economics. She is a prominent consumer satisfaction researcher and has published in leading academic journals. Her other interests include relationship marketing and service marketing.

Marc A. Tomiuk is Assistant Professor of Marketing at the Ecole des Hautes Eudes Commerciales (affiliated with the University of Montreal). He has a Ph.D. from Concordia University. His research interests are in the areas of marketing services, Consumer behavior, particularly cultural issues and emotions and measurement issues such as the applications of item response theory to scale development.

Wei Wu

Adel Al-Wugayan is Associate Professor of Marketing and Associate Dean at the College of Business Administration, Kuwait University. His research interests include cross-cultural consumer behavior and marketing ethics. He has directed numerous training and consulting programs in marketing and sales management for both private and public sectors.

Jerome D. Williams is Professor of Marketing at the University of Texas at Austin. During the 1999-2000 academic year he was the Whitney M. Young Jr. Visiting Associate Professor of Marketing at the University of Pennsylvania's Wharton School of Business. His research interests cover a number of areas in the business-to-business and consumer marketing domains, with emphasis on ethnic minority marketing. He received his Ph.D. from the University of Colorado.

Zhiyong Yang is a Ph.D. student in Marketing at Concordia University. His research interests include several aspects of consumer behavior, services marketing and cross-cultural research.

Chapter 1

Introduction

C.P. Rao

In recent years marketing as a discipline, both in theory and practice, has gone through phenomenal changes. First, traditional marketing is moving in the direction of relationship marketing. This is considered to be a major paradigm shift in marketing. Second, the traditional segmented marketing approach is being replaced by micromarketing focusing on satisfying individual customers rather than large market segments. The practice of micromarketing is facilitated by newer production technologies and communications and information processing technologies. Third, for some time the geographic scope of marketing has been expanding and global marketing is becoming more common. Global marketing, facilitated by the globalization, privatization, and liberalization forces, is sweeping the world's economies. Fourth, the cultural context of marketing is fast becoming multicultural in nature.

With the increase of consumer oriented marketing in years following post world war II years, the significance of cultural influences has been recognized in consumer behavior theory and marketing practice. Initially the importance of culture as a major environmental force shaping consumer behavior was seen in national terms. This approach was based on the assumption that in any national market there is one dominant culture and that marketers should strive to make their operations culturally compatible with the perspectives of the majority. Proponents of the 'melting pot' theory in the United States argued that in time subcultures get assimilated into the majority culture (Glazer and Moynihan 1963). However, in recent decades subcultures representing a wide variety of ethnic, race, nationality and demographic groups have asserted their identities and have fought for equality in social treatment. This recent sociological developments by which minority subcultures have asserted their identity and equality has created a new multicultural environment which is impacting every facet of business operations, including marketing.

Multiculturalism impels the need to recognize the cultural diversity of a society. From a marketing management perspective, culturally diverse environments create new challenges in recognizing, cultivating and reconciling different cultural groups' perspectives within the same market. This market frame could be a country, a region, or, in the new economic era of globalization, the whole world. Thus, multiculturalism has significance for marketing at country, regional and global levels. If we consider ethnic diversity alone, some countries such as the U.S. Canada, Malaysia, Australia and South Africa, are clearly multicultural market settings. But cultural diversity is not limited to ethnicity alone, especially for marketing purposes. In recent years, demographic and psychographic or lifestyle groups of people in ethnically homogeneous societies have also created multicultural environments. The youth culture, the feminist movement, senior citizens groups are some examples.

Multiculturalism is certainly becoming a major marketing environmental concern as countries form into regional trading blocs with different degrees of economic integration. Regional economic integration has become a major phenomenon in different parts of the world, thereby creating the need for regional marketing. These economically integrated regional markets, of which the European Union is a clear successful example, represent multicultural settings with all the concomitant marketing management challenges. Mere economic integration of countries does not automatically lead to cultural integration of various countries in that region. Hence, in operating in a regional trading bloc, marketers have to deal with multicultural marketing issues if they wish to reap the benefits of an enlarged market. In recent years, a number of researchers have pointed out the multicultural marketing challenges facing marketers in the context of the European Union.

Today's global markets are dominated by multinational corporations (MNCs) originating in different parts of the world, including third world countries. Cultural diversity and multiculturalism are the major challenges facing the MNCs in globalizing their marketing strategies and practices. In relation to globalization of markets (Levitt 1983) there is ongoing controversy over whether cultural diversity (Hofstaed 1984) or converging cultural homogeneity should form the basis for international marketing practice. In this context, international marketers are faced with contradictory developments with regard to the cultural scene in different parts of the world. At the political and social level, there is growing evidence that subcultures in many parts of the world are asserting their political and social identity, as can be seen from various ethnic conflicts. At the same time, with special reference to consumption patterns, there is growing evidence that global markets are emerging. As this trend toward global products and brands spreads and dominates world markets, some critics concerned about the adverse effects of global marketing on their own cultural identity have labeled global marketing a form of 'cultural imperialism.' These developments pose a challenge for marketers, who need to be able to develop global markets while at the same time maintaining local cultural identities, avoiding being branded as 'foreign companies' polluting diverse cultures and imposing cultural imperialism.

Despite the evolution of global markets, the international marketing literature is replete with examples of costly mistakes companies make when they fail to respond to the cultural nuances of diverse cultures (Ricks 1993). The current wisdom seems to be that global marketers, while pursuing global strategies, have to practice marketing essentially at the local level. In other words, multiculturalism and its implications should be considered in international marketing practice.

Multiculturalism as it impacts marketing theory and practice is a multifaceted phenomenon. Growing academic attention has been paid to this field. The Academy of Marketing Science has devoted conferences to this topic, and special issues of academic journals have appeared on the subject. Also, several books have been published in recent years on aspects of multiculturalism and its marketing implications (Costa and Bamossy 1995, Seelye and Seelye-James 1996, Rossman 1994, Howes 1996). These writings have made significant contributions to the field of multiculturalism and marketing, each contribution examining specific aspects of the phenomenon. Some publications focus on cultural-anthropological perspectives with an ethnographic approach. Others have taken purely a managerial perspective, providing concrete episodic examples of marketing challenges and problems posed by multiculturalism. This book takes a more integrative approach to multiculturalism and its implications for marketing. Both conceptual and empirical issues of multicultural diversity and its marketing implications are presented in the form of research studies conducted in different parts of the world. More importantly, the methodological issues of investigating multicultural market contexts have been addressed. Multiculturalism in relation to marketing is typically discussed from the perspective of consumer behavior only. But in globalized markets multiculturalism has significant implications for inter-organizational relations in the context of international marketing. These issues are also addressed here. In addition the book deals with multicultural marketing issues at various geographic levels – national, regional and global.

In the twenty first century, as populations become increasingly mobile and as other factors affect production around the globe, every country and region in the world is becoming multicultural in social composition. Such multicultural market environments call for different conceptualizations, methodologies, and empirical investigations to the needs of marketers for better performance. This perspective is central to several research studies presented in this volume, which is aimed at both the academicians and practitioners, interested in multiculturalism and its implications for contemporary marketing.

Conceptual Issues

Part I presents a number of conceptual issues germane to multicultural marketing, providing the necessary conceptual framework from which to assess empirical researching findings. Chapter 2 by Mourali, Laroche and Pons examines cultural differences in consumer susceptibility to interpersonal influence and the role of individualism. The authors argue that consumer susceptibility to interpersonal influence depends not only on individual propensities but also on cultural influences. They contend that societal values and norms systematically influence consumer susceptibility to interpersonal influence. This proposition is based on Hofstede's thesis that the relationship between the individual and the collectivity as a fundamental dimension on which societies differ. The research proposition was empirically tested in the context of French and English Canadian consumers.

Chapter 3 examines relationship between personal and cultural values and desired benefits across diverse cultures. The authors' primary research objective was to explore the interaction between cultural values and personal values in two countries with different cultural orientations. Unlike most of the studies on this topic, this research considered cultural values and personal values simultaneously. The study established the linkage between these two sets of values and consumer preferences for specific product benefits in two culturally diverse countries. The implications for international marketing are discussed.

Chapter 4 examines consumption as a function of ethnic identification and acculturation. Unlike other studies on this topic, this chapter, borrowing from cross-cultural psychology literature, argues that ethnicity indicators are hardly uni-dimensional in nature as they are determined by two correlated but distinctive factors – ethnic identification and acculturation. This chapter empirically tests the relative power of ethnic identification and acculturation in predicting lifestyle and consumption behaviors of a sample of French-Canadians. A new two-dimensional typology of ethnic consumption behaviors is introduced.

Methodological Issues

Although cross-cultural and multicultural research has been conducted for some time, concern with methodological issues is of recent origin. Researching a marketing issue in diverse cultures raises many thorny problems in terms of equivalence, reliability, and validity of research findings across cultures. Replicating studies of one culture in other cultural contexts also involves complex methodological problems. Additionally, multicultural marketing requires conducting research in diverse cultural settings within nations, regions, and at global level. Chapters 5 and 6 in Part II are devoted to these methodological issues. Chapter 5 addresses the effects of extreme response style (ERS) in cross-cultural research. Using a cross-cultural application of the Greenleaf ERS measure, the author found that black and white student populations have consistent significant differences in the proportional usage of the extreme categories at 5, 6, 7, 8, 10 point formats. The chapter discusses the implications for cross-cultural research.

Chapter 6 examines the issue of category construction (race versus ethnicity) in consumer research involving ethnic minority populations. Methodological problems with respect to establishing functional, conceptual, measurement and sampling equivalence are discussed.

Majority Versus Minority Consumer Behaviors

In spite of the recognition that a multicultural approach is preferable to the traditional majority versus minority approach to modern marketing, traditionally marketers have treated non-majority cultures as minority markets. The amount of attention marketers pay to minority markets seems to increase as social and legal recognition of equality is extended to the minority cultures in a society. This evolutionary process characterized multicultural marketing in the United States in the 60s and 70s, when considerable attention was devoted to researching white versus black consumer behaviors. By the 1980s similar marketing attention was paid to the emerging Hispanic minority in the United States, and by the 1990s marketing attention was extended to Asian-Americans. Similar trends in minority marketing can be observed in other countries such as Canada. These issues related to majority versus minority marketing are addressed in Part III.

Chapter 7 assesses the cross-cultural stability of SERVQUAL in a multicultural market by investigating the case of Canadian and Hong Kong Chinese immigrants in Canada. Assessing service quality becomes very complex in global and multicultural markets where distinct cultural groups may represent important market segments. The research results confirm that original SERVQUAL items as well as the new proposed items are useful in explaining differences in service quality perceptions.

Chapter 8 reports on research involving the influence of ethnic background on response to direct marketing strategies and on shopping mall patronage. The authors hypothesized that ethnic background would affect intention to respond to direct mail promotions of shopping malls. Research results yielded significant differences for the influence of ethnic background on attitudes toward direct marketing.

Chapter 9 reports research dealing with family level measure of acculturation for Chinese immigrants in Canada. With an exhaustive review of the pertinent literature, the authors developed an acculturation scale with three factors. The scale was then tested rigorously by both the multitriait-multimethod (MTMM) model and the correlated uniqueness (CU) model. Results showed that the scale had desirable levels of psychometric properties.

Ethnic Consumer Behaviors

As ethnic minorities continue to become more important both socially and economically, such populations represent lucrative markets. Delving deeper into the intricacies of consumer behavior will provide knowledge useful to promoting products and services. Research studies dealing with aspects of ethnic consumer behavior are presented in Part IV.

Chapter 10 presents a psycho-cultural profile of Asian immigrants in the U.S. and discusses the implications for marketing initiatives. Raval and Raval contend that culture affects the behaviors of individuals and an understanding of culturally conditioned behaviors of Asian Americans who constitute a relatively affluent market segment, can serve as a valuable tool for U.S. marketers. The authors identify universal psycho-cultural profiles of Asian Americans and suggest initiatives to reach this important market segment.

Chapter 11 explores differences in consumer behavior in Eastern and Western cultures and identities the implications of such differences for marketing a consumer durable product. The authors used People's Republic of China and the U.S as examples of Eastern and Western cultures. Empirical research data on each cultural context were used to point out the differential impact of marketing mix variables on consumer behavior.

Organizational Cultures and Relationships

Most of the earlier works on multiculturalism and its implications for marketing management focused principally on consumer behavior. However, inter-organizational relationships are critical in multicultural contexts whether they involve a country, a region, or the entire world. Organizations with diverse cultural backgrounds have to cooperate in order to carry out marketing exchanges smoothly. Especially with the focus on relationship marketing in contemporary marketing theory and practice, it behooves marketers to consider the cultural complexities in initiating, building, and sustaining inter-organizational relationships. As global marketing and global sourcing have increased in recent decades, the importance of inter-organizational relations across cultures has increased as well. As the parties to buyer-seller dyads in global marketing/sourcing often belong to diverse cultures, there is always potential for conflict and a need to be able to resolve effectively such conflicts. From these perspectives, organizational cultures and relationships in multicultural marketing contexts become significant. Part V addresses some of these issues.

Chapter 12 addresses the issue of service management effectiveness and organizational culture with special reference to the validity of the competing values model (CVM). Paulin, Ferguson, and Payaud tested the competing values model (CVM), which was originally developed in the U.S., in the context of the banking industry in France and Mexico. They found that a market-type culture, as measured by the competing values model (CVM) of organizational culture, does not reflect the desired compatibility when applied in different cultural contexts. Hence, they proposed certain modifications to the CVM and validated the modified CVM with a sample of successful French companies, thereby demonstrating the importance of a service-type culture oriented to organizational values emphasizing the client relationship. The authors also suggest scope for additional research to further validate the relevance of the modified CVM with a strong service-type culture from the perspective of achieving significantly higher service management effectiveness.

Chapter 13 proposes a cross-cultural importer-exporter relationship model. As the forces of globalization, privatization, and liberalization shape the global economy, international trade is growing by leaps and bounds. As a result harmonious importer-exporter relationships have become increasingly important for world trade. Drawing on diverse theories of importer-exporter relationships such as transaction cost analysis (TCA) and agency theory (AT), as well as extensive generic literature on buyer-seller and importer-exporter relationship development processes, the author proposes a comprehensive model that includes the key variables of dependence, trust, cooperation, satisfaction, and commitment in the development of relationships between the parties.

Global Consumer Diversity

The last section of the book is devoted to the issue of global consumer diversity. Global diversity is reflected both in the variety of cultures encountered by global marketers and the inter-cultural differences which calls for different marketing strategies to be successful in different markets. Both these types of research investigations are included in this section. In addition, the multicultural marketing problems experienced by global marketers in different parts of the world are not only from between country cultural diversity but also from within a single country multicultural diversity. This aspect of global multiculturalism is addressed in the contexts of England and Australia.

Chapter 14 explores the marketing challenges of multiculturalism in Great Britain. The authors provide a detailed profile of the multicultural nature of the British marketing environment and present a schema for cultural classification of ethnic minorities in Great Britain. Though limited to the British context, this chapter addresses the issues of researching the multicultural market and developing appropriate ethno-marketing mixes.

Chapter 15 by Chan deals with multicultural marketing issues in the context of Australia. As the ethnic composition of the Australian population is fast changing in recent years, the market potential of diverse cultural groups in Australia is increasingly recognized by marketers both global and domestic. However, the author contends that the development of multicultural marketing in Australia is still in its nascent stage. The author reviewed the latest developments in multicultural marketing in Australia by putting the issue into proper perspective and pointing out some of the misconceptions about the subject matter. In addition, the authors discussed some case histories. Finally, suggestions were made for conducting market research with ethnic communities and also how to reach such communities with appropriate promotional vehicles.

The final chapter, chapter 16, by Lee, Kwak and Cho, deals with various facets, dimensions and gaps of consumer satisfaction in the context of Korean consumers. The authors presented research exploring Korean consumers' evaluative facets which determine their satisfaction with products and services. Through appropriate and sound research procedures, the authors have identified five Korean consumer satisfaction factors. These are: purchase, service, features, image and performance. Through empirical research the perceived relative importance of these five factors in the purchase of TV products was determined. The research also reported that Korean consumers' brand switching intentions were significantly affected by their perceived gaps in service related items. The authors also discussed the academic and managerial implications of their research as well as the future research direction.

In the new millenium multiculturalism has become an established fact at various geographical levels – country, region, and global. Management, marketing or otherwise, is forced to cope with the complexities that arise in dealing with cultural diversity in work places and in markets they operate. Especially in the field of marketing, both domestic and international, multiculturalism is going to be the major challenge facing management. Although some writings have appeared dealing with the issues of multicultural marketing, this is the first attempt to focus on multicultural marketing from an integrated perspective covering various geographical levels and dealing with conceptual, methodological and managerial issues. It is hoped that this book will be valuable to both academicians and practitioners of multicultural marketing.

References

Costa, Janeen A. and Gary J. Bamossy (eds) (1995), *Marketing in Multicultural World: Ethnicity, Nationalism and Cultural Identity,* Thousand Oaks, California: Sage.

Glazer, N., D.P. Moynihan (1963), *Beyond the Melting Pot,* Cambridge, MA: Harvard University Press.

Hofstead, Geert (1984), *Culture Consequences: International Differences in Work-Related Values,* Beverly Hills, CA: Sage.

_____(1991), *Culture and Organization,* London: McGraw Hill.

Howes, David, ed. (1996), *Cross-Cultural Consumption: Global Markets, Local Realities,* London: Routledge.

Levitt, Theodore (1983), 'The Globalization of Markets,' *Harvard Business Review (May-June):* 92-102.

Ricks, David A. (1993), *Blunders in International Business,* Cambridge, MA: Blackwell.

Rossman, Marlene L. (1994), *Multicultural Marketing: Selling to a Diverse America,* New York: American Management Association.

Seelye, Ned H., and Alan Seelye-James (1995), *Culture Class: Managing in a Multicultural World,* Lincolnwood, Chicago IL: NTC Business Books.

PART I:

CONCEPTUAL ISSUES

Chapter 2

Cultural Differences in Consumer Susceptibility to Interpersonal Influence: The Role of Individualism

Mehdi Mourali
Michel Laroche
Frank Pons

Introduction

Most human behavior, including the consumption of products and services, is to a large extent shaped by the influence of others. In marketing, others have been shown to affect consumer decision processes, whether they were known or unknown to the target, present during the choice task or simply imagined (Dahl et al. 2001, McGrath and Otnes 1995, Ratner and Khan 2002). Acknowledging the ubiquitous influence of others on human decision-making, some authors have, nonetheless, suggested that people differ in their responses to social influence (e.g., McGuire 1968). The underlying concept of susceptibility to interpersonal influence has since been proposed as a general trait that varies across individuals (Bearden et al. 1989, 1990). The degree of others' influence on a person's beliefs, attitudes, and behaviors is assumed to be a function of his/her willingness to accept the mandates of the group (Kelman 1961).

The way individuals relate to the group, however, is not only affected by individual-level differences, it is also systematically influenced by cultural and societal values and norms (Hofstede 2001, Markus and Kitayama 1991, Triandis 1989). At this regard, Hofstede (2001) describes the relationship between the individual and the collectivity as a fundamental dimension on which societies differ. Along the same line of thinking, we speculate in this paper that while all humans show some willingness to accept the mandates of the group, different cultural groups show willingness to different degrees. We illustrate our hypothesis by investigating and comparing the structure, properties, and mean levels of the susceptibility to interpersonal influence scale (Bearden et al. 1989) across samples of French and English Canadian consumers. French and English Canadians were chosen because they form two culturally distinct groups, shown to differ in their levels of individualism (Hofstede 2001), which is posited here to be the cultural dimension directly impinging on the extent of consumer susceptibility to interpersonal influence.

Consumer Susceptibility to Interpersonal Influence

Consumers expect others to evaluate their choice decisions, which might lead them to choose an alternative different from the one they would have chosen in the absence of public scrutiny (Ariely and Levav 2000, Belk 1988, Ratner and Khan 2002). Ratner and Khan (2002), for instance, found that consumers incorporate more variety seeking in their public versus private decisions. The authors suggested that increased variety seeking emanates from a desire to make a favorable impression on others. Ariely and Levav (2000) also found that consumers tend to incorporate more variety in the context of public consumption. Their study, which focused on sequential choice decisions in a group, concluded that in the presence of others, a consumer has to balance his or her individual goals with the group goals, which may lead to different (more variety-seeking) choice decisions and less personal satisfaction. In yet another study, Dahl et al. (2001) found that the presence of others (real and imagined) leads to more embarrassment when purchasing an embarrassing product (a condom). The rationale was that embarrassment is driven by the concern of what others are thinking about us.

While these studies highlight the existence of manifest interpersonal influence on individual decision processes, they do not deal directly with the various types of interpersonal influence likely to take place in a given situation. In the last fifty years or so, the issue of dimensionality of interpersonal influence has received substantial interest from consumer and social psychology researchers (e.g., Bearden and Etzel 1982, Bearden et al. 1989, 1990, Burnkrant and Cousineau 1975, Deutch and Gerard 1995, Kelman 1958, 1961, Park and Lessig 1977). Generally, these authors concur that interpersonal influence could be manifested in three different forms: utilitarian, value-expressive, and informational, though utilitarian influence and value-expressive influence have frequently been grouped under the broader category of normative influence (Bearden et al. 1989, 1990).

Utilitarian influence is reflected in individuals' attempts to comply with the expectations of others in order to obtain approval or avoid disapproval (Bearden et al. 1989). Utilitarian influence operates through the process of compliance (Burnkrant and Cousineau 1975, Park and Lessig, 1977). According to Kelman (1958), compliance occurs when people adopt attitudes and behaviors in order to obtain specific rewards or to avoid specific punishments. The person, therefore, adopts group norms, values, and behaviors not out of genuine conviction of their worth, but because they are instrumental in producing a desired social outcome. Utilitarian influence is most likely to take place when the person's behavior is visible to the influencer.

Value-expressive influence, on the other hand, happens when individuals use others', values, and behaviors as a model for their own attitudes and behaviors. Value-expressiveness operates through the process of identification (Burnkrant and Cousineau 1975, Park and Lessig, 1977). Identification occurs when people adopt attitudes and behaviors in order to be associated with a satisfying, self-defining relationship with another person or group (Kelman 1958). Identification differs from compliance in that the individual actually believes in the attitudes and behaviors adopted. Therefore, value-expressive influence is likely to occur whether the person's behaviors are public or private.

The third form of interpersonal influence, informational influence, refers to people's tendency to accept information from others as credible evidence about reality (Bearden et al. 1989, Deutch and Gerard 1995). People may directly request information from knowledgeable others or may acquire it indirectly by observing the behaviors of others. Informational influence is said to operate through the process of internalization (Bearden et al, 1989, Burnkrant and Cousineau 1975), which occurs when people adopt attitudes and behaviors because their content is congruent with the individuals' value systems (Kelman 1958).

Bearden et al. (1989) developed a scale to measure all three facets of consumer susceptibility to interpersonal influence. Their analyses, however, indicated that their measures did not discriminate between the utilitarian and value-expressive dimensions. This led to a two-dimensional scale reflecting consumers' susceptibility to normative influence, including the utilitarian and value-expressive components, and their susceptibility to informational influence. Bearden et al.'s (1989) scale was further validated in several marketing studies (e.g., Bearden et al. 1990, D'Rozario 2001, Kropp et al. 1999).

Cultural Influence

The Canadian context is characterized by the coexistence of two major cultural groups, namely French Canadians and English Canadians. Numerous studies have compared consumption patterns and life-style differences between these two groups (e.g., Hui et al. 1993, Mallen 1977, Schaninger et al. 1985, Tigert, 1973). Hui et al. (1993), for example, reported that, compared to French Canadians, English Canadians were less likely to be opinion leaders, were more price conscious, and were less fashion conscious. Moreover, according to Mallen (1977), French Canadian consumers can be characterized as more sensate and more conservative than their English counterparts. The sensate trait is translated in a greater hedonistic attitude toward consumption on the part of French Canadians, whereas conservatism is seen in French Canadians' greater household and family orientation and their greater brand loyalty (Hui et al. 1993).

Several attempts have been made to explain the consumption differences between French and English Canadian consumers. Earlier work by Lefrancois and Chatel (1967) proposed that such differences could be explained by differences in the socio-economic status of the two groups. The authors noted that French Canadians were generally less educated and had lower income than English Canadians. They concluded that this difference in social class must account for the consumption differences. However, several studies have since rejected this view (e.g., Chebat et al. 1988, Palda 1967, Schaninger et al. 1985, Thomas 1975). The most widely accepted view offers culture as the main determinant of the observed differences in consumption. Mallen (1977), for instance, discusses six cultural dimensions describing the French Canadians: the rural root, the minority root, the North American root, the Catholic root, the Latin root, and the French root. He argues that these cultural roots act as determinants of the sensate and conservative traits characterizing French Canadian consumers.

Most importantly, French and English Canadians are also distinguishable on the cultural dimension of individualism. In fact, Hofstede (2001) has recently shown that French people were less individualistic and more collectivistic than British people. Given the French roots of French Canadians and the British roots of English Canadians, one could expect a similar difference in individualism between French and English Canadians.

French Canadian's lower individualistic orientation, in addition to their higher fashion consciousness and greater concern with external impressions (Hui et al. 1993), suggests that relative to English Canadians, they would be more susceptible to normative influence. That is, French Canadians are expected to have a higher need to identify or enhance their image with significant others through the acquisition and use of products and brands, and to be more willing to conform to the expectations of others regarding purchase decisions than English Canadians.

H1:   The mean level of consumer susceptibility to normative influence is higher for French Canadians than for English Canadians.

H1a: The mean level of the utilitarian dimension of consumer susceptibility to interpersonal influence is higher for French Canadians than for English Canadians.

H1b: The mean level of the value-expressive dimension of consumer susceptibility to interpersonal influence is higher for French Canadians than for English Canadians.

In a recent study comparing French and English Canadians' information search behavior, Laroche et al. (2002) found that the two groups did not vary in their susceptibility to informational influence. Similarly, we propose:

H2:   The mean level of the informational dimension of consumer susceptibility to interpersonal influence is invariant for French and English Canadians.

In building our first hypothesis, we claimed that differences in susceptibility to normative influence are, in part, due to differences in individualistic orientation. A similar argument was suggested by D'Rozario (2001) in his comparison of susceptibility to interpersonal influence between two immigrant groups in the U.S. Such an assertion, however, merits further conceptual and empirical validation. To begin with, we formally test the posited difference in individualism between French and English Canadians, based on an extension of Hofstede's (2001) findings.

H3:   French Canadian consumers will have a lower individualistic orientation than English Canadian consumers.

Individualism-collectivism has been investigated extensively in cross-cultural research (Grimm et al. 1999), with some studies having successfully related self-described personality traits and individualism-collectivism. For example, samples in individualistic cultures have averaged higher on needs for aggression, change, exhibition, independence, and uniqueness, whereas samples of collectivistic cultures have averaged higher on affiliative tendencies, interdependence, sensitivity to rejection, and needs for abasement, deference, and order (Grimm et al., 1999).

Moreover, Triandis (1995) described four central elements of the individualism-collectivism distinction: (1) a sense of self as an autonomous, independent person versus a sense of self as more connected to in-groups, (2) a priority of personal goals versus subordination of personal goals to group goal, (3) an emphasis on personal attributes versus roles and norms in guiding behavior, and (4) the maintenance of relationships for personal benefits rather than for a sense of connection and obligation. Based on these theoretical differences, one should expect some discrepancies in the way people from individualistic and collectivistic cultures respond to normative interpersonal influence. If this is the case, then consumers' individualistic orientation should have a direct negative impact on their susceptibility to interpersonal influence.

H4: Consumers' individualistic orientation will have a negative impact on their susceptibility to normative influence.

H4a: Consumers' individualistic orientation will have a negative impact on their susceptibility to utilitarian influence.

H4b: Consumers' individualistic orientation will have a negative impact on their susceptibility to value-expressive influence.

Contrastingly, susceptibility to informational influence, which reflects people's tendency to seek and accept information from interpersonal sources, is not necessarily related to individualistic orientation. Indeed, interpersonal sources have been shown to be extensively used by most consumers in their acquisition of product related information (Arndt 1967, Brown and Reingen 1987, Price and Feick 1984). Seeking product-related information from a friend or accepting an advice from a parent can help reduce the costs of information search, without compromising a person's autonomy and independence from the group, and hence does not interfere with individualistic goals. In fact, a study by Dawar et al. (1996) found that Hofstede's (1980) cultural dimensions of uncertainty avoidance and power distance were more likely to have an effect on the use of interpersonal sources than individualism-collectivism.

H5: There is no relationship between consumers' individualistic orientation and their susceptibility to informational influence.

Methodology

Sample

Data were collected using self-administered questionnaires in the Greater Montreal area. Seventeen census tracts were selected and streets were randomly chosen within each of these census areas to proceed with a door-to-door distribution of the questionnaires. A total of 500 English questionnaires and 500 French questionnaires were distributed. Four hundred and nineteen (221 French and 198 English) usable questionnaires were mailed back. The response rate of 41.9% (44.2% for French and 39.6% for English) was judged satisfactory. A detailed description of the sample is provided in Table 1.

Table 2.1   Descriptive Statistics

Variable	Range	English (%)	French (%)	Pearson χ^2	Sig. level
Gender	Male	47.1	55.7	2.657	.103
	Female	52.9	44.3		
Status	Single	21.2	25.7	9.596	.022
	Married	68.2	63.8		
	Separated	6.0	10.0		
	Widowed	4.6	0.5		
Age	Under 20	3.9	3.3	6.457	.264
	20 to 29	15.8	15.7		
	30 to 39	17.1	19.5		
	40 to 49	26.3	29.0		
	50 to 59	21.1	24.8		
	60 and older	15.8	7.6		
Income	> $30,000	10.0	11.4	4.753	.690
	$30K - <$50K	17.2	11.9		
	$50K - <$70K	21.4	20.3		
	$70K or more	51.4	46.4		
Education	Elementary	0.7	1.0	4.695	.320
	Secondary	9.3	8.6		
	College	32.7	24.8		
	University	41.3	41.9		
	Graduate	16.0	23.8		

Measures

Bearden et al.'s (1989) scale was used to assess consumer susceptibility to interpersonal influence. The original scale had 12 items: four for each of the three dimensions (utilitarian, value-expressive, and informational). As mentioned earlier, however, Bearden et al. (1989) grouped the eight items reflecting susceptibility to utilitarian and value-expressive influences to form one normative dimension. Ethnic identification was measured by one item: I consider myself English

Canadian/ French Canadian/or other. All those who responded 'other' were not considered for further analysis. The final sample included 153 English Canadians and 211 French Canadians. Finally, individualistic orientation was measured by four items, adapted from the scale of Yamaguchi (1994).

Initially, the questionnaire was developed in English. It was translated to French by a bilingual individual whose mother tongue was French. Then, it was back translated to English by a bilingual person whose mother tongue was English. The process went on until all discrepancies disappeared. All items are shown in the appendix, which also includes measures of reliability, convergent validity, and discriminant validity.

Analysis Factorial Structure of Consumer Susceptibility to Interpersonal Influence

First, using the entire sample, Bearden et al.'s (1989) 12-item scale was submitted to an exploratory factor analysis. This preliminary step indicated the presence of three factors with eigen values equal to 5.3, 2.1, and 1.1 respectively. The three factors accounted for 70.8% of the total variance explained and reflected all three facets (utilitarian, value-expressive, and informational) of susceptibility to interpersonal influence. The varimax-rotated solution (see Table 2) revealed 2 problematic items. INFL4 and INFL9 loaded substantively on more than one factor. These items were deleted for further analyses.

Table 2.2   EFA Results: Rotated Component Matrix

	Components[*]		
	1	2	3
INFL8	.822	.234	-1.616E-02
INFL6	.808	.351	-7.657E-03
INFL7	.786	.218	5.884E-03
INFL5	.674	.365	7.516E-02
INFL9	.654	-.00683	.477
INFL3	.336	.821	.119
INFL1	.109	.816	8.842E-02
INFL2	.367	.793	.114
INFL4	.522	.652	6.681E-02
INFL11	.115	.146	.878
INFL10	.00133	.00125	.848
INFL12	.0059	.115	.842

[*]Extraction Method: Principal Component Analysis. Varimax Rotation with Kaiser Normalization.

Next, confirmatory factor analyses were conducted to confirm the factorial structure of the construct. More specifically, we compared a three-factor structure, as suggested by the EFA results to a two-factor structure, as suggested by past research (Bearden et al. 1989, 1990, D'Rozario 2001).

Fit of the CFA model is assessed using the traditional chi-square χ^2 statistic and its p-value, the ratio χ^2/df, the Normed Fit Index (NFI), the Non Normed Fit Index (NNFI), and the Comparative Fit Index (CFI). Ideally the χ^2 value should be small and its associated probability value should be greater than the selected significance level. However, as this statistic is extremely sensitive to sample size and statistical power, it would reject almost every reasonable model in a great statistical power condition (Raykov et al. 1991). Alternatively, acceptable model fits are indicated by χ^2/df values smaller than 5 (Taylor and Todd 1995). As for the practical fit indices (NFI, NNFI, and CFI), they range from 0 to 1 and are derived from a comparison of the hypothesized model with the null model. Values greater than .90 are considered to indicate acceptable fit to the data (Bentler 1992).

The three-factor model displayed the following fit results: $\chi^2 = 85.5$ with 32 degrees of freedom (p < 0.01), $\chi^2/df = 2.67$, NFI = .96, NNFI = .97, and CFI = .98. The two-factor model, on the other hand, displayed poorer fit statistics: $\chi^2 = 364.9$ with 35 degrees of freedom (p < 0.01), $\chi^2/df = 2.28$, NFI = .83, NNFI = .80, and CFI = .85. A chi square difference test confirms that the three-factor structure fits the data significantly better than a two-factor structure (χ^2 difference = 279.4, df = 3, p < .01).

Convergent and Discriminant Validity

In assessing the validity of the measures, Bollen (1989) suggests a scrutiny of the factor loadings as well as the squared multiple correlations between the items and the constructs. Bagozzi and Yi (1988) suggest that factor loadings of .60 and more are indicative of convergent validity. Regarding the squared multiple correlations, values greater than .40 are suggestive of substantial shared variance with the underlying theoretical constructs (Taylor and Todd 1995).

The results, shown in the appendix, indicate that, for both samples, all ten items of susceptibility to interpersonal influence have acceptable loadings and squared multiple correlations, thus suggesting good convergent validity.

As evidence of discriminant validity, Lagrange multiplier tests revealed that no item loaded significantly on a factor for which it was not intended. A more stringent statistical test of discriminant validity, however, consists of performing a chi-square difference test between two models: one in which the correlation between two constructs is freely estimated, and one where the correlation is fixed to unity (Salisbury et al. 1996). A chi-square difference greater than 3.84 ($\alpha = .05$) would suggest that the two constructs are statistically different. The results provide strong evidence of discriminant validity of constructs for every possible pairing (see Appendix).

Measurement Equivalence

Equivalence across the French and English Canadian samples was assessed following the procedure outlined by Steenkamp and Baumgartner (1998). The first test is for configural invariance. No constraints are imposed across the groups. This test assesses whether the same simple structure of factor loadings holds across the two groups. The second test examines metric invariance. Here the factor loadings are constrained equal. A third test assesses invariance of the factor covariances and of the factor variances. Finally, a fourth test evaluates scalar invariance before latent means can be compared.

By examining various combinations of constrained and unconstrained models, we can determine the source of any differences in the way the constructs are composed and interpreted in the different cultures. Specifically, by examining the Lagrange Multiplier (LM) statistics, we can judge which individual items, if any, are problematic in using the constructs (Bollen 1989, Byrne 1994).

Results

The test of configural invariance produced a χ^2 = 128.6 with 64 degrees of freedom (p < .01), yielding a ratio χ^2/df = 2.01, suggesting a good fit to the data. The practical fit indices confirmed the model's good fit: NFI = .94, NNFI = .95, and a CFI = .97. Thus, both cultural groups exhibit the same simple factor structure.

The second test examined whether the factor loadings were equal for the two groups. The test produced χ^2 = 161.8 with 71 degrees of freedom (p < .01), χ^2/df = 2.28, NFI = .92, NNFI = .94, and CFI = .95. Although the fit indices overall indicate a good fitting model, they also show a significant decrease in fit. The chi square difference between the simple structure model and the equal loadings model was 33.2 with 7 degrees of freedom. This is significant at p < .05, and suggests a slight violation of metric invariance. A close look at the LM statistics revealed that one of the equality constraints did not hold. The loading of INFL8 on the value-expressive factor differed between the Anglo and Franco Canadian samples. Thus, only partial metric invariance of the scale of susceptibility to interpersonal influence was established (9 factor loadings out of 10). Byrne, Shavelson and Muthén (1989) argue that full metric invariance is not necessary for further tests of invariance and substantive analyses, such as comparison of factor means, to be meaningful, provided that at least one item other than the one fixed at unity (to define the scale of each latent construct) was metrically invariant. In further testing, the non-invariant parameters should be specified as unconstrained across groups. The model of metric invariance was reassessed after deleting the problematic constraint. The analysis yielded the following results: χ^2 = 148.0 with 70 degrees of freedom (p < .01), χ^2/df = 2.11, NFI = .93, NNFI = .95, and CFI = .96, which represents a significant improvement in model fit compared to the full metric invariance model: χ^2 difference = 13.8 with 1 degree of freedom, p < .05.

When equality constraints of the factor covariances and the factor variances were added to the partially metric invariant model, the analysis yielded the following model fit results: χ^2 = 163.1 with 76 degrees of freedom and p < .01, χ^2/df = 2.15, NFI = .92, NNFI = .95, and CFI = .96. Here again, the significant drop in chi-square (15.1 with 6 degrees of freedom) compared to the previous model indicates possible misspecification of at least one of the new constraints. An examination of the LM statistics revealed three mis-specified constraints. First, the variance of the first factor (utilitarian influence) was statistically different across the French and English Canadian samples. Furthermore, the covariances between the utilitarian dimension and the value-expressive dimension, and between the utilitarian dimension and the informational dimension were also different across the two groups. The presence of non-invariant factor variance and covariance implies that the correlations between the latent constructs differ for the two groups (Steenkamp and Baumgartner 1998). Indeed, a reassessment of the model after deleting the mis-specified constraints not only resulted in an improved fit of the model to the data, but also revealed significant differences between the two groups in two out of three correlations between the latent constructs.

The reanalysis yielded χ^2 = 152.3 with 73 degrees of freedom, p < .01, χ^2/df = 2.09, NFI = .93, NNFI = .95, and CFI = .96. The correlation between the utilitarian and the value-expressive factors for English Canadians was equal to .67, while it equaled .63 in the French Canadian sample. Similarly, the correlation between the utilitarian and the informational factors was .25 for the English Canadian Sample and .41 for the French Canadian sample. Correlation between the value-expressive and the informational factors, on the other hand, was invariant across the two groups and was equal to .19. Interestingly, these results show a stronger association between the normative and the value-expressive dimensions of interpersonal influence than between any one of these dimensions and the informational dimension. This is consistent with previous findings suggesting two dimensions for susceptibility to interpersonal influence (e.g., Bearden et al. 1989, 1990), though our data, as shown earlier, was better represented by a three-dimensional structure.

The last test was concerned with assessing scalar invariance. A two-group latent means model of consumer susceptibility to interpersonal influence was tested.

The goodness-of-fit statistics show the model to be a good fit to the multi-group data, as indicated by χ^2 = 162.3 with 80 degrees of freedom, p < .01, χ^2/df = 2.03, NFI = .92, NNFI = .95, and CFI = .96. The LM statistics, however, indicated that two equality constraints were mis-specified (intercepts of INFL2 and INFL11). The model was subsequently re-estimated with these intercepts freed. Removal of these constraints yielded a significant improvement in goodness-of-fit: χ^2 = 153.7 with 78 degrees of freedom, p < .01, χ^2/df = 1.97, NFI = .93, NNFI = .96, and CFI = .96. Again the difference in chi-square (8.6 with 2 degrees of freedom) is statistically significant at p < .05.

We have been successful in establishing partial metric and scalar invariance. Now we can confidently turn to hypothesis testing by interpreting the factor intercepts, which represent the differences in latent mean values. The English Canadian group was designated the reference group, and as such, had all factor intercepts fixed to zero. Table 3 shows the factor intercepts for the French Canadian group along with their associated error terms and test statistics.

Table 2.3 Latent means comparison between English Canadians and French Canadians

Factor Intercept	Estimated Value	Standard Error	Test Statistic	Conclusion
Utilitarian	.37	.14	2.73	Higher for French Canadians
Value-expressive	.36	.15	2.34	Higher for French Canadians
Informational	-.16	.17	-.91	Invariant

In support of hypothesis 1 (both H1a and H1b), table 3 shows that French Canadian consumers are more susceptible to utilitarian and value-expressive influences than their English Canadian counterparts. These results were expected based on previous findings indicating higher fashion consciousness and greater concern with external impressions for French Canadian consumers as opposed to English Canadian consumers (Hui et al. 1993), and on a speculated difference in individualistic orientation. In support of hypothesis 2, table 3 also shows that both groups have a statistically equivalent level of susceptibility to informational influence.

Differences in susceptibility to normative influence between French and English Canadians were thought to arise, mainly, from differences in individualistic orientation between the two cultural groups. The reasoning was that English Canadians were more individualistic than French Canadians, which made them less susceptible to normative influence. To test this theory, two conditions have to hold. First, we must show that English Canadians are indeed more individualistic than French Canadians (Hypothesis 3). Next, we must show that individualism has a direct negative impact on consumer susceptibility to normative influence and no effect on consumer susceptibility to informational influence (Hypotheses 4 and 5).

Hypotheses 3, 4, and 5 were tested simultaneously by fitting a structural model, depicting direct relationships between individualistic orientation and the three dimensions of susceptibility to interpersonal influence (see Figure 1), to both groups.

**Figure 2.1   Impact of Individualistic Orientation on Consumer
Susceptibility to Interpersonal Influence**

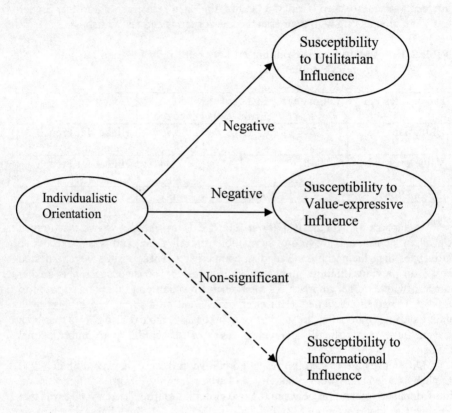

The Steenkamp and Baumgartner (1998) procedure for assessing model equivalence, described earlier, was applied to the entire structural model. The results confirmed the partial invariance of susceptibility to interpersonal influence and indicated full invariance of individualistic orientation across the two groups. The fit statistics of the final invariance model (including constraints relative to metric, structural, and scalar invariance) are: χ^2 = 242.1 with 138 degrees of freedom, p < .01, χ^2/df = 1.75, NFI = .90, NNFI = .94, CFI = .95.

Metric and scalar invariance having been established, factor intercepts can be interpreted confidently. Again, using the English Canadian group as the reference group, the factor intercept for the French Canadian group indicates whether a significant difference in the latent mean of individualistic orientation exists. Consistent with Hypothesis 3, the results (factor intercept = -.57, standard error = .17, test statistic = -3.27) show that French Canadians are significantly less individualistic than English Canadians.

Furthermore, the Lagrange Multiplier test for releasing constraints indicated that all structural paths linking individualistic orientation to each dimension of consumer susceptibility to interpersonal influence were invariant for the two groups. These paths, along with their associated errors and test statistics provide a strong test of hypotheses 4 and 5.

Individualistic orientation had a significant negative effect on consumer susceptibility to utilitarian influence (path coefficient = -.32, standard error = .09, test statistic = -3.41). This result provides full support for hypothesis 4a. Further, in support, of hypothesis 4b, individualistic orientation had a significant negative effect on susceptibility to value-expressive influence (path coefficient = -.33, standard error = .11, test statistic = -2.90). Finally, supporting hypothesis 5, individual orientation had no significant effect on susceptibility to informational influence (path coefficient = .11, standard error = .10, test statistic = 1.06).

Discussion

Consumer decision processes are often influenced by other people. Bearden et al. (1989) developed a scale to measure individual differences in consumer susceptibility to interpersonal influence. Though their scale has been widely validated with American samples, its application to non-American samples has been very limited (D'Rozario 2001). In the present study, we tested the properties, structure, and mean levels of the susceptibility to interpersonal influence construct across samples of French and English Canadian consumers. Interestingly, our analyses revealed that a three-factor representation, comprising the utilitarian, value-expressive, and informational facets of susceptibility to interpersonal influence, provides an excellent description of the data.

While, Bearden et al.'s (1989) initial exploratory factor analysis also revealed a three factor solution, further analyses of their data revealed that the utilitarian and the value-expressive dimensions were highly correlated and could not be treated as distinct factors. In our study, evidence of discriminant validity among the three constituting dimensions was readily found. Moreover, a chi-square difference test comparing a three-factor model and a two-factor model confirmed the superiority of the three-factor model.

Beyond the empirical superiority of the three-factor representation, the distinction between susceptibility to utilitarian and to value-expressive influences is theoretically useful as it recognizes that both influences operate through different processes. Utilitarian influence, for instance, operates through the process of compliance, which occurs when people adopt attitudes and behaviors in order to obtain specific rewards or avoid specific punishments (Kelman 1958). Value-expressiveness, on the other hand, operates through the process of identification, which happens when people adopt attitudes and behaviors in order to be associated with a satisfying, self-defining relationship with another person or group (Kelman 1958). Identification, therefore, is indicative of a higher degree of influence than compliance since the individual actually believes in the attitudes and behaviors adopted.

We have also argued that the extent of consumer susceptibility to interpersonal influence depends on cultural and societal values and norms. Based on previous findings highlighting consumption and lifestyle differences between French and English Canadians, we predicted and found that French Canadians were on average more susceptible to normative (utilitarian and value-expressive) influence than English Canadians. We further speculated that these differences were in part due to differences in individualistic orientation between the two groups. Though previous research has hinted on the potential role of individualism (e.g., D'Rozario 2001), this paper denotes the first attempt to empirically model its influence on the various dimensions of susceptibility to interpersonal influence. By showing that French Canadians were indeed less individualistic than English Canadians, and that individualistic orientation had a significant negative effect on both the utilitarian and the value-expressive dimensions of consumer susceptibility to interpersonal influence, we hope to have demonstrated that differences in susceptibility to normative influence between French and English Canadians are partly driven by cultural differences in individualistic orientation.

Methodologically, this study has been carefully designed to ensure a high degree of validity in the conclusions drawn. Traditionally, cross-cultural consumer research has often suffered a lack of methodological rigor. In particular, critics have denounced the lack of evidence of measurement equivalence in cross-cultural studies (Mullen 1995, Sin et al. 1999). Lack of evidence of measurement invariance casts doubts on the conclusions of a study and on the theory underlying them. In this paper we used multiple group confirmatory factor analyses, which represent the most powerful and most versatile approach to testing for cross-group measurement invariance (Steenkamp and Baumgartner, 1998). We were able to demonstrate full configural invariance as well as acceptable partial metric and scalar invariance of the scale of consumer susceptibility to interpersonal influence before moving to a confident interpretation of latent mean differences between the two groups under study.

Our study also offers a number of practical implications. First, the absence of significant differences in susceptibility to informational influence between French and English Canadian consumers suggests that word-of-mouth communications and the use of interpersonal sources of information are equally important across the two groups. Consequently, when planning their promotional activities and budgets, Canadian marketers as well as international firms present in the Canadian market need not vary the proportions of interpersonal versus impersonal communication activities and budgets across the two groups, though the content of these activities may differ significantly.

Next, French Canadians' higher susceptibility to normative influence suggests that certain products, by attaining the status of norm, could be adopted on a larger scale and would gain larger market shares in the French Canadian market than in the English Canadian market. A related issue pertains to the diffusion of innovations. French Canadians' higher susceptibility to normative influence is at the source of their greater brand loyalty, especially toward the leading brands (Kindra et al. 1994). As a result, new brands are likely to encounter greater difficulties in penetrating the French Canadian market than the English Canadian market. However, as the product moves through the later stages of its lifecycle and gains further acceptance among opinion leaders, its adoption could increase at an even faster rate than it would in the English Canadian market.

Interestingly, most of the practical implications mentioned above could be extended beyond the Canadian market to firms marketing their products and services in countries on the opposite poles of the individualism-collectivism dimensions. For instance a new brand of soft drinks may have a harder time penetrating the Chinese market than the American market, but once accepted by opinion leaders, it may reach higher market performances in China than in the U.S., especially if it succeeds in attaining the norm status.

Limitations and Future Research

Although the main objectives of the study were generally met, some weaknesses still exist. For instance, regarding the use of multi-group analyses, it should be noted that procedures for assessing construct equivalence are implemented after data collection. Therefore, this technique still does not offer a remedy to the problem of cross-cultural measurement equivalence, even though it is an extremely reliable diagnostic tool. To date, only care in the data gathering process is offered as a preventive measure for dealing with this problem (Sekaran 1983). In the present case, extreme care has been taken in the data gathering process, as the original English instrument was translated to French and back translated to English until all discrepancies disappeared. Another limitation to the use of multi-group structural equation modeling is the large sample size requirement (Bollen 1989). In this study, sample size was not a limitation because a sufficient number of observations was available given the number of parameters in the model.

This study, however, can be criticized for the way culture was operationalized. Ethnic identification was measured by a single subjective indicator. Kim et al. (1993) argued that such classification scheme ignores the varying degrees of acculturation individuals may have experienced towards either end of French-English ethnicity. Future research should investigate the role acculturation might play in influencing the structure and level of consumer susceptibility to interpersonal influence. Future research could also validate the susceptibility model in other cultural settings and explore the potential effects of other cultural dimensions such as those identified by Hofstede (1980).

References

Ariely, D and J. Levav (2000), 'Sequential Choice in Group Settings: Taking the Road Less Traveled and Less Enjoyed,' *Journal of Consumer Research*, 27 (December): 279-290.

Arndt, J. (1967), 'Word of Mouth Advertising and Informal Communication,' in *Risk Taking and Information Handling In Consumer Behavior,* eds. D. F. Cox. Boston: Harvard University, Graduate School of Business Administration, 188-239.

Bagozzi, R.P. and Yi, Y. (1988), 'On the Evaluation of Structural Equation Models,' *Journal of the Academy of Marketing Science*, Vol 16, pp. 74-94.

Bearden, W. O. and M. J. Etzel (1982), 'Reference group Influence on Product and Brand Purchase Decisions,' *Journal of Consumer Research*, 9 (September): 183-194.

Bearden, W.O., R. Netemeyer and J.E. Teel (1990), 'Further Validation of the Consumer Susceptibility to Interpersonal Influence Scale,' in *Advances in Consumer Research*, 17, 770-776.

Bearden, W.O., R. Netemeyer and J.E. Teel (1989), 'Measurement of Consumer Susceptibility to Interpersonal Influence,' *Journal of Consumer Research*, 15 (March): 473-481.

Belk, R. W (1988), 'Possessions and the Extended Self,' *Journal of Consumer Research*, 2 (September): 139-168.

Bentler, P. M (1992), *EQS: Structural Equations Program Manual*, BMDP Statistical Software, Los Angeles, CA.

Bollen, K. A. (1989), *Structural Equations with Latent Variables*, John Wiley & Sons New York, NY.

Brown, J.J. and P.H. Reingen (1987), 'Social Ties and Word-of-Mouth Referral Behavior,' *Journal of Consumer Research*, 14 (December): 350-362.

Burnkrant, R. E. and A. Cousineau (1975), 'Informational and Normative Social Influence in Buyer Behavior,' *Journal of Consumer Research*, 2 (December): 206-215.

Byrne, B. M. (1994), *Structural Equation Modeling with EQS and EQS/ Windows: Basic Concepts, Applications, and Programming*, Sage Publications, Thousand Oaks, CA.

Byrne, B. M., R. J. Shavelson and B. Muthén (1989), 'Testing for Equivalence of Factor Covariance and Mean Structures: The Issue of Partial Measurement Invariance, *Psychological Bulletin*, 105, 456-466.

Chebat, J. C., M. Laroche and H. Malette (1988), 'A Cross-Cultural Comparison of Attitudes Towards and Usage of Credit Cards,' *International Journal of Bank Marketing*, 6, 42-54.

Dahl, D. W., R. V. Manchanda and J. J. Argo (2001), 'Embarrassment in Consumer Purchase: The Roles of Social Presence and Purchase Familiarity,' *Journal of Consumer Research*, 28 (December): 473-481.

Dawar, N., P. M. Parker and L. J. Price (1996), 'A Cross-Cultural Study of Interpersonal Information Exchange,' *Journal of International Business Studies*, 57 (3rd quarter): 497-516.

Deutsch, M. and H. B. Gerard (1955), 'A Study of Normative and Informational Influence upon Individual Judgement,' *Journal of Abnormal and Social Psychology*, 51 (November): 629-636.

D'Rozario, D (2001), 'The Structure and Properties of the Consumer Susceptibility to Interpersonal Influence Scale in Two Immigrant Populations in the U.S.,' *Journal of International Consumer Marketing*, 13 (2): 77-101.

Grimm, S.D., A.T. Church, M.S. Katigbak and J.A.S. Reyes (1999), 'Self-Described Traits, Values, and Moods Associated with Individualism and Collectivism,' *Journal of Cross-Cultural Psychology*, 30 (July): 466-500.

Hofstede G.H (1980), *Culture's consequences: International Differences in Work-Related Values*, Sage Publications, Beverly Hills, CA.

Hofstede G.H (2001). *Culture's consequences: Comparing Values, Behaviors, Institutions, and Organizations*, Sage Publications, Thousand Oaks, CA.

Hui, M., A. Joy, C. Kim and M. Laroche (1993), 'Equivalence of Lifestyle Dimensions Across Four Major Subcultures in Canada,' *Journal of International Consumer Marketing*, 5 (3): 15-35.

Hui, M., M. Laroche and C. Kim (1998), 'A Typology of Consumption Based on Ethnic Origin and Media Usage,' *European Journal of Marketing*, 32 (9/10): 868-883.

Kelman, H.C (1961), 'Processing of Opinion Change,' *The Public Opinion Quarterly*, 25 (Spring): 57-78.

Kelman, H.C (1958), 'Compliance, Identification, and Internalization: Three Processes of Attitude Change,' *Journal of Conflict Resolution*, 2 (1): 51-60.

Kim, C., M. Laroche and A. Joy (1990), 'An Empirical Study of the Effects of Ethnicity on Consumption Patterns in a Bi-Cultural Environment,' in M. E. Goldberg, G. J. Gorn and R. Pollay, eds., *Advances in Consumer Research*, Vol. XVII, Provo, UT: Association for Consumer Research, 839-846.

Kindra, G.S., M. Laroche and T.E. Muller (1994), Consumer Behavior: A Canadian Perspective, second edition, Nelson Canada, Scarborough, Ontario, Canada.

Kropp, F., A.M. Lavack and S.J.S. Holden (1999), 'Smokers and Beer Drinkers: Values and Consumer Susceptibility to Interpersonal Influence,' *Journal of Consumer Marketing*, 16 (6): 536-557.

Laroche, M., M. Mourali and F. Pons (2002), 'Cultural Differences in Interpersonal Information Search: The Case of French and English Canadians,' in E. Bigné, V. Johar and S. Hassan, eds., *Proceeding of the 2002 AMS Multicultural Marketing Conference*, Volume IV, Miami: Academy of Marketing Science.

Lefrancois, P. C. and Chatel, G. (1967), ' The French Canadian Consumer: Fact and Fancy,' *The Canadian Marketer*, 2, 4-7.

Markus, H.R. and S. Kitayama (1991), 'Culture and the Self: Implications for Cognition, Emotion, and Motivation,' *Psychological Review*, 98 (2): 224-253.

McGrath, M. A and C. Otnes (1995), 'Unacquainted Influencers: When Strangers Interact in the Retail Setting, *Journal of Business Research*, 32: 261-272.

McGuire, W.J (1968), 'Personality and Susceptibility to Social Influence,' in *Handbook of Personality Theory and Research*, eds. E. F. Borgatta and W.W. Lambert, Chicago: Rand McNally, 1130-1187.

Mallen, B. (1977), *French Canadian Consumer Behavior: Comparative Lessons from the Published Literature and Private Corporate Marketing Studies*, The Advertising Executive Club of Montreal.

Mullen, M. (1995), 'Diagnosing Measurement Equivalence in Cross-National Research,' *Journal of International Business Studies*, 3, 573-596.

Palda, K. S. (1967), 'A Comparison of Consumers' Expenditures in Quebec and Ontario, *Canadian Journal of Economics and Political Science*, 33, p26.

Park, C.W. and P.V. Lessig (1977), 'Students and Housewives: Differences in Susceptibility to Reference Group Influence,' *Journal of Consumer Research*, 4 (September): 102-110.

Price, L. L. and L. F. Feick (1984), 'The Role of Interpersonal Sources in External Search: An Informational perspective,' in *Advances in Consumer Research*, Vol. 11, eds. T.C. Kinnear, Provo, Utah: Association for Consumer research, 250-255.

Ratner, R. K and B. E. Khan (2002), 'The Impact of Private versus Public Consumption on Variety Seeking Behavior,' *Journal of Consumer Research*, 29 (September): 246-257.

Raykov, T., A. Tomer and J. R. Nesselroade (1991), 'Reporting Structural Equation Modeling Results in Psychology and Aging: Some Proposed Guidelines,' Psychology and Aging, 6 (4): 499-503.

Salisbury, W.D., A. Gopal and W.W. Chin (1996), 'Are We All Working from the Same Script? Developing an Instrument to Measure Consensus on the Appropriation of an Electronic Meeting System,' in Nunamaker, J.F.Jr. and Sprague, R.H.Jr. (Eds.), *Proceedings of the Twenty-Ninth Annual Hawaii International Conference on System Sciences*, IEEE, 13-23.

Schaninger, C. M., J. C. Bourgeois and W. C. Buss (1985), 'French-English Canadian Subcultural Differences,' Journal of Marketing, 49 (Spring): 82-92.

Sekaran, U. (1983), 'Methodological and Theoretical Issues and Advancements in Cross-Cultural Research,' *Journal of International Business Studies*, 14 (2): 61-73.

Sin, L. Y. M., G. M. H. Cheung and R. Lee (1999), 'Methodology in Cross-Cultural Consumer Research: A Review and Critical Assessment,' *Journal of International Consumer Marketing*, 11 (4), 75-96.

Steenkamp, J-B. E. M. and H. Baumgartner (1998), 'Assessing Measurement Invariance in Cross-National Consumer Research,' *Journal of Consumer Research*, 25 (June), 87-90.

Taylor, S. and Todd, P.A. (1995), 'Understanding Information Technology Usage: A Test of Competing Models,' *Information Systems Research*, Vol 6 (June), pp. 144-176.

Tigert, D. J. (1973), 'Can a Separate Marketing Strategy for French Canada Be Justified: Profiling English-French Markets Through Lifestyle Analysis,' in Marketing to the French Canadian Market,' in *Canadian Marketing: Problems and Prospects*, eds., Thompson, D. N. and D. S. Leighton, Toronto: Wiley of Canada Ltd., 119-131.

Thomas, D. R. (1975), 'Culture and Consumption Behavior in English and French Canada,' in *Marketing in the 1970's and beyond, B. Stidsen, ed.*, Montreal: Administrative Sciences Association of Canada.

Triandis, H. C. (1995), *Individualism and Collectivism*. Boulder, CO: Westview.

Triandis, H.C. (1989), 'The Self and Social Behavior in Differing Cultural Contexts,' *Psychological Review*, 96 (3): 506-520.

Yamaguchi, S. (1994), 'Collectivism Among the Japanese: A Perspective From the Self,' in *Individualism and Collectivism: Theory, Method and Applications* (Cross-Cultural Research and Methodology, 18, 175-188), eds. U. Kim, H. C. Hui, C. Kagitcibasi, S. Choi and G. Yoon, Thousand Oaks, CA: Sage.

APPENDIX

Item description	Multiple Sqrd Corr		Std Loading		Std error		t-value		Alpha	
	FC	EC	FC	EC	FC	EC	FC	EC	FC	EC
Utilitarian Influence									0.89	0.79
I rarely purchase the latest fashion until I am sure my friends approve of them **(INFL1)**	0.53	0.39	0.76	0.68	-	-	-	-		
It's important that others like the products and brands I buy **(INFL2)**	0.67	0.72	0.9	0.88	0.08	0.57	13.66	4.16		
When buying products, I generally purchase those brands that I think others will approve of **(INFL3)**	0.7	0.72	0.89	0.95	0.09	0.52	13.54	4.15		
Value-expressive Influence									0.85	0.81
I like to know what brands and products make good impressions on others **(INFL5)**	0.42	0.46	0.69	0.69	-	-	-	-		
I achieve a sense of belonging by purchasing the same products and brands that others purchase **(INFL6)**	0.64	0.69	0.87	0.9	0.09	0.09	11.25	9.59		
If I want to be like someone, I often try to buy the same brands that they buy **(INFL7)**	0.51	0.65	0.74	0.82	0.08	0.08	9.73	9.1		
I often identify with other people by purchasing the same products and brands they purchase **(INFL8)**	0.68	0.37	0.87	0.6	0.08	0.07	11.2	6.55		
Informational Influence									0.8	0.88
If I have little experience with a product, I often ask my friends about the product **(INFL10)**	0.4	0.53	0.66	0.77	-	-	-	-		
I often consult other people to help choose the best alternative available from a product category **(INFL11)**	0.51	0.66	0.91	0.91	0.17	0.12	8.87	11.08		
I frequently gather information from friends and family before I buy **(INFL12)**	0.42	0.61	0.64	0.85	0.13	0.11	8.68	10.79		
Individualistic Orientation									0.69	0.77

I don't think it necessary to act as fellow group members would prefer	0.38	0.46	0.67	0.69	-	-	-	-		
I don't change my opinions in conformity with those of the majority	0.46	0.53	0.76	0.78	0.22	0.13	6.95	8.42		
I don't support my group when they are wrong	0.41	0.49	69	0.77	0.17	0.09	4.07	8.73		

Evidence of Discriminant Validity

Factor correlations constrained = 1	χ^2	Diff in χ^2 (comparison with freely estimated correlations)	Conclusion
None (Freely estimated correlations)	85.5	-	-
Utilitarian and Value-expressive	95.8	10.3	The utilitarian and the value-expressive dimensions are statistically distinct
Utilitarian and Informational	95.6	10.1	The utilitarian and the informational dimensions are statistically distinct
Value-expressive and Informational	102.3	16.8	The value-expressive and informational dimensions are statistically distinct

Differences in $\chi^2 > 3.84$ indicate that the constructs are statistically different.

Chapter 3

Examining the Relationships Between Personal, Cultural Values and Desired Benefits: A Cross-National Study

Adel A. Al-Wugayan
Carol F. Surprenant

Introduction

There is a growing concern that what is known so far about consumer behavior has been derived from research done in the US and few Western European nations, comprising less than 6 percent of world population (e.g., Adler 1983, Durvasula et. al 1993). In this regard, Adler (1983) warned that the growth of published cultural validation of western business theories has fallen far behind the fast growth of international commerce. Inevitably, such gap in international marketing literature might have led many international marketers to be less sensitive to the diverse norms, values, lifestyles, and needs of the international consumer in foreign markets.

Among the factors contributing to our failing to understand host cultures has been the general acceptance of the convergence thesis – the expectation that fast growth of international travel, telecommunication, and international media has slowly dissolved much of existing cultural differences, paving the way for the world to be dominated by a single culture (Heenan 1988). Market success in such a world culture depends on the ability to deliver products that are technologically superior relative to the competition, focusing primarily on the wants and desires of the 'typical' customer rather than on the specific preferences of the international customer (Levitt 1983). Loss of competitive edge, unexpected product withdrawals, and negative consumer sentiment may all have been symptoms for inadequate understanding of the peculiarities of that foreign market.

The present empirical study has been conducted with two main objectives in mind. The first objective is to explore the interaction between cultural values and personal values in two different nations with different cultural orientations. The national culture of Kuwait, as a part of the Arab cluster reported in Hofstede 1980 study, was characterized as having higher power distances between individuals and stronger uncertainty avoidance than the US in general. The second objective is to

Marketing and Multicultural Diversity

examine the relationship between the two kinds of cultural values and consumers' preference for specific product benefits in two culturally different countries.

Culture as a System of Values

One of the most salient imprints of a culture on its people is the shaping of consumer values. This conception of culture is more suitable for consumer research because it focuses less on cultural icons and more on mechanisms determining human behavior. Hofstede (1980), for example, defines culture as the 'collective mental programming that conditions peoples' values and perceptions'. Individuals living within a culture usually share common values and cognitive structures that profoundly impact their consumption behavior. Viewed as conceptions of the desirable learned from social and physical environment, core cultural values are social patterning that prescribe and proscribe many aspects of human behavior, including behaviors related to buying and consumption. For example, Gatignon and Robertson (1985) in a cross-national study investigating women status in different cultures found that female involvement in the work force seems to determine future sales of some products such as dishwashers (Gatignon and Robertson 1985, p. 860). Henry (1976) found a strong correlation between consumer cultural values and preference for a particular category of automobiles. In a later study, Ness and Stith (1984) found significant differences between cultural values of middle-class white and black consumers and proposed that designing customized advertising to each group is instrumental to the success of advertising campaign when targeting a mass market.

Personal Values

'Values' has been conceptualized as an organized system of centrally held beliefs based on what individuals consider to be important at various stages of their lives. Within consumer literature, consumer values were consistently shown to be a key determinant of consumer behavior (Rokeach 1973, Kahle 1983, 1986, 1996). As Clawson and Vinson (1977) put it, '...Values may prove to be one of the more powerful explanations of, and influences on, consumer behavior.' Once formed, these values influence consumer behavior in two major ways. First, values become important goals that need to be attained and fulfilled and in turn influence consumer consumption patterns and product/brand preferences. For example, when security becomes the most important value for a consumer, a major part of his or her behavior would be geared toward satisfying this pressing need. Second, values serve as moral standards upon which objects and events can be considered to be 'just,' 'right,' 'fair,' and 'appropriate' in life (Posner and Munson 1979). For example, the influence of values on personal judgment is apparent in views expressed about social issues (e.g., pro-life and pro-choice debate over abortion), in logic used to reason out arguments (economic benefits of child slavery), and in deciding whether or not to engage in specific behaviors when the situation seems conflicting (Should I gamble even though I consider it to be immoral?).

The number of personal values and its suitability for research varies greatly from one scale to another. Rokeach Value Survey (Rokeach 1973) asks respondents to rank 18 Terminal Values that represent preferred end-estate of existence and 18 Instrumental Values representing preferred mode of conduct. Utilizing RVS scale in value-measurement research has declined since it was found that human memories are incapable of ranking 18 values all presented at one time and because ranking produces ordinal data points unfit for most advanced multivariate statistical techniques. VALS II measure personal values using 34 questions about demographics and general attitudes. Researchers at SRI identified nine categories of American consumers based on their value systems; however, attempts at validating the results have failed because of the proprietary nature of the instrument. The last scale, termed List of Values (LOV), identifies nine categories of values that have been extensively validated in the literature (Beatty, Kahle, Homer and Misra 1985, Kahle 1983). Post hoc refinement of the scale resulted in accepting eight personal values commonly shared by individuals with different rank order.

Culture and Consumer Personal Values

Because humans are born into an existing culture, personal values are expected to be shaped by several cultural institutions such as family, work, school, religious institutions, and social organizations. Consider, for example, how respect for the elderly is first learned and then reinforced in many Eastern and Middle-Eastern cultures. A child who observes parents and significant others treating older people respectfully tends to behave similarly, especially when that behavior is encouraged by rewards (verbal complements and positive facial gestures) and deviation is curbed with punishment (frowning, deprivation of valued possessions or privileges).

While both are called 'values', personal values and cultural values differ with regard to a number of characteristics. One key difference is that personal values represent what is important and desirable to an individual, whereas cultural values are viewed as what society promotes as preferred and useful to the common good. These values has been accepted and carried from one generation to the next. Individuals are expected to abide by cultural values since they are realities that must be respected, yet personal values are desired modes of behavior and an end-state of existence that reflects the needs and objectives in life for an individual. Another difference is that, unlike personal values, cultural values generally lack a specific rank order of importance, and they are shared by members of a culture with varying intensity.

A stream of cross-national research on personal values tends to confirm the conceptualized effects of culture on personal values both in the United States and cross-nationally. To investigate homogeneity of personal values of US residents,

Kahle (1986) studied the rank-order of personal values possessed by a probability sample of 2,000 residents living in nine geographical locations as suggested by the Census Regions in the United States. Findings showed that the ranking of individual values differed significantly from one region to another. In a series of studies conducted on measuring cross-national differences in the ranking of personal values, several authors utilized the LOV scale to measure the ranking of eight personal values in five Western countries, namely Great Britain, Germany, Denmark, Norway, United States, and the former Soviet Union, and in one Eastern country, Japan (Cited in Kahle 1996). Citizens of various countries exhibited significant differences in what they considered to be their most important value. Unfortunately, these studies merely report the presence of variations and don't explain what creates such variations.

Cultural Framework

A particularly useful approach that has gained wide prominence in organizational behavior is studying the impact of culture on individuals' values from a National Character perspective (Clark 1990, Inkeles and Levinson 1969). Briefly defined, national character reflects the adult modal personality that is prevalent across social groups living in one nation. The characteristics of modal personality are the direct outcome of the interplay between the social environment and its members; group members consistently exhibit synchronous patterns of behaviors. Clearly, the aim of the national character is not to generate superficial stereotypes about how groups typically behave, but rather to characterize intramural values and subtle behavior traits. It is believed, therefore, that dimensions of national character be of 'higher-order abstractions that refer to stable, generalized dispositions or modes of functioning …' (Inkeles and Livinson 1969, p. 426).

The literature contains many methods that can be helpful in describing the traits of national character and can be generally classified into two main approaches: a culture-centered approach or a personality-centered approach (Clark 1990). The culture-centered approach is a deductive framework that starts with critical observation of types of social structures, artifacts, and collective behavior, and identifies common elements that help sketch the modal personality that best represents the culture. Obviously, the underlying rationale behind this approach is simply that the institutions that make up a culture must have a psychological unity and an individual personality that reflects the national unity. The personality-centered approach can be described as starting with the observation and measurement of representative random samples to generate evaluations and identify common traits of the group. It uses a modal personality to represent a culture where individual personality traits are observed, enumerated, tabulated, and aggregated. Within the personality-centered approach, actual dimensioning of predominant cultural values may take any of two methods, purely conceptualized dimensions (Kluckhohn and Stradtbeck 1961) or empirical-based dimensions (Hofstede 1980).

The first empirical effort to validate the concept of national character was started by Hofstede (1980, 1983) and has revealed significant new findings. Methodologically, Hofstede surveyed workplace values possessed by 116,000 IBM workers of various occupations in 40 countries in two-wave studies. In the first study, a factor-analysis of the data revealed that nations can be relatively positioned on a bi-polar continuum in terms of (1) how members perceive their own power relative to others', and how they relate to authority (high/low Power-Distance), (2) the relative tolerance of ambiguity, lack of life structure, and risk-taking in life (high/low Uncertainty-Avoidance), (3) the degree to which society believes that members consider gender to be a determinant of specific roles and to what extent members endorse gender-specific values (Feminine cultures vs. Masculine cultures), and (4) how strongly members relate and show concern to others (Individualist cultures Vs. Collectivist cultures).

The validity of these dimensions was demonstrated in two subsequent studies. In a follow-up study that included more countries, Hofstede conducted a factor analysis of worker responses to the same scale and managed to extract the same dimensions thereby lending more support to the validity and reliability of these dimensions. In addition, a subsequent qualitative analysis of data drawn from completely unrelated sources in these nations (e.g., data from surveys of managers' values systems training at IMEDE in Lausanne, Switzerland, and via content analysis of children's books) was found to be correlated with one or more of these dimensions (Hofstede 1980, p.11, 22).

Values and Post-Consumption Satisfaction

As consumers see it, products represent a bundle of benefits rather than a mere set of attributes. These benefits may or may not be isomorphic to the utilitarian features of the product. Vehicles, for example are perceived by consumers as not only a medium of transportation with specific mechanical features but also as a display of personal wealth or social status, as an entertainment instrument, and as a symbol about the personal life style, to name a few. Desired benefits are needs that originate from personal values. If values determine what to choose, it may be reasonable to expect that values also influence other post-consumption constructs such as satisfaction with a chosen brand, attitude toward the brand, and loyalty to the brand.

To introduce the notion of values to satisfaction, Westbrook and Reilly (1983) proposed an alternative satisfaction model to the widely accepted 'disconfirmation paradigm' (Oliver 1980), labeled the Value-Precept Disparity Paradigm (VPDP). This model reconceptualized satisfaction from simply a comparison between expected performance and perceived performance to be the difference between what is valued by the customer and what has been experienced during product use. According to the authors, the main contribution is that, unlike the disconfirmation model which is descriptive of the process, the VPDP model offers a more parsimonious explanation of the satisfaction process, and has theoretical support in the marketing literature (Westbrook and Reilly 1983). This model seems to be in agreement with the theoretical proposition of Gutman (1982) Means-End model, which postulates that consumers' desires are extracted from high-end values, and that consumers are actively seeking products that have attributes that satisfy these desires. However, when the VPDP model was empirically tested against the disconfirmation paradigm, neither models fitted the data properly (both structural models had significant χ^2).

A later study by Parakash (1984) attempted to investigate the relationship between personal values and customer expectation of product performance. Parakash factor-analyzed 18 terminal values and 18 instrumental values possessed by white and black US consumers, and then correlated these factors to consumer normative expectations of product attributes (how the product should perform). His findings revealed that consumers basically derive their normative expectations from their values, which in turn exert more influence on satisfaction than did either predictive expectations (how the product will perform) or comparative expectations (how well the brand will perform compared to similar brands). These findings are important in light of the fact that normative expectations were found to be more directly related to satisfaction than were predictive expectations.

A later study by Spreng, MacKenzie and Olshavsky (1996) used structural equation modeling to examine the relationships between consumer desires, expectations, and perceived performance, and their relative influence on overall satisfaction responses. In controlled experimental setting, participants were assigned to six experimental groups (high/low expectations, high/low desires, and high/low performance and were asked to use and evaluate their satisfaction with a Camcorder. Their findings indicated that the congruency between desires and product performance strongly influenced attribute satisfaction (structural path coefficient = .63) as opposed to disconfirmation of expectation (structural path coefficient = .34).

In light of these findings, valued benefits exhibited direct impact on post-consumption satisfaction that shape subsequent constructs such as attitude and psychological loyalty. So far, there has been no work attempting to link personal values to cultural values, and these two sets together to the consumer general preferences. Next, research hypotheses will be presented.

Hypotheses

Power Distance

This dimension reflects the presence of human inequality created by disparate distribution of wealth, unequal political influence, and varying degree of family prominence. A particularly interesting artifact of the disparity of power in a society is the development of personal status (in general, individuals who have high power usually enjoy an elevated social status and vice versa). More often than not, individuals with power and status enjoy advantages such as social respect, greater access to economic opportunities, and an ability to control others' behavior. Over time, a social equilibrium process occurs in which individuals with low power strive to eliminate the gap in status by employing one or several power expanding strategies. These strategies include enhancement of physical strengths (i.e., athletic), intellectual abilities (e.g., education, skills), accumulation of wealth (i.e., saving, investment), and possession of status-enhancing products. While each of the preceding strategies increases perceived social power, the last method is particularly popular since power enhancing effects are almost instantaneous compared to other methods. To counterbalance the effect of newly gained power by weaker individuals, high-power individuals will either increase their power or reduce another persons' attempt to gain power.

H_1: In general, consumers living in a nation with large social power distance (in our case, Kuwait) tend to value products that provide benefits that enhance status and social image more than consumers living in nations with low power distance (i.e., US).

Uncertainty Avoidance

As the label of this dimension suggests, uncertainty avoidance reflects the degree to which members of a nation tolerate role ambiguity and lack of structure in life. This can be seen as a relative measure of fear of what the future might bring a concept Hofstede labeled 'National Anxiety'. Attempting to cope with future uncertainties produced several strategies that differ in terms of scope. On the individual level, guarding against the future requires continually enhancing personal skills, talents, and abilities. On the social level, individuals will try to reduce future uncertainties by pursuing strong interpersonal relationships with others and firm interfamilial ties.

H_{2a}: In general, consumers living in a nation with low tolerance for uncertainty (high uncertainty avoidance, i.e., Kuwait) should place more importance on personal abilities and interpersonal relationships than would individuals living in a low uncertainty avoidance nation (in our case, the US).

In the context of cross-national consumer behavior, it was found that cultures do indeed differ in terms of their tolerance for future ambiguity. Within cultures, intolerance for risk can take one of many forms, including reducing risk in purchasing. In general, a major reason why consumers prefer known brand names products over generic products is the level of confidence in the quality of performance. Well-known brands establish considerable trust and awareness with extensive promotional campaigns and standing behind their claims of product quality. Taking this linkage into consideration, it is expected that:

H_{2b}: Members of a national that tend to exhibit high uncertainty avoidance (Kuwait) generally prefer familiar brands with known levels of attribute quality over unfamiliar brands than would a nation with low uncertainty avoidance (US).

The Study

Two countries with presumably heterogeneous cultural value systems were selected for this study, namely Kuwait (N=121) and the US (Rhode Island, N=120). The selection of these two countries allowed us to choose two cultures that: (1) enjoy relatively similar standards of living and comparable marketing and retail industry structures; and (2) differ in terms of their cultural orientation (Western and Middle Eastern) and in terms of their relative positioning on the Hofstede dimensions of national character. A comparative analysis of the indicators presented in Table 1 reveals the similarity between the socioeconomic conditions of the residents of both countries. Furthermore, Kuwait, as a part of a cluster of Arab countries, scored high on both power distance and uncertainty avoidance. The United States, in comparison, scored low on power distance between individuals and on uncertainty avoidance.

A new computer notebook was used as the stimulus product for both groups in this study. This product category was deemed appropriate for the purposes of this study. There has been a rapid diffusion of personal computer machines for business and household use in both countries and the college student population has been one of the target markets for notebook makers. As such, participants are expected to possess ample prior knowledge to identify what kind of benefits and attributes are wanted in a computer and to judge its performance. Second, an important objective of our model is to examine whether greater power distance leads consumers to adopt status-enhancing consumption. Because notebook computers are considered as high-end products with prices far exceeding their desktop counterparts, and because they are portable and can be carried and used in public, notebook computers qualify as a status symbol, very similar to owning a cellular phone.

Table 3.1   Comparison Between Kuwait and Rhode Island on Standard of Living Indicators and Relative Position on Power Distance and Uncertainty Avoidance

INDICATORS	RHODE ISLAND (US)	KUWAIT
Population as of 1994 (thousands)	997	1,620 (41% nationals)
Income per Capita (after tax,1994)	16,274	$ 17,490
Literacy	98 %	63%
Number of autos (Car ownership ratio)	695,310 (1.4 person/car)	778,406 (2 persons/car)
Telephone per 1000s	5-20 telephone	5-20 telephone

Scores on Two Cultural Dimensions		
Power distance (out of 110)	40	85
Uncertainty Avoidance (out of 95)	46	66

Measures

Cultural Values

Relating cultural values to personal values should be preceded by a discussion of taxonomy of relevant cultural dimensions. Although previous work on cultural values has employed different frameworks to delineate relevant cultural dimensions, the focus of this research will be limited to exploring the interrelationships between Power Distance and Uncertainty Avoidance with personal values. The approach to measuring each of these two dimensions is described below.

Power Distance Scale (PDS)

This construct was traditionally measured using 3 items mentioned in the Hofstede original scale. All of these items dealt with employee perception of the behavior of their management (i.e., 'To what extent employees are afraid to disagree with their manager?', 'What is the present decision-making style of your manager?', and 'what is the preferred decision-making style?'). It was feared that measuring such a broad societal tendency using only three items related to workplace values might be too restrictive and may not capture the true presence of power distance.

In order to improve the measurement of this cultural dimension, a broader scale has been constructed including two of the three original items and 9 additional questions related to behaviors and perceptions closely associated with these dimensions. These additional items were all derived from Hofstede's observation of the broad consequences of Power Distances in society. All questions are scored using an 11-point scale, ranging from strongly disagree (1) to strongly agree (11).

Uncertainty Avoidance Scale (UAS)

The original scale measuring the uncertainty avoidance construct was composed of opinions expressed about three statements (Rules of the company should not be broken even when it is beneficial to break it; Perceived stress on the work place; and How long does the worker intend to stay with the company?). Again, concerns about the restrictive scope of these questions to behaviors in the workplace might risk the validity of the scale when introduced to a population other than company workers. The remedial approach taken here was similar to the power distance scale, where 7 more items were added based on Hofstede's conclusions about the ramifications of high/low Uncertainty Avoidance on some aspects of social perceptions and behavior.

Personal Values

The approach taken in measuring personal values was to use an already existing scale with established reliability and validity, called the List Of Values Scale (LOV, Kahle 1983). The original scale included 9 values (need to belong, wanting to live an exciting life, need for warm relationships, making the best use of talents, wanting other's respect and recognition, enjoying pleasurable life, wanting to feel safe, maintaining sense of self-respect, and the need to become successful). Post-modification of the LOV scale yielded 8 values, blending the *need for excitement in life* and *fun and enjoyment* into one category.

The scale's author conducted extensive testing to measure its reliability. Results from two studies designed to assess LOV's reliability over a month's time reported test-retest reliability coefficients of .92 and .85 (Kahle 1996). To maximize the scale's power of detecting the magnitude of individual preferences for each value on LOV, the author suggested using positive unbalanced scaling which ranges from important to most important as endpoints. The nomological validity of the LOV scale was established when the author observed a strong association between obtained scores and many aspects of personality traits and behaviors measured by other established scales.

Relative Strength of Cultural Affiliation

This scale is composed of four items. The first two items are direct measures of cultural identification and strength of affiliation (with what culture the participant identifies, how strongly the person feels affiliated to the culture of choice, Deshpande et al. 1986). The remaining two items are indirect measures of the strength of cultural affiliation (wearing national clothes outside the country and observing social celebrations and festivities outside the country). These measures were included to detect the strength of cultural affiliation.

Results

Scale Reliability and Dimensionality

The reliability of each scale was examined by calculating Cronbach's alpha coefficient of internal consistency (see table 2), which is based on the average of inter-item correlations. According to Novick and Lewis (1967), this reliability measure is a conservative estimate of lower bound reliability of unweighted items in a scale. Even though there was no agreed-upon minimum value to judge reliability, a reasonable threshold frequently mentioned in the business literature has been set at .70, although some researchers considered alpha values below .70 to be acceptable in research of exploratory purposes (e.g., Hair et al. 1995, p. 641).

Table 3.2   Assessment of Scales' Reliability

Scale	Number of Items (Factors)		Alpha Reliability		
	Items	(Factors)	Kuwait	US	Both
Personal Values (LOV)	8	(2)	.76	.81	.77
Power Distance (PDS)	11	(5)	.53	.55	.55
Uncertainty Avoidance (UAS)	10	(5)	.51	.65	.54

Exploratory Factor Analyses with Principal Component extraction procedures were applied to all items in each scale for each sample. Scales with small alpha coefficient (below .7), namely Valued Benefits, PDS, and UAS, were further examined to uncover their factor structure. Exploratory factor analysis was employed using a Principal Component Analysis (PCA) extraction and VARIMAX orthogonal rotation procedures, using a cut-off factor loading value (L_i) value of .40 to consider a variable as an indicator of a factor.

Factor analyzing the PDS scale with VARIMAX rotational procedures revealed a multidimensional factor structure for this scale. Initial examination of the extraction sum of squared loadings table suggests that power distance scale consisted of 5 factors in each sample, with the following range of communalities; for Kuwaiti sample, .43 - .78, and for US sample, .53 - .81. Because of the exploratory nature of this study, a special effort was made to explore this dimensionality and understand the nature of each factor in each sample. Visual inspection of the VARIMAX-rotated component matrix was employed to examine the similarity of the factor structure across the two samples. Though not completely reliable, the magnitudes and signs of factor loadings were used as criteria to examine the relative similarity of internal factor structure. It was concluded, based on the following discussion, that these five factors exhibited much more similarity than distinctiveness across the two samples.

A similar factor analysis and VARIMAX rotation procedure was employed to explore the dimensionality of the UAS scale. Five factors were extracted explaining 66% and 70% of total scale variance in Kuwaiti and US samples, with communalities ranging from .39 to .71 and .56 to .88 respectively. The rotated matrix of factor loadings was closely investigated in each sample to determine the structure of retained factors.

Because of the inherently subjective nature of a visual inspection method of rotated factor loadings, it was felt that a statistical test with more discriminatory power should be performed to examine the validity of these findings. Cattell's Salient Similarity Index, s, (Cattell and Baggaley 1960) was selected for this study (see Cattell et al. 1969 for a full explanation of this method and significance tables). Of the five factors extracted from PDS, the first four factors were found to be significantly similar for the two groups (p-value for these factors were in the following order: .008, .015, .028, and < .001) while factor 5 was not (p-value = .105). The similarity testing for the first two factors extracted from UAS were found to be significant (p-value for both factors < .001) while the third factor was not (p-value = .07). Testing the significance for the last two factors was indeterminate due to the absence of table values for Hyperplane proportions below 60% and the inapplicability of interpolation methods for this case. Out of the 10 factors examined in both sets, 7 were found to be similar.

Validating Study Assumptions

In his typology of national character, Hofstede proposed that Kuwaitis should have higher power distance between individuals than their American counterparts would have in their society. His typology also portrayed Kuwaitis to be less tolerant of vagueness and lack of structure in life compared to the Americans. Results from MANOVA and simple one-way ANOVA were generally supportive of this contention, despite the failing of some items to emerge at the desired level of significance. In the following sections, measurement findings from each scale in each country are reported.

Results of (M)ANOVA on (PDS)

Multivariate Analysis of Variance (MANOVA) was run using all items in PDS as continuous dependent variables and using country as the dichotomous independent variable. Special attention was paid to insure that MANOVA assumptions were met including normality, independence among observations, and multivariate normality. Only results from the Box test showed an inequality of the variance-covariance matrix, however, this inequality is not problematic because the cell size is approximately equal (Hair et al. 1995, p. 275).

To measure the direction of this omnibus between-sample difference, all items on the scale were summed up to form a composite score (negatively framed questions were reversed) and then analyzed using one-way ANOVA. Results clearly showed that Kuwaitis score higher on power distance scale relative to Americans, (M_K=75.89 and M_{US} =70.40, main effect for country difference $F_{[1,239]}$ = 21.48, $p < .0001$).

A follow up procedure was conducted to identify differences in individual items, both in terms of magnitude and direction. Of the 11 items used to measure power distance, 5 items were found to be statistically significant in the expected direction. The remaining six power distance items were found to be in the right direction but failed to reach the .05 level of significance, which can be attributed to some loss of power due to small sample size. In conclusion, these results show that Kuwaitis differ markedly from Americans on some dimensions of power but not on the others.

Results of (M)ANOVA on UAS

The retained item pool used in constructing this scale consists of 10 main questions measuring the extent to which individuals, as a whole, tolerate role ambiguity and lack of structure in life and society. According to the classification of cultures on this dimension, Kuwait should have strong uncertainty avoidance relative to Americans. Results obtained from applying MANOVA to all items in the UAS scale tend to support this view, the main effect for country difference $F_{[10,221]}$ = 24.17, $p < .0001$, $\eta^2 = .53$). A composite score for all items, similar to the power distance scale, was analyzed in a one-way ANOVA to examine between-country differences in terms of magnitude and direction. Results revealed that Kuwaitis were less tolerant toward uncertainty (high uncertainty avoidance) when compared to Americans (M_K=75.33 and M_{US} =67.89, main effect for country difference $F_{[1,239]}$ = 41.67, $p < .0001$, $\eta^2 = .15$).

Follow up one-way ANOVAs were performed to identify the magnitude and significance of each item generated mixed results. Of the ten items employed to measure uncertainty avoidance, six were found to be significantly different at the .05 level, with mean order consistent with original hypotheses. Mean scores and significance of the remaining four items were inconsistent with the prior predictions

Marketing and Multicultural Diversity

either due to insignificant between-country differences or to significant results but in the wrong order. While it's hoped that all item scales will be consistent with the original prediction, these results lend support to differences on the UAS scale between the two countries.

Hypotheses Testing

Hypothesis One

One-way ANOVA and bivariate correlational analysis were used to test the first hypothesis as to whether consumers living in high power-distanced cultures value and consume status-enhancing products more than consumers living in cultures with relatively smaller power distances. Results obtained from running one-way ANOVA on item 9 (which measured the extent to which people are evaluated based on what they own such as clothing quality, vehicle luxury, and house elegance) showed that Kuwaitis scored higher (M_K =8.88 and M_{US} =8.12, main effect for country difference $F_{[1,239]}$ = 9.548, p < .002). To assess the relative strength between perceived power distance and the tendency to consume status-enhancing products, a bivariate correlation was computed using individuals' composite score and scores obtained on item 9. Results revealed a fair correlation coefficient (r = .279) which is significant at .001 level (Table 3).

Table 3.3   Correlating PDS and UAS with Social Image, Family Ties, and Brand Loyalty Using the Pooled Sample

VARIABLE NAME	2	3	4	5
1. Image-Enhancing Consumption	.115	.142[*]	.279[**]	.243[**]
2. Brand Loyalty		.043	.119	.146[*]
3. Strong Family Ties			.272[**]	.385[**]
4. PDS Composite Score				.376[**]
5. UAS Composite Score				1.0

[*]   Correlation is significant at the 0.05 level (2-tailed).
[**]   Correlation is significant at the 0.01 level (2-tailed).

The desirability for enhanced social image was also examined by assessing how respondents from each country differed in their preferences for reputation as a valued benefit in the notebook computer. Kuwaitis were found to place more emphasis on this benefit compared to their American counterparts at a statistically significant level (M_K =7.58 and M_{US} =6.13, main effect for country difference $F_{[1,239]}$ = 18.65548, p < .001).

Hypothesis Two

This hypothesis consisted of two parts. In the first part, it was predicted that individuals living in cultures in which intolerance of ambiguity and lack of structure in life are relatively high (i.e., Kuwaitis) would tend to place more importance on strengthening family ties to guard against future hardships (social level strategy) and making the best use of talents and abilities (individual level strategy) than others living in low uncertainty avoidance cultures (i.e., Americans). Results obtained from one-way ANOVA and correlation procedures were mixed (see table 4). On the one hand, Kuwaitis expressed more emphasis on establishing strong familial ties to guard against future hardships than did Americans (M_K=9.18 and M_{US} = 7.87, country main effect $F_{[1,239]}$ = 103.288, p < .001) while a moderate size correlation was found between UAS composite score and strengthening familial ties (bivariate r = .39, p < .01). On the other hand, no statistically significant differences were observed between the level of importance Kuwaitis and Americans assign to making the best use of their talents and abilities (M_K=9.37 and M_{US} = 9.34, country main effect $F_{[1,239]}$ = 0.047, p < .91). In the second part, it was proposed that members of the high uncertainty avoidance culture prefer purchasing familiar brands to generics. Results obtained from between-countries ANOVA were statistically insignificant (M_K=6.98 and M_{US} = 6.74, country main effect $F_{[1,239]}$ = 3.455, p < .44) and no further follow-up analysis was performed. It was, therefore, concluded that no support was found for this part.

Table 3.4   Summary Descriptive Statistics and One-Way ANOVA for Social Image, Family Ties, and Brand Loyalty: Two Countries

ITEM	GROUP	N	MEAN	SD	SE
Social Respect Derived from consuming Status enhancing products	Kuwait	120	8.88	2.12	.19
	US	121	8.12	1.66	.15
	Total	241	8.49	1.94	.13
Strengthening Family ties to guard Against the Future	Kuwait	120	9.18	1.74	.16
	US	121	7.87	1.80	.16
	Total	241	8.53	1.88	.12
Preference for well-known brands over generic	Kuwait	120	6.98	2.46	.22
	US	121	6.74	2.38	.22
	Total	241	6.85	2.42	.16

ANOVA RESULTS							
ITEM	source	SS	df	MS	F	η^2	sig.
People judge other based on the quality of their possessions	B.G.	34.7	1	34.74	9.6	.042	.002
	W.G	869.5	239	3.64			
	Total	904.2	240				
People should maintain strong familial ties to face future hardships	B.G.	103.2	1	103.2	33	.13	.00
	W.G	749.1	239	3.13			
	Total	852.3	240				
Buying well-known brands over generic brands	B.G.	3.5	1	3.455	.59	.002	.443
	W.G	1400.5	239	5.860			
	Total	1403.9	240				

Conclusions

The results of this study were found to be consistent with predictions derived from previous research on cultural values, and provided some, though not complete, evidence supporting the effects of values on some important aspects of consumer behavior. This research has also shown that, as predicted by Hofstede (1980), Kuwaitis have a higher level of power distance and uncertainty avoidance compared to their American counterparts. Moreover, the general findings of this study tend to support the existence of a relationship between personal values and cultural values, though some of the results were not as strong as was predicted. As demonstrated by results obtained from canonical correlation analysis, it was found that there is, at least, one reliable form of linear association between each of the two dimensions of national character with personal values. The somewhat small size of redundancy variance explained by the canonical root did not lend equivocal support to practical significance of this root.

Personal and Cultural Value Systems

Findings obtained from applying canonical correlation procedures uncovered at least one reliable canonical root linking relative power distance and strength of uncertainty avoidance, separately, to The absence of rotational techniques in present statistical software hindered, to some extent, the interpretation of pairs of canonical variates, so the matrix of canonical loadings was examined to aid the decision as to identify the variables forming the extracted variates in each set.

For PDS, findings from the pooled sample reveal that a higher need for social acceptance and for others' respect is positively correlated with both social and managerial power-expressive behaviors. Follow up analysis performed on the Kuwaiti sample suggests that personal values related to the desire for more social acceptance, more security, and a less exciting life were all found to be associated with power-expressive social behaviors. In contrast, the same personal values reemerged in the US sample and were associated with power-expressive behaviors, but limited to managerial context. Taken together, the pattern of these results strongly suggests that power expressive behaviors, either social or managerial, are associated with outward personal values. Yet, the strength of these results should be cautiously interpreted, because the amount of variability LOV explained by the variability of PDS was on the low side (from 2% to 4%). One explanation for observing such a small redundancy is related to the way the index is built. Because the procedure involves averaging squared correlation coefficients between a variate and the variables composing the other variate using equal weights, the large number of variables with insignificant coefficients has diluted the effects of the smaller number of variables with significant coefficients.

The canonical association between LOV and UAS was relatively stronger than the relationship observed between LOV and PDS, both in terms of magnitude of canonical roots (.52 to .64) and redundancy (4% to 9.4%). For Kuwaitis, preference for outer-directed values (belonging, warm relationship and being well respected) was associated with the magnitude and sources of uncertainty (level of worry about the future and relative intolerance of socially conflicting opinions). For the US group, mostly inner-directed values (security, accomplishment, and belonging) were found to be related to future anxiety and preference for homogenous social opinions.

These forms of association do not, however, ascertain whether people with a stronger need for social acceptance and others' respect are driven to practice more power-expressive behaviors or conversely, the presence of large power distance (and its related behaviors) leads its members to favor this subset of personal values (the same argument applies to observed relationship between LOV and UAS). Yet, it is intuitive that the latter is more likely. Through socialization, individuals learn the values, norms, and attitudes of the community, which then become a primary influence on the way individuals define themselves, their roles, and their interests at the personal level. Admittedly, answering this question requires a longitudinal analysis rather than the cross-sectional approach taken in this study.

PDS, UAS and Relative Importance of Personal Values

Main effects of country on the importance of personal values were examined using one-way ANOVA, and yielded mixed results. Citizens of both countries equally valued self-fulfillment, Kuwaitis were found to value self-respect less than Americans (consistent with earlier prediction), while Kuwaitis expressed higher desire for sense of belonging than did Americans.

Complexity of Cultural Values

The multidimensionality of factor structures of the PDS and UAS scales was viewed, paradoxically, as a point of interest and a cause for concern. Hofstedes' measurement of workplace values involved three items for each of the two chosen cultural dimensions, but clearly, the relevance (and hence the validity) of such indicators becomes questionable when applied to cultural contexts other than the organizational culture. In response, the scale was expanded by adding items measuring the social and managerial consequences of power distance and uncertainty avoidance, items that Hofstede uncovered using qualitative analyses. Given the level of association that one might expect to find between indicators and consequences of a phenomenon, it was expected that two factors would emerge, the first measuring the magnitude of each dimension and the other measuring its consequences. However, results obtained from factor analyses suggested the presence of five reliable factors in each scale, with somewhat similar, but not identical, factor structures between the two countries. The retention of a 5-factor solution in each scale was immediately followed by an extensive factor labeling process that relied heavily on both the researcher's conceptual judgment of marker item contents and on the use of more objective similarity indices to ensure factor interpretability and cross-group validity.

It could be said that the elaborate factor structure uncovered in this study indicates both the richness and the complexity of these two dimensions of national character. These findings show that the extent to which power distances exist in society should be measured at many different levels including beliefs about sources of power, attitudes toward high power, and prevalence of power expressing behaviors in society. Likewise, the emergence of a 5-factor solution in the uncertainty avoidance scale suggests a complex structure of this cultural dimension, more than what Hofstede initially had proposed and measured in his famous study. It is the contention of the present author that the measurement of relative tolerance for future risk and lack of structure in life would be greatly enhanced if a more coherent set of items can be generated and tested in future research.

Values and Wanted Product Benefits

Hypothesis one predicted that consumers in the country with high level of power distances (i.e., Kuwait) would exhibit more preference for products that provide enhanced social image compared to individuals living in countries with more power equality. The genesis of this hypothesis originates primarily from the theory of conspicuous consumption, which suggests that consumers may not consume products merely to satisfy themselves, but rather to satisfy others in their communities. But for ostentatious consumption to be prevalent in society, individuals should believe that evaluation of others based on the luxury of possession is a common practice, and more importantly, individuals should also believe that ostentatious consumption should contribute to improving their social status. As such, question 9 in the questionnaire was coined to measure the presence of this practice in both countries at an absolute level, while measuring the relative importance of creating a favorable reputation when using a mobile computer measured this phenomenon at the product level. Results generated from running one-way ANOVA procedures on these two items provided ample support for this prediction, although estimates of effect size measures (η^2) were relatively small (η^2 = .04 and .07 respectively).

Theories of conspicuous consumption behavior were divided on identifying the main motive for pursuing this overt display of wealth (Mason 1981). In his book, he explained that the old school of thought attributes leisure consumption to innate personality traits that motivate the individual to favor distinctiveness from others, while the contemporaneous school considers this form of consumption as an effort on the part of the individual to improve social status. If one subscribes to the later view, overt display of power and wealth, and hence, ostentatious consumption, would then be more likely to occur in societies with large power disparities as opposed to societies with relatively even power structure. Fortunately, because the two cultures chosen for this study do not have family or birth-restricted social classes, social mobility of individuals can be achieved by means of conspicuous spending.

Because self-reporting was the approach taken in measuring the presence of conspicuous consumption, demand artifacts and social desirability may have inhibited the full measurement of this behavior. For Kuwaitis, admitting the presence of, let alone engaging in, the practices of conspicuous consumption is susceptible to the moderating effects of religion. According to Islamic beliefs, lavish lifestyle and wasteful spending are highly discouraged, which, under the pressure of social desirability, some respondents might have been less open and candid about this behavior. This concern becomes more real in light of the fact that Kuwaitis have reported higher adherence to religion than did their American counterparts at a statistically significant level.

The second hypothesis contained two parts with two distinct predictions. In the first part, it was stated that nationals of cultures with a high level of uncertainty avoidance attempt to reduce the undesirable effects of uncertainty by enhancing personal talents and abilities and by building stronger ties with their families. In the second part, it was stated that, given that uncertainty avoidance is, in fact, a culture-wide measure of risk aversion in general, it would be expected that avoiding ambiguity in general might also affect personal preferences for familiar well-known brands over generic products with uncertain, and highly variant, quality.

Results generated from one-way ANOVA and bivariate correlational analyses (see 'Results' section) failed to provide firm support for all the predictions made in the first part of hypothesis 2. Respondents in the Kuwaiti group were found to be more concerned with building stronger ties with their families to cope with the unpredictable future, however, both Kuwaitis and Americans were equally concerned with making the best use of their talents and abilities. Similarly, no support was found for predictions made in second part of hypothesis 2.

One possible explanation for this lack of association lies with the level at which uncertainty-avoidance tendency may be operating. Anxieties generated from a high level of uncertainty are not manifested in individual level behaviors such as those related to consumption, but might be evidenced in other forms of social behaviors, such as more emphasis on familial unity.

Generally, results generated from canonical correlation were supportive of the linkages between general human values and benefits wanted at the product level. In the consumer literature, it has been theorized that values guide many aspects of human behavior, including those pertaining to buying and consumption. Gutmans' (1982) means-end chain model conceptualizes values as 'end states of existence' and products as 'means' employed to satisfy an end. Thus, it is anticipated that in a competitive market with a variety of differentiated products, product choice, and ultimately the satisfaction with that choice, are dependent on the degree of match between initial personal values and the kind of benefits provided by the product.

From this study, and from other studies reported elsewhere, it was found that the cultural background of the consumer leads to subtle differences in the degree of importance assigned to some personal values. If one accepts the argument that values indeed guide consumer behavior, it might be reasonable to expect that cross-cultural variability of importance assigned to values might very well lead to the display of different consumer behaviors, including product choice and evaluations.

References

Adler, N.J. (1983), 'Cross-Cultural Management Research: The Ostrich and the Trend,' *Academy of Management Review*, 8, 226-232.

Beatty, S.E., L. Kahle, P.M. Homer and S. Misra (1985), 'Alternative Measurements Approach to Consumer Values: The List of Values and the Rokeach Value Survey,' *Psychology and Marketing*, 2, 181-200.

Cattell, R. B. and A. R. Baggaley (1960), 'The Salient Variable Similarity Index for Factor Matching,' *British Journal of Statistical Psychology*, 13, 33-46.

_____, K. R. Balcar, J. L. Horn, and J. R. Nesselroade (1969), 'Factor Matching Procedures: an Improvement to the Index; With Tables,' *Educational and Statistical Measurement*, 29, 781-792.

Clark, Terry (1990), 'International marketing and National Character: A Review and Proposal for an Integrative Theory,' *Journal of Marketing*, October, 54 (3), 66-79.

Clawson, C. J. and D. E. Vinson, 'Human Values: An Historical and ary Analysis,' In *Contributions to Consumer Research*, 5, Keith ssociation for Consumer Research, 396-402.

A. (1992), 'An Assessment of the State of Customer Satisfaction

Measurement Research: Total and Global,' *In Marketing in the New Europe*, 44th ESOMAR Congress, Joint Session on Customer Satisfaction and Quality Management, Amsterdam, 37-48.

Deshpande, Rohit, Hoyer, Wayne, and Naveen Donthu (1986), 'The intensity of Ethnic Affiliation: A study of the Sociology of Hispanic Consumption,' *Journal of Consumer Research*, 13 (September), 214-220.

Durvasula, Srinivas, J. Craig Adrews, Steven Lysonski and Richard Netemeyer (1993), Assessing the Cross-national Applicability of Consumer Behavior Models: A Model of Attitude Toward Advertising in General, *Journal of Consumer Research*, 19 (March), 626-636.

Fornell, Claes (1992), 'A National Customer Satisfaction Barometer: The Swedish Experience,' *Journal of Marketing*, 56, 1 (January), 6-21.

_____, Michael D. Johnson, Eugene W. Anderson, Jaesung Cha, and Barbara E. Bryant (1996), 'The American Customer Satisfaction Index: Nature, Purpose, and Findings,' *Journal of Marketing*, 60, 4 (October), 7-18.

Gatignon, Hubert and Thomas S. Robertson (1985), 'A Propositional Inventory for New Diffusion Research,' *Journal of Consumer Research*, 11 (March), 849-867.

Gutman, Jonathan (1982), 'A Means-End Chain Model Based on Consumer Categorization Process,' *Journal of Marketing*, 46, Spring, 60-72.

Hair Joseph, Rolph Anderson, Ronald Tatham, and William Black (1995), *Multivariate Data Analysis with Readings*, Fourth Edition, Prentice Hall: New Jersey.

Heenan, David A (1988), 'The Case for Convergent Capitalism,' *Journal of Business Strategy*, November/December, 54-57.

Henry, W. A. (1976), 'Cultural Values Do Correlate With Consumer Behavior,' *Journal of Marketing Research*, (May), 13, 121-128.

Hernandez, Sigfredo A., Strahle, William, Gracia, Hector L. and Sorensen, Robert C. (1991), 'A Cross-Cultural Study of Consumer Complaining Behavior: VCR Owners in US and Puerto Rico,' *Journal of Consumer Policy*, 14, 35-62.

Hofstede, Geert A. (1980), 'Motivation, Leadership and Organization: Do American Theories Apply Abroad,' *Organizational Dynamics*, Summer, 9 (1), 42.

_____, (1983), 'The Cultural Relativity of Organizational Practices and Theories,' *Journal of International Business Studies*, 14 (3), 75-89.

Howard, John and J. N. Sheth (1969), *The Theory of Buyer Behavior*. New York: John Wiley & Sons.

Inkele, Alex and Daniel J. Levinston (1969), 'National Character: The Study of Modal Personality and Sociocultural Systems,' in *The Handbook of Social Psychology*, 4, 2nd eds., G. Lindzy and E. Aronson , eds., Cambridge, MA: Addison-Wesley Publishing Company.

Kahle, Lynn R. (1983), *Social Values and Social Change: Adaptation to Life in*

America. New York: Praeger.

_____, (1986), 'The Nine Nations of North America and the Value Basis for Geographical Segmentation,' *Journal of Marketing*, 50, 37-47.

_____, (1996), 'Social Values and Consumer Behavior: Research from the List of Values,' In Clive Seligman, James M. Olson, and Mark P. Zanna, eds., *The Psychology of Values: The Ontario Symposium Vol. 8*, Hillsdale, NJ: Lawrence Erlbaum Associates, 135-151.

Kluckhohn, F. R. and F. L. Strodtbeck (1961), *Variations in Value Orientations*, Westport, CT: Greenwood Press.

Kotler, Philip (1994), *Marketing Management*, New Jersey: Prentice Hall, Inc.

Levitt, R. T. (1983) 'The Globalization of Markets,' *Harvard Business Review,* May/June, 92-102.

Lowenstein, Michael, W. (1995), *Customer Retention: An Integrated Process for Keeping your Best Customers,* Milwaukee: Wisconsin, ASQC Quality Press.

Oliver, Richard L. (1980), 'A Cognitive Model of the Antecedents and Consequences of Satisfaction Decisions,' *Journal of Marketing Research*, 17, 460-469.

Mason, Roger S. (1981), *Conspicuous Consumption: A Study Of Exceptional Consumer Behavior*. New York: St. Martin's Press.

Novick M. and G. Lewis (1976), 'Coefficient Alpha and the Reliability of Composite Measurements,' *Psychometrika*, 32, 1-13.

Ness Thomas E. and Melvin T. Stith (1984) 'Middle Class Values in Blacks and Whites,' In *Personal Values and Consumer Psychology,* Robert E. Pitts and Arch Woodside, eds., Canada: DC Heath and Company, 145-151.

Parakash, Ved (1984), 'Consumer Values and Product Expectations,' In *Personal Values and Consumer Psychology*, Robert E. Pitts and Arch Woodside, eds., Canada: DC Heath and Company, 145-151.

Posner, B.Z. and J.M. Munson (1979), 'The importance of Personal Values in Understanding Organizational Behavior,' *Journal of Human Resource Management*, 18, 9-14.

Rokeach, M. (1973), *The Nature of Human Values*, New York: Free Press.

Spreng, Richard A., Scot B. MacKenzie, and Richard W. Olshavsky (1996), 'A Reexamination of the Determinants of Consumer Satisfaction,' *Journal of Marketing*, 60 (3), 15-32.

Westbrook, Robert A. and Michael D. Reilly (1983), 'Value Precept Disparity: an Alternative to the Disconfirmation of Expectation Theory of Consumer Satisfaction,' in *Advances of Consumer Research*, Richard P. Bagozzi and Alice M. Tybout, eds. Ann Arbor, MI; Association of Consumer Research, 256-261.

Yau, Oliver H. (1988), 'Chinese Cultural Values: Their Dimensions and Marketing Implications,' *European Journal of Marketing*, 22 (5), 44-57.

Chapter 4

Consumption as a Function of Ethnic Identification and Acculturation

Michael Hui
Michel Laroche
Chankon Kim

Introduction

This chapter examines consumption as a function of ethnic identification and acculturation. When comparing the consumption patterns of ethnic minorities with their mainstream counterparts, past researchers tended to take a uni-dimensional approach. In general, consumption is analyzed as a function of a linear composite of various ethnicity indicators. However, in the cross-cultural psychology literature, ample evidence has indicated these ethnicity indicators are hardly uni-dimensional in nature as they are determined by two correlated but distinctive factors – ethnic identification and acculturation. This chapter empirically tests the relative power of ethnic identification and acculturation in predicting lifestyle and consumption behaviors of a sample of French-Canadians residing in Toronto. A new two-dimensional typology of ethnic consumption behaviors will also be introduced.

The recent surge of interest in the study of ethnicity and its impact on consumer behavior reflects a belief that consumption is primarily a cultural phenomenon (Webster, 1994; Lee, 1993; Donthu & Cherian, 1992; Hirschman, 1981; Wallendorf & Reilly, 1983; Deshpande, Hoyer, & Donthu, 1986; Schaninger, Bourgeois, & Buss, 1985). A major focus of these studies has been the identification of ethnic minority group membership and finding idiosyncrasies in behaviours and attitudes, relative to those of the mainstream group, that are of importance to decision makers.

Results obtained from a recent empirical study suggest that ethnic identification and acculturation are two correlated but distinctive dimensions of ethnicity or ethnic change (Berry, 1980). Ethnic identification refers to an ethnic individual's identification with and maintenance of the original ethnic identity, or to the acquisition of cultural traits of the mainstream society. One important implication of this two-dimensional perspective of ethnic change is that ethnicity indicators commonly employed by consumer researchers may actually vary in terms of the extent to which these indicators are amenable to acculturative pressure. Indicators of ethnic identification (such as ethnic self-labeling) are ethnic behaviors that tend to change in a highly gentle pace; those that may take many years of continuous contact with the mainstream group before any significant changes would likely occur (Laroche et al., 1998). On the other hand, indicators of acculturation (such as language use/exposure) are ethnic behaviors that tend to undergo substantial changes as a result of continuous contact with the mainstream group. The first objective of this study is to provide empirical support to our argument that ethnicity indicators commonly employed by researchers are multi-dimensional in nature, with ethnic identification and acculturation as the two key underlying factors.

Arbitrary use of these indicators may result in inconsistent research findings and deter researchers from exploring the complex relationship between ethnicity and consumption. Existing evidence has shown that different ethnicity indicators may lead to different predictions of behaviors of ethnic minorities (Carvajal, 1997). It is not uncommon to have a person with an ethnic minority origin but use primarily the mainstream language in his/her daily communication (Berry, 1980; O'Guinn & Faber, 1985; Jun, Ball, & Gentry, 1993). The same person could be considered 'slightly ethnic' (as far as language is concerned) or 'strongly ethnic' (as far as ethnic origin is concerned), depending on the measure used to operationalize the construct of ethnicity. In this paper, we attempt to examine consumption as function of ethnic identification and acculturation as two distinctive factors.

As suggested by Glock and Nicosia (1964), some minority consumption behaviors are associated with the core values of an ethnic group and they are unlikely to undergo drastic acculturative changes. Ethnic identification should therefore be a more powerful predictor of this type of consumption behaviors than acculturation. On the other hand, ethnic minority individual may exhibit significant changes in some of their consumption behaviors even after some minimal contact with the mainstream group. Accordingly, acculturation should be a more powerful predictor of this type of consumption behaviors than ethnic identification. The second objective of this paper is to examine the relative power of ethnic identification and acculturation in predicting two different sets of consumption variables, one related to consumer lifestyle patterns and the other to the consumption patterns of convenience food products and alcoholic drinks. By looking into consumption as a function of ethnic identification and acculturation, we will also present a new typology of ethnic consumption behaviors.

Ethnic Identification and Acculturation

Most of the definitions of ethnicity found in the extant literature tend to agree that, at a general level, the concept refers to the character or quality encompassing several cultural indicators that are used to assign people to groupings. Besides, ethnicity is widely accepted as a dynamic and adaptable concept because cultural traits may change as a result of some large scale economic, political, and demographic trends (Paranjpe, 1986).

Existing evidence suggests that some ethnic traits tend to be more amenable to acculturative pressure than others (Laroche et al., 1996). For example, Rosenthal and Feldman (1992) proposed a distinction between 'core' elements and 'peripheral' elements of ethnicity, and suggested that the former may be less changeable than the latter over time. Their findings indeed showed that the second-generation adolescent Chinese Americans, despite their higher degree of behavioral acculturation toward American society (i.e., peripheral elements), did not differ from their first-generation counterparts in the perceived importance or positive valuation of Chinese ethnicity (i.e., core elements).

Keefe and Padilla (1987) also found that an individual's knowledge of cultural traits of the traditional culture decreased at a fast rate in the first and second generations, and continued to decrease at a slower but steady rate in the third and fourth generations. On the other hand, loyalty exhibited by the same individual toward the traditional culture decreased slightly between the first and second generations, and thereafter it remained virtually constant through the fourth generation. Keefe and Padilla (1987) concluded that: 'The loss of cultural awareness on the part of respondents is at least partially independent of ethnic loyalty, which explains why it is not uncommon to meet a third-or-fourth-generation Mexican American who does not speak Spanish and knows relatively little about his/her cultural background, but retains pride in his/her Mexican heritage and enjoys associating with Mexican people' (p.52).

A review of existing cross-cultural marketing studies suggests that there is a trend toward the recognition of the dynamic and adaptable nature of ethnicity. Departing from the traditional dichotomous conceptualization of ethnicity (i.e., one does or does not belong to an ethnic group), Hirschman (1981) argued for the need to measure a person's degree of identification to his/her group of origin. Similarly, in the investigation of consumption differences between French- and English-Canadians, Schaninger, Bourgeois, and Buss (1985) added a third 'bilingual' group to the traditional dichotomous French- and English-Canadian ethnic classification, which included individuals with varying degrees of acculturation toward either cultural group.

The multifaceted nature of ethnicity is also well reflected in the extant cross-cultural marketing literature. In addition to ethnic self-labeling, Hirschman (1981) also incorporated religion into her measure of Jewish ethnicity. In their study of Hispanic ethnicity, O'Guinn and Faber (1985) derived two different scales, a general acculturation scale and a consumer acculturation scale, which included measures of an individual's national origin, general language preference, demographic variables, and the preferred language for shopping and for using in consumer specific roles. Similar multifaceted operationalization of ethnicity can also be found in many other studies, including Valencia (1985), Lee (1993), Donthu and Cherian (1992), and Webster (1994) to operationalize ethnicity.

As mentioned earlier, all these different ethnicity facets vary in terms of the extent to which they are influenced by acculturation. For example, Laroche et al. (1998) have shown that although both language use/exposure and ethnic self-labeling are inter-related and common ethnicity indicators employed by past researchers, the prior ethnicity facet is significantly more amenable to acculturative influence than the latter ethnicity facet. Results obtained from surveying various ethnicity minority groups in Canada indicate that even for those who indicate English to be their only language use/exposure, they still very much maintain their minority self-labeling. Accordingly, language use/exposure can be considered to be more a formative ethnicity indicator while ethnic self-labeling can be considered to be more a reflective ethnicity indicator. An extreme example of reflective ethnicity indicators is ethnic origin, which is a de facto characteristic of any minority member. A tenth-generation Mexican-American would hardly be identified by others as Hispanic based on his/her physical appearance and behaviors, but s/he still cannot deny his/her Mexican ancestry, as stated by Penaloza (1994, p.35):

> … I am a tenth-generation Mexican American from San Antonio, Texas. I differ from informants [Mexican immigrants] in my color, gender, class and residence in relation to that imaginary line, the United States-Mexico border. In my family I am called Guera, a Spanish term for women who can pass as white. Because I do not physically resemble Mexican Americans, I am seldom identified as a member of this group, yet this is the group with which I identify.

If common ethnicity indicators do in fact vary significantly in terms of the extent to which an indicator is amenable to acculturative influence, these indicators will not be uni-dimensional in nature. Our first research hypothesis is therefore formulated as follows:

H1: A factor analysis of common ethnicity indicators will produce a two-factor rather than single-factor solution.

Ethnicity and Consumption

The relationship between ethnicity and consumption has drawn considerable attention from marketers.

The distinction between ethnic origin as a reflective ethnicity indicator and language of exposure to mass media as a formative ethnicity indicator is important when marketers attempt to explain and predict consumer behavior as a function of ethnicity. Some consumption activities are more ingrained in the culture of a person's group of origin and are, thus, less likely to change as a result of continuous contacts with the host group. Some other consumption traits are more prone to the influence of acculturating forces and may change even after some very minimal contacts with the majority group. For example, Lee and Tse (1994b) found that the immigrants' duration of residence in Canada has significant effects on their culture-irrelevant activities (i.e., activities that have no conflict with one's culture of origin; e.g., waxing the car) but no effect on their culture-relevant activities such as celebrating ethnic festivals. The distinction between these two types of consumption activities is analogous to that between the reflective and formative ethnicity indicators. Accordingly, culture-relevant activities should be better predicted by ethnic origin (a reflective indicator) than by language of exposure to mass media (a formative indicator) while the opposite should be true for cultural-irrelevant activities.

A typology of consumption (Table 1; the examples listed in each category are explained in the results section) is developed based on (a) the distinction between the reflective and the formative ethnicity indicators, and (b) Mendoza's (1989) four acculturation patterns: cultural resistance, cultural shift, cultural incorporation and cultural transmutation. Cultural resistance is defined as 'either active or passive [resistance] against the acquisition of alternate norms, while maintaining native customs' (Mendoza, 1989, p.373). When product consumption or a lifestyle dimension is a function of the reflective ethnicity indicator only, the product/ lifestyle can be labeled as a 'cultural resistant' one as continuous contact with the majority group will probably not change the behavior of the minority group.

Table 4.1   A Typology of Consumption Based on the Two Ethnicity Indicators

		(a) The reflective ethnicity indicator?	
		Yes	No
(b) The formative ethnicity indicator?	Yes	Cultural incorporation or cultural transmutation[a] (e.g., rye, cognac and frozen vegetables)	Cultural shift (e.g., Vodka and canned baked beans)
	No	Cultural resistance (e.g., scotch and attitudes towards housework)	Non-cultural product (e.g., dry gin and canned salmon)

[a] The difference between cultural incorporation and cultural transmutation is whether the combined effect of the reflective and the formative ethnicity indicators will result in a consumption pattern that is between or beyond the two anchors defined by the majority culture and the minority culture. For example, the consumption frequency of rye by consumers of FC origin is not expected to surpass the consumption frequency of EC regardless of their extent of acculturation. On the other hand, unacculturated FC will drink more cognac than EC but, when acculturated, FC may drink less cognac than EC.

Cultural shift refers to 'a substitution of alternative cultural norms for native customs' (Mendoza, 1989, p.373). This is similar to what Yinger (1985) and Berry (1980; Berry et al., 1992, Chapter 12) have labeled assimilation. In terms of consumption, this implies that in continuous contacts with the majority culture, minority group members will gradually change their consumption behaviors or lifestyles and will ultimately behave in ways identical to majority group members. This is the case when the consumption of a product is a function of the formative ethnicity indicator only.

Cultural incorporation indicates 'an adaptation of customs from both native and alternate cultures' (Mendoza, 1989, p.373). In other words, although minority group members may shift their consumption or lifestyle patterns toward that of the host group, assimilation of the minority group (i.e., to a pattern identical to the majority group) is rather unlikely. Cultural transmutation is 'an alteration of native and alternate cultural practices to create a unique subcultural entity' (Mendoza, 1989, p.373). This is similar to what Triandis et al. (1986) have labeled 'ethnic affirmation' or 'ethnic overshooting,' i.e., a situation where the minority group member develops a consumption or lifestyle pattern more extreme than that either of the majority group members or of their group of origin. Accordingly, when the consumption of a product or a lifestyle dimension is a function of both the reflective and formative ethnicity indicators, it can either be 'cultural incorporation' or 'cultural transmutation'. The difference between these two categories is whether acculturation will result in a behavioral pattern that is in-between (incorporation), or outside (transmutation) the two anchors defined by the majority culture and the minority culture.

Finally, when the consumption of a product is neither a function of the reflective nor the formative ethnicity indicator, the product/lifestyle can be labeled as non-ethnic as both ethnic origin and acculturation have no significant impact on that consumption pattern.

The Study

An empirical study was conducted to examine and classify various products/lifestyles as a function of two ethnicity indicators – ethnic origin (a reflective indicator) and language of exposure to mass media (a formative indicator). Specifically, using a sample of both English-Canadians (EC, the majority group) and French-Canadians (FC, the minority group), the study investigates the relative power of the two ethnicity indicators – ethnic origin and language of exposure to mass media- in predicting ethnic indicators commonly used by marketers. A number of lifestyle dimensions and the consumption frequencies of a variety of frozen/canned food items and alcoholic beverages are also analyzed as a function of the two ethnicity indicators.

The benefit of using a sample of FC and EC is that the consumption differences between the two ethnic groups are well documented in the extant literature (e.g., Mallen, 1973; Tigert, 1973; Schaninger, Bourgeois, & Buss, 1985). This is useful when products and lifestyles are selected to compare the predictive power of the two ethnicity indicators. For example, ample evidence has shown that EC and FC exhibit considerable differences in various lifestyle dimensions (e.g., attitudes toward housework, children, and generic products) and the consumption of the product items (frozen/canned foods and alcoholic beverages) included in this study. On the other hand, the relationship between EC and FC in Quebec can hardly be interpreted as from a 'mainstream-minority' perspective (Berry et al., 1992, Chapter 12). Therefore this study uses a sample of respondents drawn from the metropolitan Toronto area, as the status of FC in this area is similar to that of other ethnic minority groups.

Methodology

Source of the Data

An area sampling technique was used to secure a group of EC respondents. The method involved randomly drawing forty census tracts from the Toronto area. As the census tracts were drawn, some judgement was exercised to eliminate those with large concentrations of industrial/commercial activities and/or too large concentrations of other ethnic minorities. Within each chosen census tract, a number of streets were further selected at random and efforts were made to survey as many households on these streets as possible. The male or female head of each household was interviewed. After a brief introduction, the interviewer used a filter question to screen out those who denied themselves as being EC. The self-administered questionnaire was then left with the consenting individual to be picked up at a later time. A total of 275 households were approached in this part of the survey and this produced 150 usable questionnaires for analysis.

On account of the impossibility to locate in Toronto census tracts with a large enough concentration of French-Canadians to warrant door to door surveying, it was decided to mail both the English and French versions of the questionnaire to 2680 Torontonians with a French last name. The mailing lists were obtained from the publishers of two different French magazines, French schools and federal government offices. A total of 536 questionnaires were returned to the researchers (a response rate of about 20%), resulting in 500 usable cases for further analysis.

Measurement

Any respondent with a FC last name (i.e., when the questionnaire was obtained from the mail survey, x_1) was coded as one with FC ethnic origin. The questionnaire also included three 10-point Likert-type items (x_2 to x_4) tapping FC ethnic origin. These items, generated from interviews with various FC, attempted to capture the respondent's ancestry ('My parents are French-Canadians'), Catholic root ('I had a strong Catholic childhood upbringing'), and place of origin ('I grew up in mostly French-Canadian neighborhoods'). As far as exposure to French mass media (the formative ethnicity indicator) is concerned, each respondent was asked to estimate the distribution of his/her exposure to French (versus English) mass media including radio (x_5), newspaper (x_6) and television (x_7).

In another section of the questionnaire, there are twenty-one 10-point Likert-type items. These items, extracted from Tigert (1973), were used to measure eight different lifestyle dimensions (attitudes towards children, attitudes towards housework, fashion consciousness, price consciousness, homebody, health consciousness, brand loyalty and attitudes towards generic) on which EC and FC have been shown to exhibit considerable differences (e.g., Hui et al., 1993). The respondent also reported personal consumption frequency for 10 canned/frozen food items (canned tuna, canned salmon, canned baked beans, canned soups, canned stew, canned spaghetti sauce, frozen vegetable, frozen TV dinner, frozen pie/cake and frozen potato products) and 10 alcoholic beverages (scotch, rye, dry gin, vodka, cognac, rum, red wine, white wine, champagne and liqueurs). The above lifestyle and product items were chosen based on a review of the existing literature on the consumption differences between EC and FC. The list was not meant to be exhaustive but it comprises items representing the most frequently mentioned differences between the two ethnic groups. Demographic measures are included in the final section of the questionnaire.

Results

Questionnaires obtained from both the EC and FC respondents were used in the analysis. Structural equation modeling was employed to confirm the underlying factor structure of the four measures of ethnic origin (the reflective ethnicity indicator) and three measures of exposure to French mass media (the formative ethnicity indicator). The confirmatory factor model as shown in Figure 4.1 was tested by the program LISREL (Joreskog & Sorbom, 1989). The model produces a chi-square value of 48.56 with 13 degrees of freedom (p=.000), an adjusted goodness of fit index (AGFI) of .955, and a root mean square residual (RMR) of .032. The significant chi-square value can be attributed largely to the large sample size (n=607 after pair-wise deletion of missing cases) and the violation of the assumption of multivariate distribution as all the seven measures have primarily a bi-modal distribution (with both EC and FC respondents included in the analysis). Both the AGFI (>.900) and RMR (<.1) suggest that the model has an acceptable fit (Bagozzi & Yi, 1988). The Bentler and Bonett's (1980) incremental fit index (.982) also indicates a good fit with the confirmatory factor model. Standardized estimates of the parameters are given in Table 2.

Figure 4.1   Confirmatory Factor Model

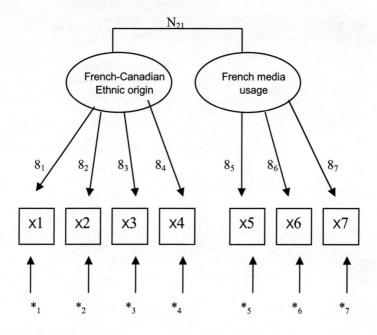

Table 4.2   Standardized Estimates of the Confirmatory Factor Model

Parameters	Estimates (t-values)
λ_1	.879[a]
λ_2	.944 (34.11)
λ_3	.759 (23.22)
λ_4	.831 (27.24)
λ_5	.780
λ_6	.724 (17.13)
λ_7	.853 (18.74)
ϕ_{11}	1.000 (10.47)
ϕ_{22}	1.000 (13.51)
ϕ_{21}	.503 (9.31)

[a] Estimates without a t-value are fixed parameters.

Lifestyles, Convenience Foods and Alcoholic Beverages

As expected, a principal component analysis of the twenty-one lifestyle items produced eight different factors with either two or three items loading on each factor (factor loading greater than .6). The eight lifestyle dimensions (with 2 or 3 indicators each), ten frozen/canned food items and ten alcoholic beverage were modeled individually as a function of FC ethnic origin, exposure to French mass media, and four socioeconomic variables: sex, age, income, and family size (Figure 4.2). This allows us to examine the predictive power of the two ethnicity indicators after controlling for the effects of the key socioeconomic factors (Schaninger, Bourgeois, & Buss, 1985). Again, although all the obtained chi-square values were significant (p=.000), the twenty-eight LISREL models appeared to have good fits as their AGFI (from .939 to .949) and RMR (from .028 to .038) are well within the acceptable levels.

The results of the LISREL analyses are summarized in Table 4.3. Five of the eight lifestyle dimensions (attitudes towards children, housework and generic brands; fashion consciousness; and homebody) are significant functions of FC origin only (i.e., the t-value of γ_1 is significant and the t-value of γ_2 is not significant), two (price consciousness and brand loyalty) are significant functions of exposure to French mass media only (i.e., the t-value of γ_2 is significant and the t-value of γ_1 is not significant) and one (health consciousness) is a function of neither ethnicity indicator. Out of the ten canned/frozen food items, four (canned tuna, baked beans and soups; and frozen potato products) are significant functions of exposure to French mass media only, two (canned pasta sauce and frozen vegetable) are significant functions of both FC ethnic origin and exposure to French mass media, and four (canned salmon and stew; and frozen TV dinner and pie/cake) are not associated with either indicator. As for the ten alcoholic beverages, six are significant functions of exposure to French mass media only (vodka, rum, red wine, white wine, champagne and liqueurs), one is a significant function of FC ethnic origin only (scotch), two are significant functions of both ethnicity indicators (rye and cognac), while one (dry gin) is not influenced by either indicator. These results indicated that any significant differences in the lifestyles of EC and FC were better predicted by FC origin than by exposure to French mass media, while the opposite was true for the differences between the two ethnic groups in the consumption of canned/frozen food items and alcoholic beverages.

Although most of the existing studies focus on product consumption differences between different ethnic groups (e.g., Hirschman, 1981; Wallendorf & Reilly, 1983; Schaninger, Bourgeois, & Buss, 1985), a number of them are more concerned with consumer values, lifestyles, and attitudes towards marketing or non-marketing activities and objects (e.g., Lee, 1993). Meanwhile, Jun, Ball and Gentry (1993) have proposed a distinction between behavioral acculturation and attitudinal acculturation. They also suggest that changes in attitudes are less likely than external forms of acculturation because values, beliefs and attitudes tend to be ingrained in the psyche of individuals from a particular culture (Lee, 1993; Lee &Tse, 1994b; Triandis, 1994, Chapter 3). Accordingly, consumer lifestyles (a mixture of values, beliefs and attitudes) should be more a function of ethnic origin (the reflective indicator) than language of exposure to mass media (the formative indicator) while the opposite is true for product consumption in general; this is supported by findings obtained from the present study.

Figure 4.2   Lifestyle and Product Consumption as a Function of Ethnic Origin and Language of Exposure to Mass Media

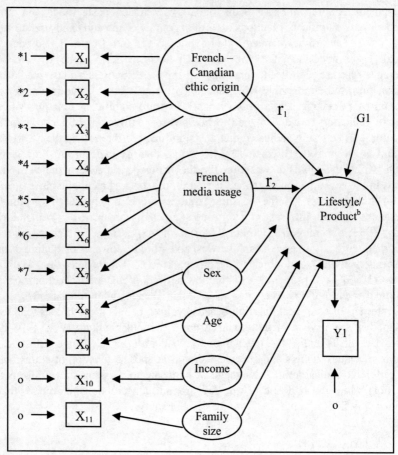

[a] Each lifestyle dimension has two or three measures. For the consumption frequency of each product, there is only one measure. For the sake of simplicity, the figure refers to the case when there is one measure for the dependent construct.

Table 4.3   Lifestyle and Consumption as a Function of Two Ethnicity Indicators

	γ_1	γ_2	χ^2			
Lifestyles[b]						
Attitudes towards:						
Children	.258 (4.23)[c]	.024 (.39)	93.8	48	.945	.029
Housework	.258 (4.23)[c]	-.040 (-.65)	118	60	.949	.032
Generic brands	-.137 (-2.22)	.037 (.59)	117	48	.944	.029
Consciousness:						
Fashion	.251 (4.14)	-.056 (-.91)	138	60	.939	.038
Price	.007 (.12)	-.151 (-2.38)	125	60	.945	.032
Health	.013 (.21)	.102 (1.52)	103	48	.947	.029
Homebody	.250 (3.45)	-.007 (-.11)	110	48	.947	.029
Brand loyalty	.045 (.67)	-.258 (-3.21)	131	60	.944	.034
Canned/Frozen Food Items						
Canned						
Tuna	-.006 (-.11)	-.103 (-1.81)	93.1	38	.945	.028
Salmon	.002 (.03)	-.047 (-.87)	93.3	38	.945	.029
Baked beans	-.036 (-.70)	-.118 (-2.18)	96.7	38	.943	.029
Canned soups	-.035 (-.67)	-.148 (-2.68)	94.5	38	.944	.029
Canned stew	-.038 (-.71)	-.037 (-.67)	96	38	.943	.029
Pasta sauce	-.088(-1.65)	-.105 (-1.91)	97.4	38	.942	.029
Frozen						
Vegetable	-.156(-3.11)	-.213 (-4.04)	100	38	.941	.030
TV dinner	.072 (1.30)	.011 (.20)	96	38	.943	.028
Pie/cake	.023 (.41)	-.053 (-.93)	96.3	38	.942	.032
Potato products	-.010 (-.19)	-.162 (-2.88)	100	38	.940	.029
Alcoholic Beverages						
Scotch	-.107(-1.98)	.070 (1.27)	87.4	38	.945	.029
Rye	-.093(-1.69)	-.110 (-1.95)	86.3	38	.945	.029
Dry gin	-.063(-1.13)	-.026 (-.46)	79.9	38	.949	.028
Vodka	-.044 (-.80)	-.128 (-2.24)	87.2	38	.945	.046
Rum	-.021 (-.39)	-.101 (-1.81)	93.9	38	.944	.029
Cognac	-.094(-1.71)	.169 (2.98)	92.5	38	.942	.029
Red wine	-.033 (-.63)	.263 (4.78)	90.7	38	.943	.029
White wine	-.032 (-.60)	.145 (2.62)	84.1	38	.947	.028
Champagne	-.037 (-.67)	.122 (2.13)	91.7	38	.942	.029
Liqueurs	-.054(-.099)	.228 (3.98)	83.6	38	.947	.028

[a] Standardized estimates after controlling for the effects of four socioeconomic indicators (sex, age, income & family size); [b] Each lifestyle dimension has 2 or 3 indicators; [c] t-value of the estimate. |t-value|>1.64,p<.1;|t-value|>1.96, p<.05.

The signs of the two path coefficients, γ_1 and γ_2, show that compared with EC, FC in general show more positive attitudes toward children but more negative attitudes towards generic products; enjoy more housework and staying at home; are more fashion conscious but less price conscious; and tend to be less loyal consumers. Except the last dimension (i.e., brand loyalty), all the findings are consistent with those obtained from past studies (Kindra, Laroche, & Muller, 1989). All the significant γ_1 and γ_2 obtained from the analysis of the canned/frozen food items have a negative sign. These results imply that FC respondents exhibit less propensity to consume convenience foods than EC respondents and this again is consistent with the findings obtained from several past studies (e.g., Mallen, 1973). By the same token, parameter estimates obtained from the LISREL analyses reveal that FC respondents tend to drink less scotch, rye, vodka and rum, and drink more cognac, red wine, white wine, champagne and liqueurs than their EC counterparts (Table 3). These results are largely in accordance with those obtained by Schaninger, Bourgeois and Buss (1985).

More importantly, our proposed typology of consumption (Table 1) suggests that when a lifestyle/product is a significant function of ethnic origin (the reflective ethnicity indicator), it can be considered as a behavioral trait that is deeply ingrained in the minority group culture and is less likely to be modified by acculturation. For example, although FC consume less of four alcoholic beverages (scotch, rye, vodka and rum) than EC, the results also suggest that acculturation is less likely to reduce the consumption discrepancies between the two ethnic groups for rye and scotch than vodka and rum. In other words, FC individuals tend to drink more vodka and rum when they become more acculturated while their consumption level of scotch and rye tend to remain relatively low even after extended contact with the EC group. This explanation received some support in a follow-up survey of 22 individuals of FC origin. Respondents tended to agree more on a 10-point scale that they would never want to drink scotch (x=7.95) and rye (x=8.55) than vodka (x=7.73) and rum (x=7.59).

Discussion and Conclusions

The proposed typology of consumption provides an explanation for past findings that, for some consumption behaviors (cultural resistant or cultural incorporation products), the acculturating group resembles the minority group; but for some other consumption behaviors (cultural shift products), the acculturating group is more similar to the majority group. Schaninger, Bourgeois, and Buss (1985) found that bilingual families (the acculturating group) behave more like English-speaking families in the type of furniture they own but are more like French-speaking families in the type of appliances and automobiles they own and in their television viewing habits. This typology suggests that consumption behavior should be examined as a function of both the reflective and formative ethnicity indicators.

Using only one of the indicators in an analysis can lead to erroneous conclusions regarding differences between two ethnic groups.

Findings obtained from this study also indicate that ethnicity indicators commonly employed by researchers may not be unidimensional. Past studies tended to compute a single consumer ethnicity index from a linear combination of measures of different ethnicity indicators that may vary considerably on the reflective-formative continuum (see, for example, Hirschman, 1981; Valencia, 1985; O'Guinn & Faber, 1985; Lee, 1993; Donthu & Cherian, 1992; Webster, 1994). However, this practice is legitimate only when these indicators are unidimensional; and a high reliability coefficient and a single factor solution do not necessarily imply unidimensionality (Gerbing & Anderson, 1988). When there is no strong evidence that these ethnicity indicators are unidimensional, researchers should keep them as separate variables in their analyses. This will allow researchers to gain a better understanding of the relationship between ethnicity and consumption.

The proposed typology of consumption is also useful for the development of strategies in a multicultural or even global marketing context. Multinational marketers can employ the typology as a basis for predicting the chances of successfully introducing a product from one cultural group to another. They should go after products that belong to the 'cultural shift' category rather than the 'cultural resistant' category. For example, our results indicate that there will be a slim chance of success if one tries to introduce a product like scotch or rye to FC living in the Toronto area. On the other hand, one needs not hesitate to market vodka and rum to FC living in the same area especially when the majority of them have lived in the area for a long period.

Finally, there is consensus that advertising appeals should attempt to portray the lifestyles and values of the target audience (Mueller, 1987; Gilly, 1988; Tse, Belk & Zhou, 1989). According to our typology, advertisers need to use different appeals when they are concerned with values or lifestyles that are primarily 'culture resistant' in nature. On the other hand, if the values and lifestyles belong to the 'cultural shift' or the 'cultural incorporation' category, standardization of advertising appeals is possible especially when most of the minority group members have had extended contacts with the majority culture. One tentative conclusion to be drawn from these results is that product consumption behaviors are more likely to be influenced by acculturation than by basic lifestyles and values. This suggests that although marketers may find a good potential in selling products across different ethnic groups living in the same area, they will still need to use different advertising appeals when dealing with different ethnic groups.

References

Bagozzi, R.P., & Yi, Y. (1988). On the evaluation of structural equation models. *Journal of the Academy of Marketing Science*, 16, 74-94.

Bentler, P.M., & Bonett, D.G. (1980). Significance tests and goodness of fit in the analysis of covariance structures. *Psychological Bulletin*, 88, 588-606.

Berry, J.W. (1980). Acculturation as varieties of adaptation. In A.M. Padilla (Ed.), *Acculturation: Theory, models and some new findings* (pp.9-26). Boulder, Colorado: Westview Press.

Berry, J.W., Poortinga, Y.H., Segall, M.H., & Dasen, P.R. (1992). *Cross-cultural psychology: Research and applications.* Cambridge, UK: Cambridge University Press.

Deshpande, R., Hoyer, W.D., & Donthu, N. (1986). The intensity of ethnic affiliation: A study of the sociology of Hispanic consumption. *Journal of Consumer Research*, 13, 214-220.

Donthu, N., & Cherian, J. (1992). Hispanic coupon usage: The impact of strong and weak ethnic identification. *Psychology and Marketing*, 9, 501-510.

Gerbing, D.W., & Anderson, J.C. (1988). An updated paradigm for scale development incorporating unidimensionality and its assessment. *Journal of Marketing Research*, 25, 186-192.

Gilly, M.C. (1988). Sex roles in advertising: A comparison of television advertisements in Australia, Mexico, and the United States. *Journal of Marketing*, 52, 75-85.

Glock, C.Y., & Nicosia, F.M. (1964). Use of sociology in studying 'consumption' behavior. *Journal of Marketing*, 28, 51-54.

Hirschman, E.C. (1981). American Jewish ethnicity: Its relationship to some selected aspects of consumer behavior. *Journal of Marketing*, 45, 102-110.

Joreskog, K.G., & Sorbom, D. (1989). *LISREL 7: User's Reference Guide.* Mooresville, IN: Scientific Software, Inc.

Jun, S., Ball, A.D., & Gentry, J.W. (1992). Modes of consumer acculturation. In L. McAlister & M.L. Rothschild (Eds.), *Advances in consumer research, Vol. 20* (pp.76-82). Provo, UT: Association for Consumer Research.

Keefe, S.E., & Padilla, A.M. (1987). *Chicano ethnicity.* Albuquerque: University of New Mexico Press.

Kindra, G.S., Laroche, M., & Muller, T.E. (1993). *Consumer behavior.* Scarborough, Ontario: Nelson Canada.

Laroche, M., Kim, C., Hui, M.K., & Joy A. (1996). An empirical study of multidimensional ethnic change: The case of the French Canadians in Quebec. *Journal of Cross-Cultural Psychology*, 27, 114-131.

Laroche, M., Kim, C., Hui, M.K., & Tomiuk, M.A. (1998). Test of a nonlinear relationship between linguistic acculturation and ethnic identification. *Journal of Cross-Cultural Psychology*, 29, 418-433.

Lee, W. (1993). Acculturation and advertising communication strategies: A cross-cultural study of Chinese and Americans. *Psychology and Marketing*, 10, 381-397.

Lee, W., & Tse, D.K. (1994a). Changing media consumption in a new home: Acculturation patterns among Hong Kong immigrants to Canada. *Journal of Advertising*, 23, 57-70.

Lee, W., & Tse, D.K. (1994b). Becoming Canadian: Understanding how Hong Kong immigrants change their consumption. *Pacific Affairs*, 67, 70-95.

Mallen, B. (1973). The present state of knowledge and research in marketing to the French-Canadian market, in D.N. Thompson & D.S. Leighton (Eds.), *Canadian marketing:*

Problems and prospects (pp.98-112). Toronto: Wiley of Canada.

Mendoza, R.H. (1989). An empirical scale to measure type and degree of acculturation in Mexican-American adolescents and adults. *Journal of Cross-Cultural Psychology*, 20, 372-385.

Mueller, B. (1987), Reflections of Culture: An Analysis of Japanese and American Advertising Appeals, *Journal of Advertising Research*, 27 (June-July), 51-59.

O'Guinn, Thomas C. and Timothy P. Meyer (1984), Segmenting the Hispanic Market: The Use of Spanish-Language Radio, *Journal of Advertising Research*, 23, 9-16.

_____ and Ronald J. Faber (1985), New Perspectives on Acculturation: The Relationship of General and Role Specific Acculturation with Hispanics' Consumer Attitudes, in *Advances in Consumer Research*, Vol. 12, eds. Elizabeth C. Hirschman and Morris B. Holbrook, Provo, UT: Association for Consumer Research, pp. 113-117.

Paranjpe, A.C. (1986), *Ethnic Identities and Prejudices: Perspectives from the Third World*, the Netherlands: Leiden.

Phinney, J. (1990), Ethnic Identity in Adolescents and Adults, *Psychological Bulletin*, 108, 499-514.

Rosenthal, D.A., & Feldman, S.S. (1992). The nature and stability of ethnic identity in Chinese youth: Effects of length of residence in two cultural contexts. *Journal of Cross-Cultural Psychology*, 23, 214-227.

Schaninger, Charles M., Jacques B. Bourgeois, and W. Christian Buss (1985), French-English Canadian Subcultural Consumption Differences, *Journal of Marketing*, 49 (Spring), 82-92.

Stayman, Douglas M. and Rohit Deshpande (1989), Situational Ethnicity and Consumer Behavior, *Journal of Consumer Research*, 16 (December), 361-371.

Tigert, Douglas J. (1973), Can a Separate Marketing Strategy for French Canada be Justified: Profiling English-French Markets Through Life Style Analysis, in *Canadian Marketing: Problems and Prospects*, eds. Donald N. Thompson and David S. Leighton, Toronto: Wiley of Canada, pp. 119-131.

Triandis, Harry C. (1994), *Culture and Social Behavior*, New York: McGraw-Hill.

_____, Yoshihisa Kashima, Emiko Shimda and Marcelo Villareal (1986), Acculturation Indices as a Means of Confirming Cultural Differences, *International Journal of Intercultural Relations*, 12, 43-70.

Tse, David K., Russell W. Belk, and Nan Zhou (1989), Becoming a Consumer Society: A Longitudinal and Cross-Cultural Content Analysis of Print Ads from People's Republic of China, Hong Kong, and Taiwan, *Journal of Consumer Research*, 16 (March), 457-472.

Valencia, Humberto (1985), Developing an Index to Measure Hispanicness, in *Advances in Consumer Research*, Vol. 12, eds. Elizabeth C. Hirschman and Morris B. Holbrook, Provo, UT: Association for Consumer Research, 118-121.

Wallendorf, Melanie and Michael Reilly (1983), Ethnic Migration, Assimilation, and Consumption, *Journal of Consumer Research*, 10 (December), 293-302.

Webster, Cynthia (1994), Effects of Hispanic Ethnic Identification on Marital Roles in the Purchase Decision, *Journal of Consumer Research*, 21 (September), 319-331.

Yinger, Milton J. (1985), Ethnicity, *Annual Review of* Sociology, 11, 151-180.

PART II:

METHODOLOGICAL ISSUES

Chapter 5

The Effects of Extreme Response Style on a Likert Response Format in Cross-Cultural Research

Irvine Clarke III

Introduction

Markarian explains that 'as the cultural and racial makeup of the population changes, the development, marketing and selling of many products and services is taking a more multicultural bent' (p.127). In their effort to respond to the growing cross-cultural needs, marketing researchers are finding alternate methodology issues transported to the forefront of consideration. One relevant cross-cultural marketing methodological consideration is extreme response style (Samiee and Jeong 1994). Cross-cultural quantitative marketing research often compares the individuals of differing cultures in their responses to various items of interest. However, cultural difference can also influence the manner in which subjects respond to these research efforts (Albaum et al. 1987; Bocker 1988; Chun, Campbell and Yoo 1974; Green and White 1976; Yu et al. 1990). For example, if members of one culture have an inherent inclination to respond using only the extreme response categories of a scale (ERS), while other cultures routinely display an inhibited response style, comparisons of differences between the groups could be distorted. Consequently, the confounding of genuine effects could improperly sway conclusions based on these instruments (Hui and Triandis 1985a, b).

Although most marketers concerned with response bias believe that these variables act as a form of systematic bias, some researchers have strived to lesson the importance of response styles and counseled that extremeness in response is of slight weight in the total variation of the subject (Gove and Geerken 1976; Peabody 1962; Rorer 1965). They contend that the methodological limitations of the current literature prohibits it from demonstrating the relationship between response bias and systematic bias. Consequently, many market researchers erroneously 'hope' away the effects and fail to consider response styles in the research designs for cross-cultural research. This chapter looks at ERS to investigate the possibility of detecting ERS bias and using a variation of Likert response formats to minimize cultural differences.

Implications

The identification of extreme response patterns is a purposeful marketing methodological consideration, since ERS can distort group averages and limit the validity of cross-cultural marketing survey results (Marin, Gamba and Marin 1992). The bias element in ERS can beguile the use of inferential statistics and market segmentation at the aggregate-level (Greenleaf 1992a; Gurwitz 1987; Heide and Gronhaug 1992). Marketers comparing cultural groups with differing response styles may incorrectly make claims based on observed differences that are strictly attributed to a culturally driven extreme response style bias.

As ERS is a systematic, consistent and stable response set, the implications for marketers are broad. Shapiro et al. (1976) explains:

> ... extreme response style problems are not just oddities or occasional matters. They occur frequently even in carefully controlled research. Unless they are properly noted and treated they may lead to errors in the analysis and interpretation of research findings (p.362).

The possible consequences of ERS are sufficient to confound the use of inferential statistics. Standard deviation and variance are biased by the response set and misrepresent research relying on the use of these rating scales. ERS artificially increases the within group variance, leading to a corresponding increases in type II error (Hui and Triandis 1985).

Additionally, ERS skews frequency distributions toward the outermost regions, increasing the standard deviations and reducing correlations. For example, figure one contains both a group (1) without ERS and a group (2) exhibiting ERS. Initially, assume that the two groups have similar construct attitude and only differ in their response style. ERS becomes visible in a comparison of the distribution patterns between groups.

Figure 5.1   Distribution

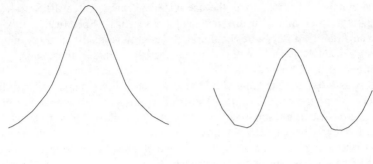

Group 1: No ERS   Group 2: ERS

The distribution for group two flattens and exhibits a greater standard deviation, which would concurrently create reduced correlations. These weaker correlations modify beta-coefficients and cause a reduction in explained variance (R^2). In measures where the means between items are greatly dissimilar, the damaging effects of ERS are even more pronounced (Heide and Gronhaug 1992). Additionally, ERS group two displays larger variance, directly affecting the size of item intercorrelations, thereby distorting true factor structure or cluster solutions (Chun, Cambell and Yoo 1974; Greenleaf 1992a; Hui and Triandis 1989). ERS can alter eigenvalues, in factor analysis, sufficient to create an incorrect factor interpretation in the data set (Heide and Gronhaug 1992). Preeminently, the two groups, possessing identical construct attitude, will appear statistically dissimilar, solely from extreme response style.

Extreme response style can pose serious problems to segmentation analysis. Multivariate statistical segmentation methods will typically group individuals with similar response styles, forming a segment based on distinctive behavioral characteristics rather than directly related to the question content. Although the segment will share certain basic characteristics, a style of response, marketers are likely to find such a segment useless for targeting actions (Gurwitz 1987).

Moreover, correlations of ERS scores between test groups become meaningless, since response styles bias the correlations (Cronbach 1946; Greenleaf 1992a). Lastly, since ERS is consistent, it may heighten reliability, but lower the validity of the test (Cronbach 1946). Overall, a strong ERS bias could induce market researchers into erroneous inferences from a cross-cultural data set. For example, traditional marketing research techniques such as segmentation analysis or multidimensional scaling to estimate consumers' preferences, perceptions and product evaluations could be deceived by the bias component in ERS across cultures.

This study investigates the issue of cross-cultural ERS; specifically analyzing these differences across scale response formats. Hence, the primary objectives of the study are: (1) to investigate black/white cultural differences in response styles in a

Likert-type format, (2) to identify scale formats that have equal proportions of ERS between cultures, (3) to examine the use of Greenleaf's 16-item ERS scale, with varying response formats, in different cultural settings. Specifically, this study investigates if ERS differs across cultural/ethnic groups in sufficient magnitude to evoke significant differences in the outcomes of cross-cultural comparisons. A cross-cultural test of the Greenleaf ERS measure would demonstrate its applicability to marketers as a test for the bias. If it is able to detect ERS, marketers may find it necessary to vary the number of response categories, adjust with a covariate or even investigate the use of a response style correction (Greenleaf 1992a; Gurwitz 1987). Also, it inquires whether ERS within groups and between groups, can actually be reduced by adding response categories. Previous studies, utilizing measures not designed for ERS, have suggested that varying the number of response categories can compensate for culturally influenced ERS. Finally, this study seeks to further the development of cross-cultural measurement instruments, by identifying *a priori* scale formats which reduce the intrinsic bias of ERS between groups, thereby, increasing the validity of the cross-cultural survey results (Heide and Gronhaug 1992). The results indicate that cross-cultural marketing researchers should carefully consider the impact of extreme response style on their research.

Background

Marketers have long acknowledged the difficulties associated with response styles. Wells (1961) explained that since the response style pattern is not related to the content of the research questions, the bias imposed when style overcomes information contaminates the results of measurements of attitudes. The problem of cultural response styles for self-rating scales is often singled out as the primary consideration in pancultural analysis (Leung and Bond 1989; Stening and Everett 1984).

Oskamp (1977) defines response styles as 'systematic ways of answering which are not directly related to the question content, but which represent typical behavioral characteristics of the respondents' (p.37). The four most common response styles, yea-saying/ nay-saying, social desirability, centrism and extremism, have been recognized for decades (Couch and Keniston 1960; Cronbach 1946; Wells 1961) and have been concretely demonstrated to '... influence measures of abilities, attitudes, opinions, beliefs, and personality, and thus be the source of response effects' (Heide and Gronhaug 1992). Yet, the vexing nature and the possibility that response bias could invalidate '... much (if not most) of the work...' (Gove and Geerken 1976) has lead researchers to treat them as a nuisance variable and ignore their influence (Gurwitz 1987; Wells 1963).

The special case of extreme response bias was recognized by Cronbach (1946) as one of the major response classes and thereby became one of the most discussed response styles. Extreme response style is classified as the tendency for some individuals to consistently use the extreme ends of response scales in a multiple response category format. Subsequent research found ERS to be consistent, stable and a valid response set over time (Bachman and O'Malley 1984b; Berg 1953; Berg and Collier 1953; Das and Dutta 1969; Greenleaf 1992b; Hamilton 1968; Littrell 1971; Merrens 1970; Peabody 1962; Rundquist 1950; War and Coffman 1970).

Literature Review

Traditionally, both cross-cultural (Clark 1990) and ERS literature have focused on either individual personality mechanisms or the general aspect of culture. The personality approach is inductive while the cultural approach remains deductive (Samiee and Jeong 1994). Both streams of research, however, offer insight into the ERS phenomenon and suffer from the same methodological limitations of measurement instruments. Yet, the two research flows provide the theoretical basis of this study and thereby merit discussion.

Personality

Most of the work to date has investigated the links between ERS tendencies and personality variables (Borgatta and Glass 1961; Kloot, Kroonenberg and Bakker 1985; O'Donovan 1965; Peabody 1962; Warr and Coffman 1970). The researchers have focused on the personality characteristics exhibited by subjects who use an extreme response style. Specifically, experimenters have investigated ERS relationship with: level of adjustment (Norman 1969; Soueif 1958; Zax, Gardiner and Lowry 1964), involvement (Biggs and Das 1973; Warr and Coffman 1970), mood states (Lorr, McNair and Fisher 1982; Lorr and Wunderlich 1980), deviancy (Berg and Collier 1953), tolerance to ambiguity (Brengelmann 1960; Merrins 1970; Soueif 1958), anxiety (Berg and Collier 1953; Crandell 1965; Innes 1977; Iwawaki and Zax 1969; Lewis and Taylor 1955; Norman 1969; Zax, Gardiner and Lowy 1964), authoritarianism (Schutz and Foster 1963; Zuckerman, et al. 1958) pathology (Arthur 1966; Iwawaki and Zax 1969) and social interest (Crandell 1982).

Several areas of research have focused on the relationship between ERS tendencies and other factors. For example, ERS has been studied in relation to: sex (Crandell 1973; Emmerich 1971; Light, Zax and Gardiner 1965), age (Emmerich 1971; Greenleaf 1992b; Light, Zax and Gardiner 1965), cognitive development (Emmerich 1971), and intelligence (Das and Dutta 1969; Hamilton 1968; Light, Zax and Gardiner 1965). While there is a fair amount of literature on this perspective, the majority of this research has not focused on cross-cultural application. Since marketers often focus on aggregate traits of groups, the cultural dimensions of extreme respondence were deemed meritorious of augmented cross-cultural examination. The personality perspective provides the foundation for a broader cultural exploration of ERS.

Culture

Cross-cultural differences in ERS are found in various settings, subcultures and across ethnic groupings (Das and Dutta 1969; Hui and Triandis 1989; Marin, Gamba and Marin 1992; Shapiro, et al. 1976; Triandis and Triandis 1962; Zax and Takahashi 1967; Hamilton 1968). Shapiro et al. (1976) and Triandis (1972) concur that extreme response styles are common in cross-cultural work and may reflect a '... cultural difference in the subject's willingness to use the extreme ends of the scale' (Leung and Bond 1989, p.136). Chun, Cambell and Yoo (1974) illuminate the importance to marketers studying across cultures:

> Cross-cultural differences in ERS would be of interest either as a reflection of cultural differences on substantive dimensions or for its implications for the methodology of cross-cultural research, or both (p.466).

Differences in extreme response style have been found for Hispanics (Hui and Triandis 1985; Marin et al. 1992), Koreans (Chun, Cambell and Yoo 1974), Moroccans (Shapiro et al. 1976), Germans (Brenelmann 1960), Greeks (Triandis and Triandis 1962) and Japanese (Zax and Takahashi 1967).

Since the United States serves as a cultural meeting ground, these cross-cultural ERS differences could even appear between cultural groups within the country. For example, the African-American, or black, the most sizable ethnic minority in the United States, is generally viewed as a distinctive cultural group in American society (Peter & Olson 1994). Consequently, '... the vast majority of racially oriented consumer research has focused on black-white consumer differences' (Shiffman & Kanuk 1987, p.520). Periodically, ERS response styles have been used to explain the group differences in black/white cultural comparisons. Bachman and O'Malley (1984a, b) demonstrated that blacks and whites have differences in response styles to self-esteem measures. Berg and Collier (1953) also found that black males use the extreme scales on the PRT more often than whites. Blacks are also more likely than whites to employ the extreme response categories on differing Likert-type questions on self-esteem. This is predominant in those scales with an agree-disagree format (Bachman and O'Malley 1984a, b). 'Put the other way around, whites are more likely than blacks to qualify their responses on such scales' (Bachman and O'Malley 1984a, p.506). Either perspective yields the same conclusion: the degree of ERS bias inferredly varies between black and white groups.

To rectify this bias, in a cross-cultural comparison, Bachman and O'Malley (1984b) recommend the use of collapsed scoring to minimize the effects of ERS. The authors found that when they used a truncated scoring method, the average black-white difference in self esteem scores were eliminated. However, a truncated scoring approach lessens item variance, inter-item correlation, and index reliability, thereby creating a measure that is less sensitive to the authentic changes in the construct of interest. Collapsed scoring techniques designed to compensate for ERS could reduce the information content and alter conclusions, yet still entail the undesirable bias of ERS in a 'condensed form'. Triandis (1972) even advocates the use of correlational techniques as a method for controlling ERS bias in cross-cultural research. However, correlations are themselves inherently biased by ERS, making them equally inappropriate for this purpose.

These limitations make the truncated scoring method and correlational techniques undesirable to many multi-cultural researchers, suggesting a more desirable option of identifying scale response formats with equal ERS tendencies between cultures. Cronbach (1946; 1950) advises test designers to avoid research designs that these styles 'infest'. Thus, an *a priori* approach, of matching ERS equivalent scales', would allow researchers to develop measurement instruments that insure the assessment of the construct across cultures, devoid of the statistical bias of culture specific ERS.

Scaling Issues

Clearly, the Likert scale is affected by ERS (Albaum & Murphy 1988; Bachman and O'Malley 1984; Biggs and Das 1973; Crandell 1982; Greenleaf 1992a; Peabody 1962; Warr and Coffman 1970). At the forefront of Likert ERS discussion is the effect of the number of scale intervals. Past research suggests that cultural differences exist in the use of number of categories for response judgements (Hui and Triandis 1989; Wright et al. 1978). Display of ERS bias is reportedly related with the number of response intervals available to the respondent. In other words, different numbers of response intervals may display differing levels of response bias (Greenleaf 1992a). If the relationship holds true, the number of intervals in the scale may influence the degree of bias present, affecting the overall quality of the research (Hui and Triandis 1989; Kloot, Kroonenberg and Bakker 1985). However, the effect of scale intervals has shown contrasting results in contemporary ERS research (Albaum 1988; Albaum and Murphy 1988; Berg and Collier 1953; Biggs and Das 1973; Borgotta and Glass 1961; Biggs and Das 1973; Hui and Triandis 1985; Peabody 1962; Schwarz et al. 1985).

Hui and Triandis (1989), in a cross-cultural ERS study, suggest that additional response categories would be capable of encompassing the entire subjective range, resulting in reduced use of the extreme response style. A scale with finer gradations allows subjects, with differing judgement styles, more possibilities of matching their subjective categories within the scale range. They found that the amplitude of ERS became analogous between Hispanic and Non-Hispanic subjects at 10-points. However, Wyer (1969) argues that 'response style variables ... were not related to category widths' (p.114). Cronbach (1950) warned that increasing the number of response alternatives merely enhances the potential for response style without meaningful gains in information. He even suggested that response alternatives be limited to a two-choice format to compensate for ERS bias. Cox (1980) summarizes, that the appropriateness of response categories will vary with the circumstances of the research. Generally, limiting category widths between five and nine is recommended when respondents are sophisticated in their use of stimuli, since scales have decreasing reliability, with only small gains in information content, as the number of categories increases (Cox 1980; Matell and Jacoby 1971; McKelvie 1978; Miller 1956). Perhaps, this variety of recommendations can be explained, in part, by the use of assorted tests designed to measure different constructs or the circumstances of the item discussion. Yet, Cronbach, Wyer, and Hui & Triandis all agree that additional empirical investigation of scale formats is warranted in various cultural arenas to assess the implications of ERS. Samiee and Jeong (1994) even call for additional cross-cultural research that 'might employ alternative formats of responses or measurement methods in questionnaires that minimize the impact of ERS' (p.213).

Generally, the use scales possessing an even number of response intervals has been found to minimize the effects of some response styles in various cultures by forcing the respondent away from a neutral position. Theoretically, forced-choice scales should have little effect on ERS since respondents merely agree most strongly with the worded items themselves (Greenleaf 1992b). Yet, even numbered scales force choice, thereby, removing some components of central tendency and merit specific investigation.

Current Research Limitations

Most of the past ERS research, including both the personality variable and cultural postures, reports the same basic methodological limitation: the measurement instrument is not intended or designed to measure ERS. Rather, researchers have estimated ERS with multi-item measures conceived for different objectives. Since these scales typically have high inter-item correlation, to ensure the measurement of the desired construct, ERS scores are easily confused with the content of the items. Therefore, the psychometric tests themselves may influence the response style, since they are fashioned to measure some alternate construct. Relationships once thought to be associated with ERS may in fact be unique to the thesis of the instrument (Merrens 1971). ERS conclusions could be explained by item content variance rather than the reported extreme responses style (Biggs and Das 1973; Greenleaf 1992b; Hamilton 1968; Jones and Rorer 1973; Wyer 1969). This fundamental methodological limitation has made it convenient for skeptics to discount the earlier research relating culture and ERS. Recognizing this concern, important questions are raised: Are cross-cultural differences in ERS unique to the psychometric test or more generalizable across cultures? Are the scaling suggestions limited to the particular measurement instrument?

It is important to note that most response styles will have maximal occasion to operate when stimulus content is missing (Hamilton 1968). Therefore, the use of a scale that specifically measured ERS, while reducing external content cues, would offer a more accurate assessment of ERS than any of the previous research. As long as the content specific limitation remains, researchers cannot be sure that the ERS conclusions implied in the prior studies are valid. In response, Greenleaf (1992b) developed a summated index with low inter-item correlation and approximate equal extreme response proportions, aimed at the discovery of ERS. The measure was used to test the stability of ERS, autonomous from item specific content bias, across the adult population of the U.S., between 1975 and 1987, through the DDB Needham Worldwide Consumer Mail panel. The six-interval Likert response ERS scale was able to detect that individuals differing on age, education and income would have 'considerably different' (p.345) ERS scores. The internal analysis by split halves (Lord and Novick 1968) used to assess validity for the ERS measure 'compared favorably' between the observed reliability (ρ =.637) and the estimated benchmark reliability (R=.637).

An application of this scale would provide for advancement in marketing knowledge; since, existing research on effects of culture and response format, in relation to ERS, have universally not used an ERS specific measure with uncorrelated items and approximately equal response proportions. To demonstrate a reliable method of testing for ERS across cultures and ethnic groups, while identifying ERS equal Likert response would make cross cultural research design and analysis more accurate.

Methodology

The data in this study were obtained from anonymous, in-class responses to the summated 16-item, self administered Greenleaf ERS Likert-type Questionnaire (see Appendix 1) among undergraduate business students at two universities in a major Mid-Atlantic metropolitan area during a three month period in the winter of 1993. Demographic information was solicited on the same instrument. Subjects marked directly on the questionnaire and ethnic origin was registered through a self-recorded statement following the U.S. census designations. No compensation was offered. The questionnaire took approximately 15 minutes to complete.

A student sample was selected to facilitate a consistent sampling frame on educational level, age and income; all variables identified as contributing factors in ERS (Greenleaf 1992b). Although student samples cannot be viewed as representative of the larger population, they constitute comparable cross-cultural populations, meeting the primary requirement of matched-groups for cross-cultural measures (Douglas and Craig 1983; Parameswaran and Yaprak 1987). Ethnic groups were selected based on cultural proximity, since 'more robust results are likely to emerge when cultures selected for investigation share some relevant attributes' (Samiee and Jeong 1994, p. 214). 527 usable responses were returned and included in the analysis. A total of 274 black and 253 white subjects participated in the project.

The study blocked on two independent variables: ethnic group (blacks and whites) and response scale format (3,5,6,7,8,9,10 point). Formats were selected based on Cox's (1980) recommendation of 'reasonable range' with the 3 and 10 formats suggested from ERS specific studies (Hui & Triandis 1989). Response scale formats were randomly assigned among subjects. Respondents' ERS score were calculated as the proportion of items answered on the most extreme single positive and negative points of each scale. Summated scores, for matched response formats, were compared between black and white respondents using an independent sample test of differences between two proportions. In addition, proportional tests were administered within groups. Absolute inter-item correlations, summated across response formats are reported.

Results

The application of the Greenleaf 16-item ERS scale with varying response formats displayed a positive level of robustness. The initial consideration of the absolute inter-item correlations from this study would indicate that the measure remains relatively constant across response formats. The average absolute inter-item correlation coefficient, controlling for form, was .0887 with a maximum of .2676 (see Appendix 2). These results approach the average absolute inter-item correlation of .071 and maximum of .186 reported by Greenleaf (1992b). Even with altered response formats, the 16 items maintained the necessary low level of intercorrelation for a sound ERS measure.

The cross-cultural/cross-ethnic setting provides some interesting insights. Blacks, on average, exhibited higher levels of ERS on all scale formats. Statistically significant differences were found between blacks and whites for 5,6,7,8,10-point formats based on a univariate test of difference between two proportions with independent samples.

Figure 5.2   Black/White ERS

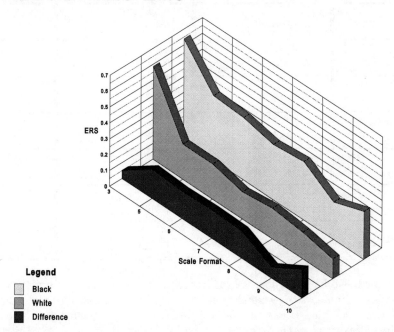

However, a 3-point scale exhibited no significant difference in levels of ERS between blacks and whites. The findings support the early works by Cronbach (1946; 1950) suggesting that fewer response points reduce the opportunity for cross-group bias. It would appear that a 3-point scale has equal levels of ERS for both whites and blacks, albeit at higher levels than alternate formats. Higher levels may be attributed to this study's operational definition of ERS, whereby, on the 3 point scale, all non-neutral responses were treated as extreme. Within groups, the 3 point scales exhibit differences in ERS from the other formats.

Figure 5.3   Cross-ethnic Comparison

Response Format	Black Proportion	n	White Proportion	...n	Significant At 90 percent
3	0.6672	36	0.5855	38	
5	0.4046	38	0.2214	35	*
6	0.3924	36	0.2214	35	*
7	0.3484	40	0.1701	36	*
8	0.3659	41	0.1932	33	*
9	0.2355	43	0.1679	35	
10	0.3031	40	0.125	41	*

It should also be noted that the difference in the use of extreme points becomes consistent for blacks and whites beyond the 3-point interval. The full scope of analysis of variance multiple range tests with a significance level .05, within groups, found no support for differences between 5,6,7,8,9 scale formats for whites and 5,6,7,8,10 scale formats for blacks. This would suggest that the degree of ERS bias is not appreciably reduced by the addition of response categories. The relative flatness of the difference curve would imply that the total degree of ERS does not change over response formats. The slight downward slope of the group proportions should be expected, as more subjective categories are included in the proportions.

Overall, the use of even numbered scales appears to have little impact on the level of ERS. When ERS is defined as the extreme end points, a slight alteration from the pattern of minimal decline may be noticed. In other words, a forced-choice scale could exhibit a somewhat higher degree of ERS, however, not at a statistically significant level. Within groups, the level of ERS exhibited between odd and even-point scales was found insignificant. No significant differences were indicated by all analysis of variance multiple range tests with a significance level .05. These results indicate that even numbered scales have negligible effect on ERS bias.

Certainly the most arresting result is that statistically significant differences can be found between black and white groups solely from ERS bias. That is, market researchers may find meaningful differences between the groups founded on the response set variations. Hence, extremeness in response is not the insignificant variation suggested by Peabody (1962) in cross-cultural comparisons. It is possible to find differences between ethnic groups based entirely on ERS. The implications of such a finding are that researchers may be reporting statistically significant differences between blacks and whites, on a particular construct of interest, which may actually reflect difference in ERS bias displayed by the groups using that response format. The difference in ERS between blacks and whites is robust enough to cause the reported affects attributed to a genuine construct. For example, market researchers may be erroneously reporting differences in product preferences, consumer attitudes or perceptions, between black and white consumers that are really attributable to ERS.

The study does provide some groundwork for the development of a culture specific ERS adjustment measure between black and white student samples. Whites, on average, consistently reported a 0.1585 lower level of ERS difference on Likert-type scales, at 5 and above-point levels. The consistency of the difference allows researchers to develop adjustment norms for ERS bias in black/white student comparisons. Yet, it should be noted that information might be lost in such an aggregate adjustment process (Greenleaf 1992a).

Limitations

Since the sample groups were limited to undergraduate students, age, income and level of education, were similar for participants. All three demographic characteristics have proven to influence ERS. While these characteristics of the sample group where deemed desirable for this paper's cultural tenor, to adjust future research solely based on these results would ignore the possibility of interaction effects of these variables. Thusly, caution is advised in the extrapolation of the results of this study beyond the established parameters. Study replication on a broader sampling frame would provide additional insight into subcultural response styles. Further research is merited on ERS interaction between cultural influences and personal characteristics.

A further limitation can be found in the application of the Greenleaf 16-item ERS measure. The instrument was designed to be used uniquely as a 6-item measure (Greenleaf 1992b). Altering the response scale formats may influence the reliability of the instrument and additional validation of the measure using the various response formats discussed above is warranted. While this study does indicate potential for altering formats, its exploratory nature prescribes further investigation into the correlations and equal extreme response proportions, prior to using the Greenleaf 16-item measure with other than a six-interval response format.

Discussion

The findings support the works of Bachman & O'Malley (1984a, b) suggesting that black students may exhibit higher levels of ERS than white students on Likert-type scales. The conclusions support the concept that ERS varies between ethnic and cultural groups. Therefore, considering the effects on inferential statistical analysis, marketers are advised to consider ERS and its consequences in the reporting of cross-cultural examinations.

Importantly, marketers must recognize that comparisons of subcultural groups, on a domestic level, may present the same response style difficulties usually reserved for international/cross-cultural discussions. The results of this domestic study fit the cultural response style relationships characteristically postulated in international cross-cultural essays. Geographic borders are not the key element in the identification of cultural response styles. ERS has been demonstrated to vary between subcultural groups within the same geographic region. Marketers involved in any level of cross-cultural research are advised to test for ERS. When significant differences are found, marketers must develop *a priori* ERS equal scale response formats or employ a *post hoc* response style adjustment technique (Cunningham, Cunningham and Green 1977; Greenleaf 1992a; Gurwitz 1987) to accrue meaningful results.

In the present study, it is shown that ERS differences between groups are reduced by using a 3-point scale. Scales with more categories did not result in a meaningful between- groups reduction of ERS. Cox (1980), in a succinct review of the literature, portrayed scales as have decreasing reliability, with only small gains in information content, as the number of categories increases. From these studies it is possible to deduce, for cross-cultural marketing research, the addition of response categories may further compound problems in group comparisons while achieving only minimal gains in information. Researchers may be better served by pursuing limited subjective categories as cross-cultural ERS norms are established.

Future Research

The range of difficulties associated with extreme response style might lead a researcher interested in cross-cultural marketing research to believe that there is little that can be contributed to controlling the ERS bias. This is not the case. Three levels of advancement are necessary: identification, understanding and control.

Initially, the continuous identification, through empirical methods designed for this purpose, of cultural ERS would enhance the scholarly work in this field. As ERS has been shown to have profound consequences on statistical analysis, and cultural groups display varying levels of the bias, cross-cultural marketing researchers should routinely report ERS information as they would any other statistical measure. The continuous reporting of the response style bias would facilitate the establishment of cultural ERS norms. Future cross-cultural research would benefit from the enhanced knowledge of the degree of bias in the statistical analysis. Cross-cultural knowledge is enriched, as more recent studies build on the foundation of prior research to achieve a higher level of methodological sophistication (Aulakh and Kotabe 1993; Nasif et al. 1991; Robert and Boyacigiller 1986; Sekaran 1983). As there is no flawless cross-cultural research, the formation of cultural ERS norms could guide future researchers in the development of culture appropriate research designs and analysis techniques.

Since this study has shown it is possible to find significant differences between cultural groups solely through ERS bias, the routine reporting of ERS would prohibit researchers from making claims of significant differences between groups based on research constructs, when the differences are truly the result of divergent cultural ERS bias.

The second level of ERS study should enhance understanding. While this study finds ERS differences between the two groups studied, it does not address the issue of explaining why these differences exist. While Bachman and O'Malley (1984a) suggest that black/white ERS differences may be attributed to '... subcultural differences in language use or style' (p.503), certainly, more study is justified, in various cultural settings to discern the exact cultural determinants of ERS. A base for future research in this area may be found in the 'personality characteristic' literature or in a cross-cultural explication like Hofstede (1980). Enhanced knowledge of how cross-cultural subjects stretch their subjective categories to meet the available response categories would improve marketing research efforts.

Finally, cross-cultural researchers are not likely to be solely satisfied with the identification of ERS in their data set. Control of the bias element inherent in the response style would be of special interest to marketers. An additional interesting area for exploration would be an application of the ERS correction described by Greenleaf (1992a) or ipsative rescaling (Cunningham, Cunningham and Green 1977; Gurwitz 1987) to minimize the consequences of response set bias. In instances when an *a priori* matching of ERS equal response sets is not appropriate or available for cross-cultural marketing research, the *post hoc* modification may prove proper. The choice of approach is likely to be determined by the specific research constraints. Regardless of the corrective procedure, one aspect is certain: disregarding the effect of ERS on cross-cultural marketing research could have a notable influence on the validity of research findings.

Conclusions

Significant difference in extreme response style between black and white subcultures can be found using the Greenleaf 16-item ERS measure. The extent of difference varies with the number of response categories, suggesting that black and white students consistently differ in their adaption of subjective range in relation to the quantity of response items available. But, the addition of response categories beyond the 5-point level does not appear to appreciably effect the difference between groups. This suggests that the addition of response categories beyond 5 will not reduce differences in ERS.

Statistically significant differences can also be found between black and white groups based solely on ERS. The implications of this finding are broad. Heretofore racial comparisons, using Likert-type scales with 5 or more response categories, may merely be reporting differences in response styles rather than the construct depicted. Marketing recommendations based on cross-ethnic quantitative Likert-type attitude research needs to be questioned for ERS.

The most important conclusion drawn from this study is that ERS is empirically shown to vary across cultures. Greenleaf's ERS Measure can be used as a test for cross-cultural ERS. This study clearly illustrates that differences can exist between subcultures in a single domestic market. Cross-cultural marketing researchers could easily draw erroneous conclusions, based on ERS effects, if the bias is invariably considered negligible. Therefore, extreme prudence is recommended in the fitting of ERS equivalent measures in cross-cultural investigations.

References

Albaum, Gerald and Brian D. Murphy (1988), 'Extreme Response On A Likert Scale,' *Psychology Reports*, 63, 501-2.

Albaum, Gerald and Linda Golden, Brian Murphy, and J. Strandskov (1987), 'Likert Scale and Semantic Differential: Issues Relevant to Cross-Cultural Research,' in *Proceedings of the Second Symposium on Cross-Cultural Consumer and Business Studies*, C.F. Keown and A.G. Woodside, eds., 113-6.

Arthur, Artur Z. (1966), 'Response Bias in the Semantic Differential,' *British Journal of Socialand Clinical Psychology*, 5, 103-7.

Aulakh, Preet S. and Masaaki Kotabe (1993), 'An Assessment of Theoretical and Methodological Development in International Marketing: 1980-1990,' *Journal of International Marketing*, 1(2), 5-28.

Bachman, Jerald G. and Patrick M. O'Malley (1984a), 'Yea-Saying, Nay-Saying, and Going to Extremes: Black-White Differences in Response Styles,' *Public Opinion Quarterly*, 48(Summer), 491-509.

_____ (1984b), 'Black-White Differences in Self-Esteem: Are They Affected by ResponseStyles?,' *American Journal of Sociology*, 90(3), 624-39.

Berg, I.A. (1953), 'Personality and Group Differences in Extreme Response Sets (ERS),' *Education and Psychological Measures*, 13, 164-169.

Berg, Irwin A. and Joanne S. Collier (1953), 'Personality and Group Differences in Extreme Response Sets,' *Educational and Psychological Measurement*, 13, 164-9.

Biggs, J.B. and J.P. Das (1973), 'Extreme Response Set, Internality-Externality and Performance,' *British Journal of Clinical Psychology*, 12, 199-210.

Bocker, Franz (1988), 'Scale Forms and Their Impact on Ratings' Reliability and Validity,' *Journal of Business Research*, 17, 15-26.

Borgatta, Edgar F. and David C. Glass (1961), 'Personality Concommitants of Extreme Response Sets,' *Journal of Social Psychology*, 55, 213-21.

Brengelmann, J.C. (1960), 'Extreme Response Set, Drive Level, and Abnormality in Questionnaire Rigidity,' *Journal of Mental Science*, 106, 171-86.

Chun, Ki-Taek, John B. Campbell and Jong Hae Yoo (1974), 'Extreme Response Style In Cross-Cultural Research: A Reminder,' *Journal of Cross-Cultural Psychology*, 5(December),465-80.

Clark, Terry (1990), 'International Marketing and National Character: A Review and Proposal for an Integrative Theory,' *Journal of Marketing*, 54(October), 66-79.

Cox, Eli P. (1980), 'The Optimal Number of Response Alternatives for a Scale: A Review,' *Journal of Marketing Research*, (November), 407-22.

Crandell, James E. (1982), 'Social Interest, Extreme Response Style, and Implications for Adjustment,' *Journal of Research in Personality*, 16, 82-9.

_____ (1973), 'Sex Differences in Extreme Response Style: Differences in Frequency ofUse of Extreme Positive and Negative Ratings,' *Journal of Social Psychology*, 89, 281-93.

_____ (1965), 'Some Relationship Among Sex, Anxiety, and Conservatism of Judgement,' *Journal of Personality*, 33, 99-107.

Cronbach, Lee J. (1950), 'Further Evidence on Response Sets and Test Design,' *Educational and Psychological Measurement*, 10, 3-31.

_____ (1946), 'Response Sets and Test Design,' *Educational and Psychological Measurement*, 6, 475-94.

Cunningham, William H., Isabella C.M. Cunningham, and Robert T. Green 1977), 'The Ipsative Process to Reduce Response Set Bias,' *Public Opinion Quarterly*, 41, 379-84.

Das, J.P. and Tapati Dutta (1969), 'Some Correlates of Extreme Response Set,' *Acta Psychologica*, 29, 85-92.

Douglas, Susan and C. Samual Craig (1983), *International Marketing Research*, Englewood Cliffs, NJ: Prentice-Hall, Inc.

Emmerich, Walter (1971), 'Cognitive Mediation of Development Trends in Extreme Response Choice,' *Developmental Psychology*, 5(3), 540.

Gove, Walter R. and Michael R. Geerken (1976), 'Response Bias in Surveys of Mental Health: An Empirical Investigation,' *American Journal of Sociology*, 82(6), 1289-317.

Green, Paul E. and Phillip D. White (1976), 'Methodological Considerations in Cross-NationalConsumer Research,' *Journal of International Business Studies*, 7, 81-87.

Greenleaf, Eric A. (1992a), 'Improving Rating Scale Measures by Detecting and Correcting Bias Components in Some Response Styles,' *Journal of Marketing Research*, 29(May), 176-88.

_____ (1992b), 'Measuring Extreme Response Style,' *Public Opinion Quarterly*, 56, 328-51.Gurwitz, Paul M. (1987), 'Ipsative Rescaling: An Answer to the Response Set Problem In Segmentation Analysis,' *Journal of Advertising Research*, (June/July), 37-42.

Hamilton, David L. (1968), 'Personality Attributes Associated With Extreme Response Style,' *Psychological Bulletin*, 69(3), 192-203.

Heide, Morten and Kjell Gronhaug (1992), 'The Impact of Response Styles in Surveys: A Simulation Study,' *Journal of Market Research Society*, 34(3), 215-30.

Hofstede, Geert (1980), *Cultures Consequences: International Differences in Work-Related Values*, Newbury Park: Sage Publications.

Hui, C. Harry and Harry C. Triandis (1989), 'Effects of Culture And Response Format on Extreme Response Style,' *Journal of Cross-Cultural Psychology*, (September), 296-309.

_____ (1985), 'The Instability of Response Sets,' *Public Opinion Quarterly*, 49(Summer), 253-60.

Innes, John M. (1977), 'Extremity and 'Don't Know' Sets in Questionnaire Response,' *British Journal of Social and Clinical Psychology*, 16, 9-12.

Iwawaki, Saburo and Melvin Zax (1969), 'Personality Dimensions and Extreme ResponseTendency,' *Psychological Reports*, 25, 31-4.

Jones, Richard R. and Leonard G. Rorer (1973), 'Response Biases and Trait DescriptiveAdjectives,' *Multivariate Behavioral Research*, 8(July), 313-30.

Leung, Kwok and Michael Harris Bond (1989), 'On the Empirical Identification of Dimensions for Cross-Cultural Comparisons,' *Journal of Cross-Cultural Psychology*, 20(2), 133-51.

Lewis, N.A. and J.A. Taylor (1955), 'Anxiety and Extreme Response Preferences,' *Psychological Reports*, 15, 111-6.

Light, Carole S., Melvin Zax and Dwight H. Gardiner (1965), 'Relationship of Age, Sex, and Intelligence Level to Extreme Response Style,' *Journal of Personality and Social Psychology*, 2, 907-9.

Littrell, Roland (1971), 'Effects of Extreme Response Style and Stimulus Word Attributes on Free Association,' *ERIC*, 1-14.

Lord, Frederic M. and Melvin R. Novick, with contributions by Allen Birnbaum (1968), *Statistical Theories on Mental Test Scores*, Reading, MA: Addison-Wesley.

Lorr, Maurice, Douglas M. McNair and Seymour Fisher (1982), 'Evidence for Bipolar Mood States,' *Journal of Personality Assessment*, 46(August), 432-6.

Lorr, Maurice and Richard A. Wunderlich (1980), 'Mood States and Acquiescence,' *Psychological Reports*, 46, 191-5.

Marin, Gerardo, Raymond J. Gamba and Barbara V. Marin (1992), 'Extreme Response Style and Acquiescence Among Hispanics: The Role of Acculturation and Education,' *Journal of Cross-Cultural Psychology*, 23(December), 498-509.

Markarian, Margie (1994), 'Cultural Evolution,' *Sales and Marketing Management*, May, p.127.

Matell, M.S. and J. Jacoby (1971), 'Is There an Optimal Number of Alternatives for Likert-scale Items? Study I: Reliability and Validity,' *Educational and Psychological Measurement*, 31, 657-674.

McKelvie, S.J. (1978), 'Graphic Rating Scale: How Many Categories?,' *British Journal of Psychology*, 69, 185-202.

Merrens, Matthew R. (1971), 'Personality Correlates of Extreme Response Style: A Function of Method of Assessment,' *Journal of Social Psychology*, 85, 313-4.

_____ (1970), 'Generality and Stability of Extreme Response Style,' *Psychological Reports*, 27, 802.

Miller, George A. (1953), 'The Magical Number Seven, Plus or Minus Two: Some Limits of Our Capacity for Processing Information,' *Psychological Review*, 63(March), 81-97.

Nasif, Ercan G., Hamad Al-Daeaj, Bahman Ebrahimi and Mary S. Thibodeaux (1991), 'Methodological Problems in Cross-Cultural Research: An Updated Review,' *Management International Review*, 3(1), 79-91.

Norman, Russell P. (1969), 'Extreme Response Tendency as a Function of Emotional Adjustment and Stimulus Ambiguity,' *Journal of Consulting and Clinical Psychology*, 33(4), 406-10.

O'Donovan, Denis (1965), 'Rating Extremity: Pathology or Meaningfulness?,' *Psychological Review*, 72(5), 358-72.

Oskamp, S. (1977), *Attitudes and Opinions*, Englewood Cliffs, N.J.: Prentice-Hall.

Parameswaran, Ravi and A. Yaprak (1987), 'A Cross-National Comparison of Consumer Research Measures,' *Journal of International Business Studies*, 18(Spring), 35-49.

Peabody, Dean (1962), 'Two Components in Bipolar Scales: Direction and Extremeness,' *Psychology Review*, 69, 65-73.

Peter, J. Paul and Jerry C. Olson (1994), *Understanding Consumer Behavior*, Irwin: Bur Ridge, Illinois.

Roberts, K.H. and N.A. Boyacigiller (1986), 'Cross-National Organizational Research: The Grasp of the Blind Men,' *Research in Organizational Behavior*, 6, 423-475.

Rorer, L.G. (1965), 'The Great Response-Style Myth,' *Psychological Bulletin*, 63, 129-56.

Rundquist, Edward A. (1950), 'Response Sets: A Note on Consistency on Taking Extreme Positions,' *Educational and Psychological Measurement*, 10, 97-9.

Samiee, Saeed and Insik Jeong (1994), 'Cross-cultural Research in Advertising: An Assessment of Methodologies,' *Journal of the Academy of Marketing Science*, 22(3), 205-17.

Schultz, Richard E. and Robert J. Foster (1963), 'A Factor Analytic Study of Acquiescent and Extreme Response Set,' *Educational and Psychological Measurement*, 23, 435-47.

Schwarz, Norbert, Hans J. Hippler, Brigitte Deutsch and Fritz Strack (1985), 'Response Scales: Effects of Category Range on Reported Behavior and Comparative Judgements,' *Public*

Opinion Quarterly, 49 (Fall), 388-95.

Sekaran, U. (1983), 'Methodological and Theoretical Issues and Advancements in Cross-Cultural Research,' *Journal of International Business*, Fall, 61-73.

Shapiro, Alvin H., Lorne Rosenblood, Geoffrey M. Berlyne and John Finberg (1976), 'The Relationship of Test Familiarity to Extreme Response Styles in Bedouin and Moroccan Boys,' *Journal of Cross-Cultural Psychology*, 7(3), 357-64.

Shiffman, Leon G. and Leslie Lazar Kanuk (1987), *Consumer Behavior*, Third Edition, Prentice-Hall Inc.: Englewood Cliffs, New Jersey.

Soueif, M.I. (1958), 'Extreme Response Sets as a Measure of Intolerance of Ambiguity,' *British Journal of Psychology*, 49, 329-34.

Stening, B.W. and J.E. Everett (1984), 'Attributions for Promotion and Demotion In the U.S.and India,' *Journal of Social Psychology*, 122,151-6.

Triandis, H. C. (1972), *The Analysis of Subjective Culture*, New York: John Wiley.

Triandis, H.C. and L.M. Triandis (1962), 'A Cross-Cultural Study of Social Distance,' *Psychological Monographs*, 76, 21.

Van der Kloot, William A., Pieter M. Kroonenberg and Dini Bakker (1985), 'Implicit Theories of Personality: Further Evidence of Extreme Response Style,' *Multivariate Behavioral Research*, 20, 369-387.

Warr, Peter B. and Thomas C. Coffman (1970), 'Personality, Involvement and Extremity of Judgement,' *British Journal of Social and Clinical Psychology*, 9, 108-21.

Wells, W.D. (1963), 'How Chronic Overclaimers Distort Survey Findings,' *Journal of Advertising Research*, 3(2), 8-18.

_____ (1961), 'The Influence of Yeasaying Response Style,' *Journal of Advertising Research*, 1(4), 1-12.

Wright, G.N., L.D. Phillips, P.C. Whalley, G.T. Choo, K.O. Ng, I. Tan and Wisudha (1978), 'Cultural Differences in Probabilistic Thinking,' *Journal of Cross-Cultural Psychology*, 9, 285-99.

Wyer, Robert S., Jr. (1969), 'The Effects of General Response Style on Measurement of Own Attitude and the Interpretation of Attitude-Relevant Messages,' *British Journal of Socialand Clinical Psychology*, 8, 105-15.

Yu, Julie H., Charles F. Keown, Laurence W. Jacobs and Kyung-Il Ghymn (1990), 'Cross-Cultural Considerations in Attitude Scale Methodology,' *Proceedings of the Third Symposium on Cross-Cultural Consumer and Business Studies*, 293-301.

Zax, Melvin, Dwight H. Gardiner and David G. Lowy (1964), 'Extreme Response Tendency as a Function of Emotional Adjustment,' *Journal of Abnormal and Social Psychology*, 69(6), 654-7.

Zax, Melvin and Shigeo Takahashi (1967), 'Cultural Influences on Response Style: Comparisons of Japanese and American College Students,' *Journal of Social Psychology*, 71, 3-10.

Zuckerman, M., J. Norton and D.S. Sprague (1958), 'Acquiescence and Extreme Sets and Their Role in Tests of Authoritarianism and Parental Attitudes,' *Psychiatric Research Reports*,10, 28-45.

Appendix 5.1 Extreme Response Style Measure (Greenleaf 1992b)

1. When I see a full ashtray or wastebasket, I want it emptied immediately.

2. I am a homebody.

3. Television is my primary form of entertainment.

4. No matter how fast our income goes up, we never seem to get ahead.

5. I try to avoid foods that are high in cholesterol.

6. Advertising insults my intelligence.

7. Investing in the stock market is too risky for most families.

8. Everyone should use a mouthwash to help control bad breath.

9. TV commercials place too much emphasis on sex.

10. A college education is very important for success in today's world.

11. My days seem to follow a definite routine - eating meals at the same time each day, etc.

12. I like to visit places that are totally different from my home.

13. I work very hard most of the time.

14. I like to feel attractive to members of the opposite sex.

15. I will probably have more money to spend next year than I have now.

16. I eat more than I should.

Chapter 6

Methodological Issues in Ethnic Consumer Survey Research: Changing Consumer Demographics and Implications

William K. Darley
Jerome D. Williams

Introduction

Demographic changes are so profoundly redefining American Society at every level including the ethno-cultural composition of the United States (Nasser 2004) that marketers are exploring new ways of dealing with the increasingly diverse marketplace. As diversity increases in the marketplace, it becomes questionable whether theories developed and tested within the dominant consumer group (i.e., Euro-Americans) can be appropriately applied to ethnic minority consumer groups (e.g., African-Americans and Asian-Americans) who perhaps differ in terms of household compositions, values, lifestyles, self-perceptions, and aspirations (Gilly 1993; cf. Riche 1990). Unfortunately, many researchers naively assume that research methods can be transferred wholesale among racial and ethnic populations (Adams and Adams-Esquivel, 1981; Dauten and Menendez, 1984; Williams, 1995; Garcia and Gerdes 2004).

Different racial groups have different histories and, for a variety of reasons, may respond differently to market-related questions. In fact, a recent Yankelovich Monitor indicates that Hispanic and African-American consumers share many points of view that white consumers do not. They differed in terms of (a) their perceptions about participation in activities that celebrate culture and heritage, (b) their need to preserve family-cultural traditions, and (c) the attributes they considered important in deciding where to shop (reported in *Marketing News*, March, 2004, p.13).

Relatively little attention has been paid to the relevance of race and ethnicity in marketing and consumer research. Methodological problems with respect to race and ethnicity can occur at all levels of the research process.

Hence, this chapter seeks to provide a much needed examination and clarification of the common methodological problems encountered in consumer research within and across ethnic minority populations. In addition, it seeks to sensitize cross-ethnic marketing researchers to problems that should be considered if valid and reliable findings are to emerge. We draw on a diverse literature to provide consumer researchers with a comprehensive and integrative discussion of the relevant methodological issues relating to consumer research within and across ethnic minority populations. Specifically, the paper examines these problems with respect to category construction, as well as functional, conceptual, measurement, sampling, and data collection equivalence. It also poses some guidelines for future consumer research with ethnic consumers.

The population of the United States is expected to reach almost 309 million by 2010 (Nasser 2004). Much of this growth is expected to come from non-white minority groups. Whereas in 1980, one in every five Americans in the United States was either of African-American, American Indian, Asian-American or Hispanic ancestry, in 1990 one in every four had such a minority background. Hispanic is an umbrella term for people from Mexico, Central America, South America, and the Caribbean and represents over 20 separate nationalities (Webster 1996). By the year 2050, the non-white minority groups' figure will climb to almost one in every two (Nasser 2004).

These changes are reflected in state, urban and inter-generational data. For example, in the age bracket above 70 years old, the ratio of whites to ethnic minorities is 5.5 to 1 but under the age of 20, it is one to one today. In California, 50% of babies born today are Hispanic and in Miami, 87% of the newly born, are of ethnic origin (Keefe 2004).

For the years 2000, 2010, 2020, and 2030, the percentage of United States population projections for African-American, Asian-American, and Hispanic groups are as follows: African-Americans (12.2%, 12.6%, 12.9%, 13.1%); Asian-Americans (3.3%, 4.8%, 5.7%, 6.6%); and Hispanics (11.4%, 13.8%, 16.3%, 18.9%), respectively (United States Department of Commerce 1996). The number of Hispanics is expected to grow to 103 million by 2050, with population share of 24% (Nasser 2004). Table 6.1 provides additional information about the United States population.

Table 6.1   Percent Distribution of U.S. Population by Race and Hispanic Origin (1990-2050)

Year	Total (in 000s)	Not of Hispanic Origin				Hispanic Origin[3]
		White	Black	American Indian[1]	Asian[2]	
1990	249,402	75.6%	11.8%	0.7%	2.8%	9.0%
2000	274,634	71.8%	12.2%	0.7%	3.3%	11.4%
2010	297,716	68.0%	12.6%	0.8%	4.8%	13.8%
2020	322,742	64.3%	12.9%	0.8%	5.7%	16.3%
2030	346,899	60.5%	13.1%	0.8%	6.6%	18.9%
2040	369,980	56.7%	13.3%	0.9%	7.5%	21.7%
2050	393,931	52.8%	13.6%	0.9%	8.2%	24.5%

[1] American Indian represents American Indian, Eskimo, and Aleut.
[2] Asian represents Asian and Pacific Island.
[3] Persons of Hispanic origin may be of any race.

Adapted from *Population Projections of the United States by Age, Sex, Race, and Hispanic Origin: 1995 to 2050* (pp.25-1130), U.S. Department of Commerce, February 1996.

As Euro-Americans steadily declines in the United States and cities such as New York, Chicago, and Los Angeles take on a more diverse character, the racial and ethnic reconfiguration of the United States will become more and more apparent. Already we are seeing a shift in the relative composition of the major ethnic groups. African-Americans are no longer the largest majority minority group; Hispanics supplanted African-Americans as the largest minority group in 2002 (Nasser 2004). The far-reaching implications of these demographic changes give reason for foresighted concern as we discern their significance for research methodology and attempt to articulate the new demographic realities in our consumer research methods.

Category Construction: Race versus Ethnicity

In general, researchers refer to race and ethnicity interchangeably when identifying and categorizing people by background (Betancout and Lopez 1993). However, the accepted definitions of race and ethnicity suggest these are considered different, although related, social categories. Race is based on socially constructed definitions of physical differences and is a meaningful social category in and by itself. In contrast, ethnicity is usually defined as membership in a subcultural group on the basis of country of origin, language, religion or cultural traditions different from the dominant society (Banton 1987; Baxter and Sansom 1972; Hutchison 1988).

Also, ethnic identification is usually expressed with varying intensity, from passive acquiescence to active participation and from denial to passionate commitment. Smith (1980) and Weinreich (1986) suggest three plausible ethnic identification measurement domains: (a) natal measures consisting of birthplace of self, siblings, natural parents, grandparents, and relatives; (b) subjective measures consisting of self-identification of preferred ethnic group, assessment of own acculturative status, real and aspired self-image, value preferences, role models and preferred reference groups, ego-involvement in group, and attitudes towards outgroups; and (c) behavioral measures comprising language usages including settings where used, friendship and acquaintance affiliative patterns, participation in cultural and religious activities, music and food preferences, and membership in mutual benefit societies. Each of the three domains contain variables that can shed insight into the personal preferences of an individual.

Some researchers view subjective self-labeling as the only valid measure of ethnicity because it represents the individuals internal beliefs and, therefore, reflects a person's cultural reality (Cohen 1978; Hirschman 1981). Nonetheless, there is great diversity among racial and ethnic minority group members as to what is most appropriate when self-selecting a category (Williams, 1995). The primary cultural identification may be different from the self-perceived ethnicity. For example, eight different responses were provided by African-American college students when they were asked to identify their race in an open-ended question (Jewell, 1985). The results of this study showed that (a) 73.5 percent identified themselves as 'Black' and (b) the remaining 26.5 percent used a variety of cultural designations or racial appellations: Black American, 9.2 percent; Negro, 6.9 percent; Afro-American, 4.6 percent; Black-Negro, 2.3 percent; Mixed, 1.1 percent; Colored, 1.1 percent and Negro-Indian, 1.1 percent. These differences in nomenclature may reflect real differences in perspectives.

Country of origin, immigration status, language and level of acculturalization add to the diversity within racial and ethnic populations. For example, Hispanics are far from being monolithic. About three quarters are of Mexican, Puerto Rican and Cuban ancestry. This proportion is however declining as other Latino nationalities continue to migrate to the United States (Garcia and Gerdes 2004). Hispanics define themselves differently, in part, through language preference: English-dominant, Spanish-dominant or bilingual (Vence 2004).

Since 1980, the identification of Hispanic groups has been based on single and different indicators: Spanish surname, country of origin, paternal ancestry, and Spanish spoken at home (Deshpande, Hoyer, and Donthu 1986). These indicators suggest disagreement about the nature of Hispanic ethnicity. The label 'Hispanic' may also be used by two researchers but operationalized differently. Even when the same label is used by researchers, the results produced may be misleading and contaminated by terminological and operational confusion (Hayes-Bautista 1980). Hence, Marin and Marin (1991, p.30) have suggested that a reliable operationalization of the label 'Hispanic' can be obtained by producing indices that consider (a) birthplace of self and parents, (b) self-identification, and (c) ancestry. However, Deshpande, Hoyer, and Donthu (1986) suggest using the strength of ethic identification or intensity of ethnic affiliation as a measure of ethnicity because within the same general group, differences between individuals of varying identification exist. In addition, Dauten and Menendez (1984) have suggested that to sharpen the screening procedure, it is best to ask respondents if they listen to Spanish broadcast media at least five hours per week.

Tanaka et al. (1998) also have noted that each of the following approaches (ancestry/national origin, cultural characteristics, and self-identification) depend on single-item probes and are inherently unreliable markers of Asian American ethnicity. Thus, they have argued that consistent with a multiple indicator approach to the identification of Asian-American ethnicity, an investigator should employ these markers in combination to define the ethnicity construct.

A related issue is how people of mixed racial background respond to ethnic identity scales or how to categorize such individuals into discrete racial/ethnic cells. For example, the U.S. Census Bureau has estimated that about 7% of adult Americans would identify themselves as multiracial, and by 2050, the percentage of U.S. population that claims mixed ancestry (i.e., some combination of black, white, Hispanic and Asian) will likely triple to 21% (Puente and Kasindof 1999). Beginning with the 2000 census, the U.S. Census Bureau is ending the deceptively simple statistical picture of U.S. racial characteristics. Instead of forcing each person listed to identify himself or herself in just one racial category, the census is allowing multiple choices. The new classification could have a profound impact on marketing. For example the child of a mixed African American and Caucasian marriage, who previously was reported as either black or white, will have the choice of being reported in a new category. Based on the current choice of 15 categories, the categories jump significantly if just two choices are made, and become intractable if more than two categories are checked. Although future statistics on race are expected to be more accurate and will allow marketers to gain a better understanding of multiculturism and the potential for growth among different consumers categories, the new statistics could be difficult to compare with older statistics, especially if many people make multiple choices (Teinowitz 1998).

In sum, confusion at the ethnicity or racial level could affect sampling quality and result in unrealistic findings. Thus, it is important to (a) distinguish between race and ethnicity, (b) provide the logic behind our ethnic groupings or racial categorization, and (c) employ a multiple indicator approach in identifying ethnicity. It is equally important to characterize the community of research interest more carefully and precisely (Nevid and Maria 1999). In keeping with anthropologists' recent views, Deshpande, Hoyer, and Donthu (1986) suggest that ethnic identification should use a combination of subjectivist and objectivist procedures, a pre-specified set of ethnic categories of research relevance needs to be developed and after testing the validity of these categories, individuals should be asked to ascribe categories to themselves. It is also important to pay attention to the unique norms and values that characterize a particular ethnic group (Hirschman 1981; Deshpande, Hoyer, and Donthu 1986; Valencia 1985).

Common Methodological Problems

In this section, we present the methodological problems associated with consumer research of ethnic minority populations. In particular, the issues of functional, conceptual, measurement, and sampling equivalence, as well as problems relating to data collection procedures, are examined.

Functional Equivalence

Functional equivalence examines whether a given activity, product, or behavior serves the same role or function in different ethnic groups. If similar consumer activities, products, or services serve dissimilar functions or purposes in different ethnic groups, then observed differences may be due to lack of functional equivalence. Hence, their parameters cannot be used for comparison purposes. The following example is presented to illustrate the potential of non-functional equivalence:

> In a study measuring networking, interpersonal communication, and word-of-mouth communication, the role of the barbershop or beauty shop would not be functionally equivalent between African-Americans and whites. In simple terms, for whites, a barbershop serves the function of a place to get a hair cut, while for the African-American, in many instances, it serves the function of a place to find out what is going on in the community. Getting a hair cut may be secondary.

Hence, functional equivalence must be established at levels involving (a) the time of consumption, (b) the purpose for which the product or service will be used, and/or (c) the social settings in which a product is consumed or an activity or service is performed. Without this equivalence, no valid cross-ethnic comparisons may be made (Usunier 1996).

Conceptual Equivalence

A basic issue in ethno-cultural research is whether concepts used within an ethnic group or across ethnic groups have equivalent meaning. Cross-ethnic studies and studies that have included significant numbers of individuals from different ethnic groups have assumed that the measures employed are universally applicable to all ethnic minority groups; these measures have been endorsed as valid by virtue of precedence. Nonetheless, problems of conceptual equivalence may occur in cross-ethnic consumer research because of the conceptual differences of certain socio-psychological constructs. Whereas many basic concepts are seemingly universal across ethnic groups, their underlying dimensions may be unequally weighted or articulated in the total construct.

To illustrate the potential of non-conceptual equivalence, the following examples are presented:

1. Income: To Hispanics, the concept 'income' is limited to earnings (i.e., wages and salary) derived from working on a job. Thus, they tend to under-report their income by excluding various types of transfer payments and earnings from investments. In contrast, income for whites tends to have a broader meaning encompassing earnings from all sources. This lack of equivalence of the income concept is compounded by differences in the time frame used to conceptualize income. Hispanics are more accustomed to thinking about their income in shorter time frames (e.g., monthly terms) as opposed to 'annual' terms (Hernandez and Kaufman 1990).

2. Coupons: The concept 'coupon' may be perceived differently by low income Hispanics. To some low income Hispanics, the term coupon (coupon) is commonly associated with food stamps (cupones de alimentos) and government handouts (Hernandez and Kaufman 1990). The majority population, however, sees coupons as a means of saving money on their grocery bill.

3. Brand loyalty: The concept of brand loyalty can mean different things to different ethnic minority groups. Most studies on Hispanic purchase behavior have utilized self-report data collected through consumer surveys (Mulhern and Williams 1995). While self-report data is advantageous for investigating consumer attitudes and perceptions, it can be problematic because consumer self-reports do not always correspond to actual purchase behavior. When asking whites and Hispanic consumers about their degree of brand loyalty, there is a high likelihood that two different concepts are being evaluated. Brand loyalty among Hispanics may be a reflection of reluctance to change to an unfamiliar brand (Garcia and Gerdes 2004) rather than a strong preference for a brand. The same could be true for other ethnic minority groups. For example, among Asians the concept of saving face, a concept somewhat foreign to most whites, may be tied to responding to a question dealing with changing brands.

4. Self-esteem: Much of the early work on self-esteem among African-Americans drew upon the studies dealing with photographs and line drawings of African-American and white children, clowns, and chickens, or choices between African-American and white dolls, and most of the traditional work on African-American self-esteem today can be traced back to these studies. However, equating self-esteem with the ability of an African-American child to select an African-

American doll over a white doll was flawed conceptually. For African-American children, most of whom had never even seen an African-American doll, it was simply a matter of selecting a doll with which they were more familiar. While the conceptual approach may have been appropriate for white children, it was not conceptually equivalent for African-American children.

5.   Innovativeness: Consumers are generally viewed in a positive light when they are said to be more innovative. However, for ethnic minority consumers, innovativeness in purchasing a new product may not have the same conceptual meaning as for non-minority consumers. The social marketing literature has a number of examples of marketers exploiting ethnic minorities (e.g., Uptown cigarettes with higher levels of nicotine, PowerMaster with higher levels of alcohol). Over the years, among ethnic minority consumers, this has created a degree of skepticism toward many marketers. What may be viewed as being less innovative among whites, may actually, among ethnic minority consumers, be a manifestation of a prudent shopper who is avoiding being taken advantage of by marketers. Similarly, Hispanics, particularly among more recent immigrants, may be insulated from a consistently high level of competitive advertising messages, which could lead to continued purchasing of the same brands. Therefore, they may prefer 'tried and true' brands as a means of protecting themselves against inferior goods, and hence may appear less innovative.

In sum, researchers have to try to use concepts or constructs that have equivalent meaning. Careful pretesting can ensure conceptual equivalence across ethnic groups.

Measurement Equivalence

Cross-Ethnic Equivalence The emic approach posits that attitudinal and behavioral phenomena are expressed in a unique way in each ethnic group. In contrast, the etic approach is primarily concerned with identifying universals across ethnic groups. Whereas measurement instruments adapted to each ethnic group (the emic approach) offer more reliability with greater internal validity than instruments applicable to several ethnic groups (the etic approach), the emic approach is at the expense of cross-ethnic comparability and external validity (Usunier 1996). Thus, an emic approach allows a researcher to do uni-ethno-cultural rather than comparative research. On the other hand, an etic approach allows comparisons across ethno-cultures, but subtle elements of the phenomena under study are likely to be missed or misinterpreted.

A number of emic ethnic identity scales have been developed for African-Americans. These emic scales commonly use questions unique to this group in order to extract ethnic identity. Examples of such items are as follows: Do you celebrate Martin Luther King's birthday? Do you belong to the NAACP? Do you subscribe to Ebony magazine? A similar approach can be used for any ethnic group. For example, see the scale developed by Valencia (1985) to measure 'Hispanicness'.

When researchers want to make comparisons among different ethnic groups, they use some type of etic approach rather than the emic scales. The simplest and most direct approach is a single item measure such as 'How strongly do you identify with your racial/ethnic group?' This is similar to the measure used by Hirschman (1981) to measure Jewish ethnicity. However, this approach can become problematic because of measure equivalence issues.

To illustrate the potential for non-cross-ethnic equivalence, the following example is provided:

> When using a scale to measure the strength of ethnic identity, the mean for ethnic minority groups, compared to whites, is almost invariably higher, and has significantly less variance. So, when one uses categories of 'high identifiers' and 'low identifiers' for African-Americans and Euro-Americans, for example, it may be difficult to find many 'low identifiers' among African-Americans. Some of this may have to do with distinctiveness theory, which suggests that the more an individual is in the minority, the more emphasis s/he places on ethnic identity. So for Euro-Americans, an ethnic identity scale may not even have a meaning because as the majority group, it is difficult to strongly identify with something taken as the norm or given. For ethnic minorities, however, expressing strong feelings about identifying with their group is akin to voicing opposition to what is perceived as the norm being imposed upon them by the majority group. Hence, there is a much stronger tendency for higher ratings (Phinney and Alipuria 1990).

In addition to single-item measures, there is a strong need for the development of relevant etic (ethno-culture-free) multi-item measures for meaningful cross-ethnic findings and to establish cross-ethnic equivalence. Such measures will allow for cross-ethnic comparability and enhance external validity. For example, Phinney (1992) has developed the Multigroup Ethnic Identity Measure, which is based on the elements of ethnic identity that are common across groups. Examples of items included in the 20-item scale are as follows: I have a clear sense of my ethnic background and what it means to me; I feel a strong attachment towards my own ethnic group; I have a lot of pride in my ethnic group and its accomplishments. Because Phinney's (1992) scale focuses on the elements of ethnic identity that are common across groups rather than on the unique elements that distinguish particular ethnic groups as used in the emic approaches, it is more suitable for cross-group comparisons.

Metric or Scalar Equivalence

Metric equivalence is concerned with whether the psychometric properties of data from different ethnic groups exhibit the same coherence or structure (Malhotra, Agarwal, and Peterson 1996) and centers on whether the same metric can be used to measure the same concept in two or more ethnic groups (Okazaki and Sue 1995). Metric equivalence is often overlooked or assumed without empirical validation in research with minorities.

Hernandez and Kaufman (1990) recommend the truncation of a multi-point scale (e.g., a 5-point scale) to a 3-point scale for survey research studies involving special groups with low literacy levels who may not be familiar with the very fine shades of meaning of the questions asked (Stanton, Chandran, and Hernandez 1982). Watson

(1992) also asserts that normal semantic 'agree-disagree' does not work with older Asian respondents and odd-interval scaled instruments inevitably attract the central or neutral response due to a desire not to cause any offence. Hence, Watson (1992) argues in support of the four point-scales for this group.

Referring to Hispanics, Hernandez and Kaufman (1990) also suggest the use of meaningful and appropriate categories. For instance, the conventional categories in the marital status question (single, married, divorced, separated, widowed) may have to be modified to include 'cohabitation' as an additional category. Similarly, categories for income may have to be structured such that more categories are included at the low end rather than at the high end of the income continuum because the median household income may be lower for many members of minority groups than for the rest of the population (Hernandez and Kaufman 1990).

The disparity in mean income among the different ethnic groups becomes problematic when comparisons are made. One approach that compares levels-of-income across ethnic groups is based on what economists sometimes refer to as the relative income hypothesis (Cicarelli 1974). This approach maintains that consumption depends on the level of a group's income relative to the income of the peer group with which it identifies, and not the absolute income level. Therefore, rather than comparing high and low income groups from different ethnic groups based on an absolute level of income, one could compare, for example, a high income group of whites to a high income group of Hispanics at different income levels. This is the approach used in the Mulhern and Williams (1995) study to account for the disparity in the relative mean incomes of the respective ethnic groups. To illustrate the potential of non-metric equivalence, the following example is given:

> For barrio Hispanics, the multi-point scales appear to be somewhat complicated for respondents to understand and are completely foreign (Hernandez and Kaufman, 1990).

In sum, it is important that the scales used are meaningful and appropriate to the target ethnic population. It is equally important to assess whether the instruments designed to measure the relevant constructs are cross-ethnically invariant. If evidence supporting a measures invariance is lacking, conclusions based on the scales are at best ambiguous and at worst misleading.

Translation Equivalence

Another measurement issue concerns the use of translated instruments. When participants are unable to read or understand English versions of the instrument, translation becomes necessary. Usunier (1996) identified four subcategories of translation equivalence: (a) lexical, (b) grammatical-syntactical, (c) idiomatic, and (d) experiential. Lexical equivalence is that which is provided by dictionaries. Grammatical-syntactical equivalence is concerned with how (a) words are ordered, (b) sentences are constructed, and (c) meaning is expressed in a language. An idiom is a linguistic usage that is natural to a group. Experiential equivalence is about what words and sentences mean for people in their everyday experiences (Usunier 1996).

In ethno-cultural consumer research, idiomatic equivalence and experiential equivalence are most likely to be problematic. Even when the same language is used to reach different segments of the population issues of translation equivalence can arise. For example, in a study of Ebonics, also known as African-American Vernacular English or Black English, there were significant differences not only between blacks and whites grouped by ethnic identity on familiarity and usage of Black English, but also between blacks who identified highly with their ethnic background and blacks who did not identify highly with their ethnic background (Williams and Grantham, 1999). The following example is provided to illustrate the potential problems with translation equivalence:

> The meaning of *bastante* (enough) in Spanish corresponded more closely to the English word moderately than did *moderamente* (moderately), the literal translation (Jones and Kay 1992).

Several translation techniques that are acceptable for achieving translation equivalence have been prescribed: translation by committee (two or more bilingual/bicultural individuals independently translate the instrument and the versions are compared); double (back) translation [i.e., one bilingual/bicultural translator translates the measure from English into the target language (e.g., Asian language); a second translator translates this version back into English, and the English versions are compared]; and decentering (a version of double translation in which both languages are considered important [i.e., the original English language version of the instrument also can be modified]) (Marin and Marin 1991).

Sampling Equivalence

Sampling Unit Because the role of respondents in the buying decision and the external influences on the choice processes vary across ethnic groups, it is important to assess sampling units' equivalency for comparison purposes. The male-female social roles, role of children, and the presence of single or dual parent families influence individual and household decision making differently in various ethnic groups. Hence, the role and responsibility of the subject must be considered in its appropriate context.

Noteworthy is the assumed homogeneity of racial and ethnic minority consumers. For example, most early consumer behavior studies of African-Americans focused primarily on the low-income, generally women, in urban areas, and often generalized the results to all African-American consumers. Also, consumer behavior studies have traditionally treated blacks as a homogenous, monolithic group (Robinson and Rao 1986; Reid, Stagmaier, and Reagan 1986; Williams 1989; Williams and Qualls 1989). The following examples are presented to illustrate the assumed homogeneity of black consumers:

1. An empirical study on perception of television commercials compared children from white middle-class schools and neighborhoods with children from black

inner city schools and neighborhoods to reach conclusions about differences between blacks and whites (Donohue, Meyer, and Henke 1978).

2.   In an ethnographic study, the inner city community was advocated as the setting to pursue research on the effects of ancestry and kinship on consumption practices among blacks since the ghetto community was viewed as the most typical setting for the black community (Hirschman 1985).

Not acknowledging heterogeneity within ethnic minority groups can create problems for analyses of the data and interpretation of the findings.   Trimble (1990/91) refers to the use of labels such as Asian-American, African-American, and 'Latino' as 'ethnic glosses' that lead one to homogenize very distinct ethnic minority populations.   For example, Marin and Marin (1991) note that ignoring differences within Hispanic populations can lead to using a methodology so faulty that it renders the results uninterpretable or misleading.   These issues also apply to other ethnic groups.   To enhance the validity of findings, Trimble (1990/91) suggests three remedies to the ethnic gloss: (a) eliminating the use of the ethnic gloss, (b) requiring researchers to provide more accurate and detailed information in describing subjects, and (c) exploring the development of ethnic identification and ethnic origin measures and using results to reorganize and redistribute sample frames.

Non-probability Samples   Intercept strategies are advocated for sampling minority consumers.   These strategies involve questioning subjects at churches, at recreation centers, on the street or at the mall, and other retail centers while making sure to include racial minorities in their proportion to the general population (Phillips, 1993). The intercept strategies suffer from lack of generalizability.   In addition, because Hispanics tend to shop as a family, only brief questioning or short surveys will minimize the imposition of an intercept (Adams and Adams-Esquivel, 1981).   In addition, mall intercepts do not capture data on 'non-Americanized' Latinos or new immigrants (Garcia and Gerdes 2004).

Sampling from college populations is an option used by some researchers; the college population offers a relatively large captive pool.   Nonetheless, students are hardly representative of any ethnic minority group.   The lack of generalizability of results from the college population has led some researchers to sample from ethnic minority communities.   Such sampling relies on captive sampling or snowball sampling in intact ethnic groups (Okazaki and Sue 1995).   In addition, sampling from ethnic minority communities also has been criticized for its lack of external validity (Sasao and Sue 1993).   However, using a focused numeration approach such as geodemographic national ethnic sampling (e.g., ACORN, PINPOINT, MOSAIC) to select areas of highly known ethnic concentration appears practically effective. Within such areas, broad quota controls are set on gender, age, and ethnic origin; localized samples are easier to interview as interviewers can be sent directly to areas of high concentration (Watson 1992).

Probability Samples   Without representative sampling, one cannot generalize to the larger group, calculate the sampling error or make valid population inferences.   To enhance the validity and credibility of ethno-cultural consumer research, probability samples are used. Still, acquiring representative samples of adequate size poses a methodological challenge.

Evidence suggests that a modification of Waksberg's (1978) method of random digit dialing may be applied to a wide range of sample surveys of ethnic minority populations (Blair and Czaja 1982). Waksberg's (1978) design is a two-stage method for selecting probability samples of the general population using random digit dialing; a modification of Waksberg's procedure that enables the researcher to locate ethnic minority populations that cluster geographically (Blair and Czaja 1982). This approach was found efficient in obtaining samples of African-Americans from highly clustered subgroups living in urban areas (Blair and Czaja 1982), as well as feasible and useful for research and evaluation purposes among Hispanics (Marin, Marin, and Perez-Stable 1990).

Another approach suggested by Hernandez and Kaufman (1990) is to use a two-stage area sampling. First, using city planning maps, residential blocks which serves as clusters in each neighborhood are selected; more blocks are selected from the larger census tracts. Second, the city maps are used to select residential addresses. Third, the residential addresses within each block are counted and a table of random numbers is used to pick the residential addresses for the sample. Finally, the households for the interviews are selected in the field.

Data Collection Equivalence

Data Collection Techniques Hernandez and Kaufman (1990) point out that telephone surveys may not be appropriate to reach Hispanics because of low telephone ownership, high incidence of unlisted numbers, and poor response rates. First, using the telephone to contact prospective subjects is far more of a problem with the Hispanic group than with non-Hispanic segments. Second, using random digit dialing to locate Hispanic households in large metropolitan area results in a 20 percent hit rate of working numbers. Third, sampling from those listed with Hispanic last names may not be helpful because 30 percent of the Spanish-origin population do not have Spanish last names and in husband-wife households where the husband has a Spanish name, 46 percent of the wives were not of Spanish origin (Meyer 1990; Suroco 1989).

Futhermore, Hernandez and Kaufman (1990) indicate that a mail survey may not be appropriate because of illiteracy and low response rates. Personal interviews do not gather complete response among Mexican-Americans and the lack of complete response raise serious issues about the reliability, validity, and overall utility of the data collected.

Reliance on telephone and mail surveys do not yield representative cross-sections of African-Americans. Phone polling, in particular, is not very effective in urban areas because of the general suspicion that African-Americans have about those seeking personal information. Because minority consumers tend to be clustered, as opposed to being randomly distributed, the random-digit-dialing techniques simply do not work. Random dialing typically yields a sample that is only 6 percent to 8 percent African-Americans, roughly half the level of African-American representation in the general population. In addition, African-Americans in the sample would tend to have values more in line with white suburbanites (Phillips 1993). Nonetheless, because of the large number of African-Americans with unlisted numbers and their general suspicion about giving out data, personal interviews are the most effective manner to reach this population (Miller 1993).

Also, Internet surveys do not capture data in minority groups. For example, a recent December 2003 report from Neilsen/NetRating Inc. suggests that only a third of the major ethnic groups- Hispanic, African-American and Asian-American – living in the United States go online now regularly (Vence 2004). Garcia and Gerdes (2004) note that Internet surveys do not capture data in 'non-Americanized' Hispanics or new immigrants.

To ensure equivalence and comparability of data collection methods across ethnic groups, Malhotra, Agarwal, and Peterson (1996) suggest reliance on telephone surveys when there is high sample control, difficulty of locating subjects at home, inaccessibility of homes, unavailability of a large pool of trained interviewers and unavailability of mailing lists. Personal interviews should prevail when there is high sample control, unavailability of mailing lists, low penetration of telephones, low level of literacy or high proportion of the population with good reading skills, and face-to-face communication preference. Mail survey method should be preferred when there is difficulty in locating respondents at home, inaccessibility of homes, unavailability of a large pool of trained interviewers, and low penetration of telephones.

Differences in Response Style

Ethnicity also can influence respondents' feelings about and willingness to answer certain questions (Ford and Norris 1991). Liu (1982) reported response errors were much higher for both immigrant and native-born Asians than for the native-born, middle class, white populations, and that the former groups may politely distort their true feelings, opinions, and even the facts. Ying (1989) also found that age, gender, and education were related to the non-response within Chinese-Americans. Nandi (1982, p.89) states that the most intriguing aspect of in-depth interview situations with Asian-Americans is the seeming inconsistency of responses, which may, at times border on contradiction. It is not uncommon to find the Asian simultaneously attracted to and repulsed by some aspect of a person, symbol, value, or system. In the context of Chinese, Japanese, or Indian philosophic values which view an absolute system of values with uneasiness. This dualism among Asian Americans is likely to pose a major challenge to conventional research techniques in both gathering and interpretation of data.

Values characteristic of Hispanic culture may influence respondents' behavior in an interview (Ford and Norris, 1991, p.544). For example, Hispanic-American respondents may be motivated to answer all questions even if they do not understand or wish to answer particular questions because of 'simpatia' (i.e., the valuing of positive and cooperative interpersonal relations with others). The tendency toward 'yea-saying' on selected attitude items was found to be higher for the Hispanic group than for the general population (Aday, Chiu, and Andersen 1980).

In addition, the macho code encourages men to restrain from any display of emotions and to maintain emotional distance and the machismo / marianismo gender stereotypes may lead women to feel restricted in offering their opinions especially if such opinions differ from their husbands (Javier 1995). Also, African Americans may appear guarded and less disclosing than other groups because of the sensitivity of many African Americans to the past exploitations by the majority white culture (Nevid, Rathus and Green 1997).

In fact, research with African-Americans and Hispanic-Americans (e.g., Hui and Triandis 1989; Marin and Marin 1991) suggests that members of ethnic minority groups who answer scaled items tend to exhibit (a) extreme response styles (Garcia 1991) and (b) an acquiescent response style (i.e., agreement with items regardless of their content). However, these response sets have been found to be moderated by the educational and acculturation levels of the research participants (Marin, Gamba, and Marin 1992), a view supported by research on Asian-Americans (e.g., Smith 1990).

Biases Resulting From the Relationship With the Interviewer

A practical concern is who should interview ethnic respondents in cross-ethnic studies. Sternlieb (1968) asserts that the ethnic background of the interviewer influences both the completion rate and the quality of material received in personal interviews. Referring to Hispanics, Marin and Marin (1991, p.60) also have noted that the use of same-ethnicity research personnel enhances the quality of the research data and increases the rate of participation. In a recent article, Webster (1996) reports that response quality was affected significantly by interaction effects of respondent and interviewer ethnicity. Ethnically, homophilous interviews generated the highest response quality. Both Hispanic and Anglo respondents deferred to an interviewer of a different ethnic background when questioned about the interviewers culture, but not when the questions were non-cultural, albeit sensitive. Because a bias can be induced by unsuitable interviewers (Nandi 1982; Watson 1992), it may be necessary to have (1) ethnic matching for cultural sensitive topics, (2) gender matching (e.g., for people of male-dominated societies or people with strong patriarchial feelings) depending on the ethnic origins of the respondents, and (3) both gender matching and ethnic matching where difficulties are likely to exist in the form of language and cultural barriers.

Context Equivalence of Data Collection

Contextual equivalence refers to elements in the data collection context that have an influence on the response given to a question (Usunier 1996). Because questions are never culture-free or context-free, the socio-cultural context of the questions should be considered. For example, Usunier (1996) notes that questions dealing either directly or indirectly with social prescription need to allow for response elaboration without the respondent feeling too embarrassed. In addition, such responses should be screened to determine if responses reflect reality or what is socially desirable. In-depth interviews may be necessary to determine subject's true views on such questions. Table 2 summarizes the key topics covered in this section of the chapter.

Table 6.2   Methodological Issues

METHODOLOGICAL ISSUES		
Problem	Definition	Example
A. Category construction and population focus	Identifying and classifying individuals into group membership.	Eight different responses of African-American college students when asked to identify their race. Different ways of identifying Hispanics.
B. Functional equivalence	The extent to which different products, services, or consumer activities serve similar functions in different ethnic groups.	The role of barbershop for African-Americans. It serves as a place to find out the latest information.
C. Conceptual equivalence	Equal meaning of concepts.	Meaning of 'income' for Hispanics. Income is limited to wages and salary.
D. Measure equivalence		
. Cross-ethnic equivalence	Whether an instrument is adapted to a specific ethnic group is applicable across ethnic groups.	Using a scale to measure the strength of ethnic identity. The mean of ethnic minority groups compared to whites is almost invariably higher.
. Metric equivalence	The assumption that the same metric can be used to measure the same concept in two or more ethnic groups.	The use of a multi-point scaled or odd-interval scaled instrument among different ethnic minority groups.
. Translation equivalence	Whether ideas, concepts, and idioms can easily be expressed in the language of the different ethnic group being studied.	The meaning of *bastante* (enough) in Spanish corresponds more closely to the English word moderately than does *moderamente* (moderately), the literal translation.

Problem	Definition	Example
E. Sampling equivalence		
. Sampling unit/choice of respondent	Selecting unit of analysis.	The different roles of individuals in different ethnic groups.
. Probability samples	Getting a representative sample of adequate size.	Waksberg's two stage method of selecting probability sample.
. Nonprobability samples	A subjective sampling procedure.	Convenience samples, sampling from college populations, snowball sampling.
F. Data Collection equivalence		
. Response style	Willingness to answer certain questions and how questions are answered.	Tendency toward 'yes-saying' found among Hispanics.
. Biases resulting from relationship with the interviewer	The effect of the interviewer on the responses of the interviewee.	Non-response may be magnified when immigrant minority populations are confronted by official looking well-mannered interviewer.
. Data collection context	The effect of the context on the responses.	Questions dealing with social prescription.
. Data collection techniques	How the data is collected.	For Hispanics, female interviewers should speak to female housewives or interviews should be conducted in the evening, when the man of the house is likely to be home.

Adapted from Douglas and Craig (1984, p.95) and Usunier (1996, p.143).

Recommendations or Guidelines

We delineate specific suggestions for category construction, conceptualization, sampling, data collection, and data analysis. We also address ethnocentric concerns. These suggestions are offered to encourage additional consumer research in minority populations.

Category Construction Considerations

Race and ethnicity should be properly defined and operationalized. Its proposed relationship to consumption variations should be presented. To allow for comparisons and appropriate hypotheses, authors should try to (1) use accurate descriptions rather than catchall terms in common use, (2) discuss, in the methods section, the logic behind their 'ethnic' groupings, (3) state explicitly how such classifications were made, (4) use terms that are as descriptive as possible and reflect how the groups were demarcated (McKenzie and Crowcroft 1996, p.1054; *British Medical Journal* 1996, p.1094), and (5) describe the contextual characteristics of ethnic minority samples. In addition, it is important to employ a multiple indicator approach in identifying ethnicity (Tanaka, Ebreo, Linn, and Morera 1998).

Conceptual Considerations

Research conducted in minority populations should not be done without first (a) examining or re-examining the basic assumptions, (b) developing culturally sensitive conceptual models, and (c) determining empirically the meaningfulness of substantive concepts for the minority ethnic groups (Jackson, Tucker, and Bowman 1982). More meaningful ethno-cultural insights will be produced if findings are linked to existing theories or converged into a new one.

Studying the minority consumer markets may require new methodological approaches with a different set of questions and different sample structures than are currently employed. Sasao and Sue (1993) suggest a three-dimensional approach or a culturally anchored framework where one considers the interaction among (a) the type of research questions, (b) the selection of methods, and (c) the cultural complexity (i.e., the extent to which an ethno-cultural group is defined in a larger ecological context at the individual and collective level). In designing and conducting research in ethnic cultural communities, these three elements interact to determine a study's design and its outcome and, thus, must be examined simultaneously, as well as weighed against each other to obtain scientifically valid research results (Sasao and Sue, 1993).

The research questions should also have a clear relationship to the purpose of the study and should be influenced by the existing knowledge and by the theoretical tools that can be applied to these questions. The methods employed should enable the researcher to answer the questions and also handle plausible validity threats to these answers (Maxwell 1998). In addition, the relevant ethno-cultural aspects of the group should be defined within the appropriate ecological context, and attempts should be made to employ ethnic-specific, culturally appropriate or relevant research methodologies.

Sampling Considerations

Rather than relying on convenience samples, we may have to understand the characteristics of ethnic minority respondents in a more complete way by employing probability sampling techniques. The two-stage sampling strategy could be successfully adapted for ethnic minority groups (Blair and Czaja 1982; Hernandez and Kaufman 1990; Marin, Marin, and Perez-Stable 1990; Takana, et al. 1998).

Samples should be checked for equivalence in terms of basic socio-economic and other salient characteristics that may affect the findings. Because the median age of some ethnic groups (e.g., Hispanics and African-Americans) is lower than that for the general population, it has been suggested that age quotas for the research project be adjusted downward (Dauten and Menendez 1984). In case the samples are not comparable, Malhotra, Agarwal, and Peterson (1996) recommend that the analysis be conducted on various subsamples to assess the impact of differences in terms of identified variables. Any lack of comparability in the samples should be noted, reported as a limitation, and incorporated into the interpretations of the data (Collins 1992).

Standard survey samples should include enough representative minorities so that within subgroups differences can be observed or analyzed. This would (a) avoid oversimplifying many of the differences within any subgroup, (b) avoid false claims of homogeneity within a subgroup, (c) decrease the margin of error, (d) enhance the reliability of results, and (e) allow for subgroup breakdown and statistical analyses (Smith 1993).

The research report should contain sufficient specification of the sample and the sampling methodology to allow cross-validation or replication and cross-study comparisons. When reporting results of ethno-cultural consumer studies researchers should strive to address questions such as (a) whether the population from which the ethno-cultural sample was drawn was consistent with the population of interest for the study, (b) whether the methods for selecting subjects had biased the sample, and (c) whether the estimates or sample statistics were sufficiently precise for the study's purpose (Henry 1998).

Data Collection Considerations

To reduce non-response in ethnocultural consumer research, questions asked should be relevant, and meaningful, and phrased in a form acceptable to the ethno-cultural group. Open-ended questions should be included to provide an opportunity to explore untapped aspects of the phenomenon under study and to allow for the discussion of the research experience. The latter would provide a check on the validity of the data (Ying 1989). Referring to Hispanics, (Garcia and Gerdes 2004) recommend that when conducting a survey, the researchers should allow respondents to select their own language preference. This allows the researcher to obtain a more accurate reflection of the marketplace.

Because of historical exclusion, ethnic groups tend to be less prepared to participate in research projects. Thus, interviewers should (a) be prepared to carefully explain the purpose of the study and what respondents can expect, (b) concentrate on straightforward questions, and (c) allow respondents an opportunity to use the language with which they are most comfortable (Dauten and Menendez 1984).

Data Analysis Considerations

The level of analysis (i.e., whether to use intra-ethnic group analysis or inter-ethnic group analysis) should be of concern (Malhotra, Agarwal, and Peterson 1996). In intra-ethnic group analysis, the data is analyzed separately within each ethnic group. The goal of intra-ethnic group analysis, in general, is to gain a better understanding of the relationships and patterns existing within that group. If the researcher is interested in a specific ethnic population, the researcher should at a minimum report some basic indicants of psychometric rigor (i.e., reliability, validity, and factor structure).

In inter-ethnic group or across-ethnic group analysis, the data of all the ethnic groups are analyzed simultaneously. The data is aggregated and analyzed for each ethnic group. The goal of inter-ethnic group analysis, in general, is to assess the comparability of findings from one ethnic group to another. Hence, similarities across ethnic groups and differences in means, variances, as well as distribution across ethnic groups should be assessed. In addition, all the commonly used statistical techniques should be applied. If the researcher is interested in comparisons across ethnic minority populations, then at a minimum, he or she should also examine the distribution of scale items across ethnic groups to detect possible range restrictions and outliers and should use the same factor analytic method across groups to evaluate conceptual equivalence (Ben-Porath 1990; Okazadi and Sue 1995).

Interpretation of simple between-group differences is complicated to the extent that intra-group heterogeneity exists. Thus, it is important to control within-group variations, the level of acculturation, level of racial identity, social class, and generational status (Ponterotto 1988). Many of these variables interact. If they are not measured, acknowledged, and/or controlled, these sources of intra-group diversity could become a source of measurement error and could obscure significant inter-group differences (Collins 1992).

Recently, Steenkamp and Baumgartner (1998) have recommended several guidelines for assessing measurement invariance and for establishing measure equivalence that are applicable across ethnic groups. Their framework is based on the multigroup confirmatory factory analysis model and applies to situations in which data is obtained in different ethnic minority populations; and the same set of items is used to operationalize the construct(s) of interest. Accordingly, if the purpose is to explore the basic meaning and structure of the construct cross-ethnically, then the same pattern of factor loadings must be present in the different ethnic groups. If the loading is cross-ethnically significant, evidence is obtained that the item is related to the underlying construct in each ethnic group. Second, if the purpose is to make quantitative comparisons of means across ethnic groups, then metric and scalar invariance for at least two items per construct (or per factor in the case of multidimensional constructs) is required. Otherwise, comparing scores cross-ethnically is meaningless since the scales are fundamentally different across groups. Finally, if the purpose is to examine structural relationships with other constructs in a nomological net, full or partial metric invariance has to be established because the scale intervals of the latent constructs have to be comparable across ethnic groups (Steenkamp and Baumgartner 1998).

Whether the data should be standardized or not is equally important. Standardized variables within each ethnic group are easier to interpret and the standardization produces a common metric, which permits comparison of the effects of different independent variables. In contrast, unstandardized variables allow for valid comparisons across ethnic groups and structural invariance is much more stable for unstandardized data than on standardized data. Malhotra, Agarwal, and Peterson (1996) recommend that (a) general etic comparisons across ethnic groups should be based on unstandardized data, assuming that construct equivalence has been established and (b) emic comparisons within an ethnic group should be made on the basis of standardized data.

Ethnocentric Considerations

Similar to investigators in other disciplines (Senior and Bhopal 1994), consumer researchers should recognize the potential influence of ethnocentricity (i.e., tendency to view one's own culture as the basis for comparing other cultures). Ethnocentricity may impinge on development of the hypothesis, the research design, and the methodology, as well as on the presentation and interpretation of the results. Wherever possible, researchers, interviewers, and respondents should share a common frame of reference. When this is not possible, the researcher should strive for closer contact with the data sources to monitor the effect of such differences on conceptual equivalence and non-response errors. At the very least, a personal experience in the field should help in the interpretation of the data from an ethno-culturally relevant perspective.

Working closely with marketing specialists from the minority communities will be helpful in interpreting the data from such research efforts. In addition, expert ethnic consultants or individuals who possess a high degree of cultural understanding and empathy should be involved in evaluating the conceptual equivalence of measures prior to data collection (Okazadi and Sue 1995).

Conclusion

In a literature search of the major academic marketing journals (i.e., *Journal of Marketing, Journal of Marketing Research,* and *Journal of Consumer Research*) from 1987-1992, Gilly (1993) found that minority issues received virtually no attention. Only one article could be found in the *Journal of Consumer Research* that examined Hispanics and none could be found which addressed the needs of African-American or

Asian-Americans (Gilly 1993, p.375). Williams (1995) also conducted a content analysis of *Journal of Consumer Research, Journal of Consumer Psychology,* and *Psychology and Marketing* for their publication periods. Only 3.4 percent of the total number of articles had a racial or ethnic minority focus and only 2.3 percent of the total number of subjects were identified as racial or ethnic minorities.

The recent surge of papers critically assessing the state of knowledge on various marketingtopics suggests that a process of reappraisal is taking place in the marketing field (Silk 1993). This reappraisal should be extended to consumer research on ethnic minority populations. Attention to the aforementioned methodological issues will (a) lead to improvements in the design and conduct of consumer research on ethnic minority populations and (b) result in advances in knowledge concerning ethnic minority consumer populations.

Whereas methods that explore mean differences among ethnic minority groups are interesting, a process-oriented approach that attempts to understand the ethnically specific factors that contribute to consumer behavior outcomes will contribute greatly to our body of knowledge (Tanaka, et al. 1998). To allow for the verification of scientific truths about the consumer behavior of ethnic minorities, we need to sort out what we know from what we do not know. Thus, what we know about the marketplace and our market generalizations would have to be updated, modified, or broadened to include all ethnic minority populations. Significant research is also needed to define precisely what constitutes a minority consumer to clearly identify when being a minority versus non-minority makes a difference (Williams 1995).

It is our hope that the foregoing discussion would stimulate critical thinking about the research methods employed in minority consumer markets and would contribute to an increased desire for a better understanding of our culturally diverse marketplace. When we directly confront the challenges inherent in applying our marketing theories and concepts in a culturally diverse marketplace, we are likely to produce better theories and stronger marketing generalizations. Including ethno-cultural variables in marketing and consumer research will help to establish the boundaries and limitations of our marketing knowledge.

References

Aday, Lu Ann, Chiu, Grace Y., and Andersen, Ronald, Methodological Issues in Health Care Surveys of the Spanish Heritage Population. *American Journal of Public Health*, 70 (April, 1980): 367-374.

Adams, Loretta H., and Adams-Esquivel, Henry, Experts Dispel Myths, Provide Tips on Conducting Hispanic Market Research. *Marketing News*, 14 (June 12, 1981): 16.

Banton, Michael P., *Racial Theories*, New York: Cambridge University Press, 1987.

Baxter, Paul, and Sansom, Basic, *Race and Social Difference: Selected Readings*, Baltimore: Penguin Books, 1972.

Ben-Porath, Yossef S., Cross-Cultural Assessment of Personality: The Case of Replicatory Factor Analysis, In *Advances in Personality Assessment*, James N. Butcher and Charles D. Spielberger, eds., Lawrence Erlbaum Associates, Hillsdale, N.J. 1990, 27-48.

Betancourt, Hector, and Lopez, Stephen Regeser, The Study of Culture, Ethnicity and Race in American Psychology. *American Psychologist*, 48 (June, 1993): 629-637.

Blair, Johnny and Czaja, Ronald, Locating a Special Population Using Random Digit Dialing. *Public Opinion Quarterly*, 46 (Winter, 1982): 585-590.

British Medical Journal, Ethnicity, Race, and Culture: Guidelines for Research, Audit, and Publication. *British Medical Journal*, 27 (April, 1996): 1094.

Cicarelli, James, On Income, Race, and Consumer Behavior. *The American Journal of Economic and Sociology*, 33 (3, 1974): 243-247.

Cohen, Ronald, Ethnicity: Problem and Focus in Anthropology. *Annual Review of Anthropology*, (7, 1978): 379-403.

Collins, R. Lorraine, Methodological Issues in Conducting Substance Abuse Research on Ethnic Minority Populations. *Drug & Society*, 6 (1-2, 1992): 59-77.

Dauten, Dale and Menendez, Teresa, Hispanic Research is Comparable to General Research-Provided Differences are Respected. *Marketing News*, 18 (February 17, 1984): 18.

Deshpande, Rohit, Hoyer, Wayne D., and Donthu, Naveen, The Intensity of Ethnic Affiliation: A Study of the Sociology of Hispanic Consumption. *Journal of Consumer Research*, 13 (September, 1986): 214-220.

Donahue, Thomas, R., Meyer, Timothy P., and Henke, Lucy L., Black and White Children: Perceptions of TV Commercials. *Journal of Marketing*, 42 (October, 1978): 34-40.

Douglas, Susan P. and C. Samuel Craig, Establishing Equivalence in Comparative Consumer Research. In *Comparative Marketing Systems*, Erdener Kaynak and Ronald Savitt, eds., Praeger Publishers, New York, 1984, pp. 93-113.

Ford, Kathleen and Norris, Anne, Methodological Considerations for Survey Research on Sexual Behaviors: Urban African-American and Hispanic Youth. *The Journal of Sex Research*, 28 (November, 1991): 539-555.

Garcia, Juan and Roberto Gerdes, To Win Latino Market, Know Pitfalls, Learn Rewards. *Marketing News*, (March 1, 2004): 14, 19.

Garcia, Carlos E., Consider Side-by-side Research for Hispanics and Non-Hispanics. *Marketing News*, 25 (September 16, 1991): 15.

Gilly, Mary, Studies of Women and Minorities in Marketing Research. *AMA Winter Educators' Conference Proceedings*, (1993): 375.

Handleman, David, The Organization of Ethnicity. *Ethnic Groups*, 1 (June, 1977): 187-200.

Hawkins, Del I., Best, Roger J., and Coney, Kenneth A., *Consumer Behavior: Building Marketing Strategy*, Irwin/McGraw-Hill, Boston, 1998.

Hayes-Bautista, David E., Identifying 'Hispanic' Populations: The Influence of Research Methodology on Public Policy. *American Journal of Public Health*, 70 (April, 1980): 353-356.

Hernandez, Sigfredo A., and Kaufman, Carol J., Marketing Research in Hispanic Barrios: A Guide to Survey Research. *Marketing Research,* 2 (March, 1990): 11-27.

Henry, Gary T., Practical Sampling. In *Handbook of Applied Social Research Methods*, Leonard Bickman and Debra J. Rog, eds., Sage Publications, Thousand Oaks, CA, 1998, 101-126.

Hirschman, Elizabeth C., Primitive Aspects of Consumption in Modern American Society. *Journal of Consumer Research*, 12 (September, 1985): 142-154.

Hirschman, Elizabeth C., American Jewish Ethnicity: Its Relationship to Some Selected Aspects of Consumer Behavior. *Journal of Marketing*, 45 (Summer, 1981): 102-110.

Hutchison, Ray, A Critique of Race, Ethnicity, and Social Class in Recent Leisure-Recreation Research. *Journal of Leisure Research*, 20 (1, 1988): 10-30.

Jackson, James S., M. Belinda Tucker, and Phillip J. Bowman, Conceptual and Methodological Problems in Survey Research on Black Americans. In *Methodological Problems in Minority Research*, William T. Liu, ed., Occasional Paper 7, Pacific/Asian American Mental Research Center, 1982.

Javier, R.A., Machismo/Marianismo Stereotypes and Hispanic Culture. In J. Nevid, S.Rathus, and L. Fichner-Rathus (eds.), *Human Sexuality in a world off Diversity*, Needham Heights, MA: Allyn & Bacon, Inc.,1995, 174-175.

Jewell, K. Sue, Will the Real Black Afro-American, Mixed, Colored, Negro Please Stand Up: Impact of Black Movement Twenty Years Later. *Journal of Black Studies*, 16 (September, 1985): 57-74.

Jones, Elaine G., and Kay, Margarita, Instrumentation in Cross-Cultural Research. *Nursing Research*, 41 (May/June, 1992): 186-188.

Liu, William T., *Methodological Problems in Minority Research*, Occasional Paper No. 7, Pacific/Asian American Mental Health Research Center, 1982.

Malhotra, Naresh K., James Agarwal, Mark Peterson, Methodological Issues in Cross-Cultural Marketing Research. *International Marketing Review*, 13 (5, 1996): 7-43.

Marin, Geraldo, Gamba, Raymond J.K., and Marin, Barbara V., Extreme Response Style and Acquiescence Among Hispanics: The Role of Acculturation and Education. *Journal of Cross-Cultural Psychology*, 23 (December, 1992): 498-509.

Marin, Gerardo and Marin, Barbara VanOss, *Research With Hispanic Populations*, Sage Publications, Newburry Park, CA.,1991.

Marin, Gerardo, Marin, Barbara VanOss, and Perez-Stable, Eliseo J., Feasibility of a Telephone Survey to Study a Minority Community: Hispanics in San Francisco. *American Journal of Public Health*, 80 (March, 1990): 323-326.

Marketing News, Common Ground: Hispanic and African American Consumers Share Many Points of View that White Consumers Don't, (Yankelovich Monitor, Yankelovich Partners, Inc.). *Marketing News*, (March 1, 2004): 3.

Maxwell, Joseph A., Designing a Qualitative Study. In *Handbook of Applied Social Research Methods*, Leonard Bickman and Debra J. Rog, eds., Sage Publications, Thousand Oaks, CA., 1998, 69-100.

McKenzie, Kwame and Crowcroft, N.S., Describing Race, Ethnicity, and Culture in Medical Research. *British Medical Journal*, 312 (April, 1996): 1054.

Meyer, Timothy P., Hispanic Consumer Behavior and the Development of Advertising Copy: The Advantages of Qualitative Research Techniques. In *Proceedings of the 1990 Conference of the American Academy of Advertising*, Patricia Stout, ed., The University of Texas at Austin, Austin, Texas, 1990, RC-157-RC-162.

Miller, Cyndee, Research on Black Consumers: Marketers With Much At Stake Step Up Their Efforts. *Marketing News*, 19 (September, 1993): 1, 42.

Mulhern, Francis J., and Williams, Jerome D., A Market Response Analysis of Shopping Behavior in Hispanic Areas. *Journal of Retailing*, 70 (3, 1995): 231-251.

Nandi, Proshanta K., Surveying Asian Minorities in the Middle-Sized City. In *Methodological Problems in Minority Research*, William T. Liu, ed., Occasional Paper 7, Pacific/Asian American Mental Research Center, 1982.

Nasser, Haya El, Census Projects Growing Diversity. *USA Today*, (March 18, 2004): 1.

Nevid, Jeffrey S. and Nelly L. Sta. Maria, *Multicultural Issues in Qualitative Research*, *Psychology & Marketing*, 16 (4, 1999): 305-325.

Nevid, Jefferry S., S.A. Rathus and B.V. Green, *Abnormal Psychology in a Changing World*, Upper Saddle River, NJ: Prentice Hall, 1997.

Okazaki, Sumie, and Sue, Stanley, Methodological Issues in Assessment Research With Ethnic Minorities. *Psychological Assessment*, 7 (September, 1995): 367-375.

Phillips, Carolyn, Data Gap: When it Comes to Understanding Black Consumers, Most Companies Are Surprisingly Ignorant. *Wall Street Journal*, (February 19, 1993): R. 18.

Phinney, Jean S., and Alipuria, Linda Line, Ethnic Identity in College Students from Four Ethnic Groups. *Journal of Adolescence*, 13 (June, 1990): 171-183.

Phinney, Jean S., The Multigroup Ethnic Identity Measure: A New Scale for Use With Diverse Groups. *Journal of Adolescent Research*, 7 (April, 1992): 156-176.

Ponterotto, Joseph G., Racial/Ethnic Minority Research in the Journal of Counseling Psychology: A Content Analysis and Methodological Crique. *Journal of Counseling Psychology*, 35 (4, 1988): 410-418.

Puente, Maria and Kasindorf, Martin, Blended Races Making a True Melting Pot, *USA Today*, (September 7, 1999): 1A, 13A.

Reid, Irvin D., John Stagmaier, and Carmen C. Reagan, Research Design Used to Describe and Explain Black Consumer Behavior. In *Cultural and Subcultural Influences in Consumer Behavior in Marketing Conference Proceedings*, Robert E. Pitts, ed., American Marketing Association, Chicago, 1986.

Riche, Martha Farnsworth, Demographic Change and Its Implications for Marketing Research. *Applied Marketing Research*, 30 (3, 1990): 23-27.

Robinson, Patricia A., and Rao, C.P., A Critical Review and Reassessment of Black Consumer Behavioral Research. *Proceedings: Southwestern Marketing Association Conference*, 1986, pp. 9-13.

Sasao, Toshiaki, and Sue, Stanley, Toward a Culturally Anchored Ecological Framework of Research in Ethnic-Cultural Communities. *American Journal of Community Psychology*, 21 (6, 1993): 705-726.

Senior, Peter A., and Bhopal, Raj, Ethnicity as a Variable in Epidemiological Research. *British Medical Journal*, 309 (July, 1994): 327-330.

Silk, Alvin K., Marketing Science in a Changing Environment. *Journal of Marketing Research*, 30 (November, 1993): 401-404.

Smith, A. Wade, Survey Research on African-Americans: Methodological Innovations. In *Race and Ethnicity in Research Methods*, John H. Stanfield, II and Rutledge M. Dennis, eds., Sage Publications, Newbury, CA., 1993, 217-229.

Smith, Bradford M., The Measurement of Narcissism in Asian, Caucasian, and Hispanic American Women. *Psychological Reports*, 67 (1990): 779-785.

Smith, Tom W., Ethnic Measurement and Identification. *Ethnicity*, 7 (1980): 78-95.

Stanton, John L., Chandran, Rajan, and Hernandez , Sigfredo A., Marketing Research Problems in Latin America. *Journal of the Market Research Society*, 24 (2, 1982): 124-139.

Steenkamp, Jan-Benedict E.M., and Baumgartner, Hans, Assessing Measurement Invariance in Cross-National Consumer Research. *Journal of Consumer Research*, 25 (June, 1978): 78-90.

Sternlieb, George, Household Research in the Urban Core. *Journal of Marketing*, (January, 1968): 25-28.

Suruco, Gonzalo R., Sampling and Non-Sampling Errors in Hispanic Population Telephone Surveys. *Applied Marketing Research*, 29 (Summer, 1989): 11-15.

Tanaka, Jeffrey S., Angela Ebreo, Nancy Linn, and Osvaldo F. Morera, Research Methods: The Construct Validity of Self-Identity and Its Psychological Implications, in *Handbook of Asian American Psychology*, Lee C. Lee and Nolan W.S. Zane eds., Sage Publications, Thousand Oaks, CA., 1998.

Teinowitz, Ira, Multinational Marketing, *Advertising Age*, (November 16, 1998): S1, S22.

Triandis, Harry C., *The Analysis of Subjective Culture*, New York: Wiley-Interscience, 1972.

Trimble, Joseph E., Ethnic Specification, Validation Prospects, and the Future of Drug Use Research. *International Journal of the Addictions*, 25 (2A, 1990/1991): 149-170.

U.S. Department of Commerce, *Population Projections of the United States by Age, Sex, Race, and Hispanic Origin: 1995 to 2050*, Department of Commerce, Washington D.C., February, 1996, 25-1130.

U.S. Department of Commerce, *Statistical Abstract of the United States*, Government Printing Office, Washington, D.C., 1995.

Usunier, Jean-Claude, *Marketing Across Cultures*, 2nd Edition, Prentice Hall, London, 1996.

Valencia, Humberto, Developing an Index to Measure 'Hispanicness'. In *Advances in Consumer Research*, Vol. 12., Elizabeth C. Hirschman and Morris B. Holbrook eds., Association for Consumer Research, Provo, UT., 1985, 118-121.

Vence, Deborah L., You Talking to Me? Experts offer Best Practices in Multicultural Marketing. *Marketing News*, (March 1, 2004):1,9,10.

Vobejda, Barbara, Hispanic Youths Outnumber Blacks: Federal Report Reveals Crest of Wave That Will Reshape U.S. Demographic Mosaic. *Washington Post*, (July 15, 1998): A02.

Waksberg, Joseph, Sampling Methods for Random Digit Dialing. *Journal of American Statistical Association*, 73 (March, 1978): 40-46.

Waldrop, Judith, You'll Know If It's the 21st Century When.... *American Demographics*, 12 (December, 1990): 22-27.

Watson, Michael A., Researching Minorities. *Journal of the Market Research Society*, 34 (October, 1992): 337-344.

Webster, Cynthia, Hispanic and Anglo Interviewer and Respondent Ethnicity and Gender: The Impact on Survey Response Quality. *Journal of Marketing Research*, 33 (February, 1996): 62-72.

Weinreich, Peter, The Operationalization of Identity Theory in Racial and Ethnic Relations, In *Theories of Race and Ethnic Relations*, John Rex and David Mason, eds., Cambridge University Press, Cambridge, England, 1986, pp. 299-320.

Williams, Jerome D. and Kimberly Dillon Grantham, Racial and Ethnic Identity in the Marketplace: An Examination of Nonverbal and Peripheral Cues? In *Advances in Consumer Research*, Vol. 26, Eric J. Aknould and Linda Scott, eds., Association of Consumer Research, Provo, UT., 1999, 451-462.

Williams, Jerome D., Book Review of Race and Ethnicity in Research Methods. *Journal of Marketing Research*, 32 (May, 1995): 239-243.

Williams, Jerome D., Reflections of a Black Middle-Class Consumer: Caught Between Two Worlds or Getting the Best of Both? In *Advances in Consumer Research*, Vol. 19, John F. Sherry and Brian Sternthal, ed., Association for Consumer Research, Provo, UT., 1992, pp. 850-855.

Williams, Jerome D. and Qualls, William J., Middle-Class Black Consumers and Intensity of Ethnic Identification. *Psychology & Marketing*, 6 (4, 1989): 263-286.

Ying, Yu-Wen, Non-response on the Center for Epidemiological Studies-Depression Scale in Chinese Americans. *International Journal of Social Psychiatry*, 35 (Summer, 1989): 156-163.

PART III:

MAJORITY VERSUS MINORITY CONSUMER BEHAVIORS

Chapter 7

Assessing the Cross-Cultural Stability of SERVQUAL in a Multi-Cultural Market: The Case of Canadian and Hong Kong Immigrant Banking Customers

Colleen Collins-Dodd
Mabel Fung

Introduction

To achieve high levels of perceived service quality, it is necessary to know one's customers, understand their needs, and ultimately, how they assess service quality. The problem becomes more complex in global and multicultural markets where new immigrants represent important market segments. In many communities, immigrant enclaves exist and, in some cases, thrive. The traditional 'Chinatowns' of San Francisco and Vancouver are being updated in the suburbs with Chinese malls. Hence, even if a firm is not concerned about 'going global' cross-cultural issues may be important in local multicultural markets.

Because consumers' perceptions of service quality are in part based upon their personal attitudes and value systems, culture, as one of the broadest influences of values and attitudes, can be expected to influence perceptions of service quality (Zeithaml, Berry and Parasuraman, 1991). Hence, we also expect culture to influence the performance of service quality measurement instruments as well.

Scales developed in a single cultural context often perform quite differently when applied outside the original context – producing scale artifacts due to the instability of the construct as well as market- induced differentials (Douglas and Craig, 1983; Hui and Triandis, 1985; Parameswaran and Yaprak, 1987). So-called 'soft' scales, such as SERVQUAL, are especially vulnerable to problems of reliability (Davis, Douglas and Silk, 1981). Studies of cross-national/ cultural commensurability of other scales have shown mixed results, with some scales exhibiting very similar reliabilities across contexts and others sensitive to the nationality of respondents (e.g. Durvasula, Andrews, Lyonski and Netemeyer, 1993 – attitudes toward advertising; Netemeyer, Durvasula and Lichtenstein, 1991

– evaluation of CETSCALE; Parameswaran and Yaprak, 1987; Zaichkowsky and Sood, 1989 – Personal Involvement Inventory).

This chapter will examine the cross-cultural psychometric properties of SERVQUAL, just as recent research has focussed on its generalizability across industries (for a recent review see Dabholkar, Thorpe and Rentz, 1996). The objective of our research is to assess the stability of the SERVQUAL scale when it is applied to both Western and Asian cultures. Content and construct validity, in addition to reliability, will be addressed.

We have chosen to examine the stability of a modified SERVQUAL scale in a banking context across two cultures: long-term resident Canadians of Western ancestry and recent immigrants to Canada from Hong Kong. With the impending return of Hong Kong to China in 1997, migration from Hong Kong to many Pacific Rim countries, such as Canada, the United States and Australia, has reached historic proportions.

SERVQUAL

It is an indication of the importance of the SERVQUAL scale (Parasuraman, Zeithaml and Berry, 1985, 1988, 1991) that so many others have sought to test and adapt the scale to ensure its usefulness and generalizability. Three properties of the scale have received the most critical attention.

First, the dimensionality of SERVQUAL has not been consistent across replications. In their original exploration of the perception of service quality, Parasuraman, Zeithaml and Berry proposed ten dimensions or aspects that defined the construct (1986). These dimensions were translated into survey items and refined and combined into five dimensions (Parasuraman et al., 1988). Other researchers have found mixed support for the five dimensional structure (e.g. Babakus and Boller, 1992; Carman, 1990; Cronin and Taylor, 1992; Finn and Lamb, 1991; Parasuraman et al., 1994).

Second, the conceptualization of SERVQUAL as a difference score between measured expectations and measured perceptions has been found to be problematic on statistical grounds (Brown, Churchill and Peter, 1993) as well as with respect to concurrent validity (Babakus and Boller, 1992; Cronin and Taylor, 1992; Parasuraman et al., 1994). Therefore, there appears to be a consensus developing around using measures of service performance perceptions rather than a calculated difference score. In addition, because the negatively worded items have tended to load together suggesting method variance, more recent applications are using only positively worded statements (Parasuraman et al., 1991; Babakus and Boller, 1992).

Third, the reliability of the scale has generally been found to be acceptable. Reliability of the subdimension scales ranges from .51 to over .90 (Babakus and Boller, 1992; Cronin and Taylor, 1992; Carman, 1990; Parasuraman et al., 1991). This provides support for the relationship among the items used but does not necessarily support the validity of any particular dimensional structure.

Culture

Culture has fascinated researchers, ecclesiastics, travellers and traders. The essence of a culture is its values. Psychologists define culture as 'ideals about what is desirable' (Athos and Coffey, 1968, p.100) and 'abstract ideals, positive or negative, not tied to any specific object or situation, representing a person's beliefs about modes of conduct and ideal terminal modes' (Rokeach, 1968, p.124). Marketing researchers have confirmed the importance of cultural influences on consumer behavior (Jain, 1993), through the influence of values on consumers' evaluations of products and services (Johnston, 1987).

Chinese Value Orientations

Chinese cultural values, based primarily on Confucian doctrine, are largely formed around interpersonal relationships and social orientations rather than personal or individual ideals. These traditional values persist, despite the rapid social and economic changes in Chinese societies (Yau, 1988). The desire for harmony with nature, with others and with the past are guiding values. Thus we tend to see a focus on long-term relationship building in business and social interactions. Chinese are not as interested as Westerners in single transaction relationships, and are more willing to invest time and effort to build life long relationships (Tung, 1982, 1991). In return, they expect their partners to reciprocate their efforts. The concept of *guanxi* in business embodies both empathy and reciprocity. Within the relationship, one goes beyond familiarity and friendship to view the situation from the other's perspective and then make allowances for the situation, assuming that the other partner will do the same.

The other component of the Chinese 'man-to-nature' orientation involves the concept of *yuarn*, or the predetermination of relationships with other things or individuals. They tend to attribute failure of products/ services to fate. In addition, 'the doctrine of the Mean', another important Confucian value, admonishes that 'The gentleman ... rectifies himself, and seeks for nothing from others ... He does not murmur against Heaven, nor grumble against men' (from Confucius, in Legge 1960, quoted by Yau, 1988). On the other hand, behavioral norms for individuals are very strict. Propriety, consideration for others, politeness and rule obeying are part of the interdependence among individuals which also includes reciprocity and 'face'. Seeing oneself as highly interdependent emphasizes the need to maintain the group's respect and public shame is highly avoided.

Yau has identified several important implications for service quality based upon his review of Chinese cultural values (1988). First, we would be surprised to hear complaints from Chinese customers – either they accept the failure as fate, and even if they did not, it would be inappropriate to comment. The manager who passively waits for customer feedback is unlikely to get any. Second, while they may view product failures as a result of fate, they would be very sensitive to personal service 'failures', such as lack of courtesy and would not overlook such behaviors, severing the relationship even though they would make no complaint to the responsible individual or their supervisor. Third, the need to maintain 'face' is accompanied by a desire for privacy and confidentiality in sensitive service situations such as banking. Fourth, the interdependence, relationship and reciprocity aspects suggest that Chinese customers value reputation and standing in the community. They like to deal with their familiar service personnel and they expect flexibility and 'favours' from service providers as a measure of empathy and understanding. However, once a relationship has been established, the Chinese exhibit tremendous loyalty – even across generations. Finally, the strong sense of community creates very powerful opinion leaders and word-of-mouth effects, thus, the effects of good or bad service encounters for an influential individual can be greatly magnified in the broader community.

Therefore, we would not be surprised to see differences in the evaluation of service quality between our two groups but we must also consider whether the scale used to measure those differences is appropriate for both groups. For example, Hofstede and his colleagues developed a widely used scale to measure cultural characteristics across nations (Hofstede, 1983). After several years in use, they found it necessary to extend their cultural values scale to capture Confucian values missing from the original framework (Hofstede and Bond, 1988). The new dimension reflects differences in time orientation and the concept of saving face. Interestingly, Hong Kong is among the highest on this dimension, while Canada is at the opposite end. Without this dimension, Canadian and Hong Kong cultures might have appeared more similar than they are. This example raises concerns that the same may be true in the case of SERVQUAL. Because multicultural applications were not explicitly considered in the scale development, cross-cultural generalizability should be tested before SERVQUAL is used in multicultural or cross-cultural applications.

Measurement Equivalence

Before we can perform useful cross-cultural research in the services area, we need measures which demonstrate equivalence-- domain/ functional equivalence, operational /instrument equivalence and measurement/ scalar equivalence. The measures should have the same conceptual and operational meaning, as well as metric properties, in order to be useful in assessing theoretical relationships across cultures (Davis et al., 1981; Hui and Triandis, 1985; Parameswaran and Yaprak, 1987; Singh, 1995).

Main Equivalence

Content validity of a measure is established by demonstrating that the items used to measure the concept represent its complete domain (Churchill, 1979). Literature reviews and qualitative approaches were used to develop the items for the original SERVQUAL scale (Parasuraman et al., 1988). But, because the research was conducted by Westerners in the Western world, it is possible that when we apply the scale to measure service quality outside that context, the domain is no longer adequate.

Operational and Item Equivalence

Operational equivalence requires that the same procedure is used to measure the construct across cultures. For example if a survey instrument is used within one culture, a survey should be used in other cultures. Ideally, survey administration should be same across cultures, but this may not be possible for technological reasons (for example, availability of telephones) or literacy limitations. Item equivalence is achieved through careful translation and back translation of the instrument (Nasif, Al-Daeaj, Ebrahimi and Thibodeaux, 1991; Hui and Triandis, 1985).

Scalar Equivalence

Scalar or psychometric equivalence is the most difficult equivalence to achieve. Reliability equivalence, internal structural congruence (i.e. similar factor structures), and nomological congruence can be assessed using techniques similar to those used for construct validation in general. Multiple-group extensions of confirmatory factor analysis and structural equations are among the methods recommended for scale development and assessment (Gerbing and Anderson, 1988; Mullen, 1995; Singh, 1995).

Method

Data Collection

Banking was selected as the context for this study in order to provide continuity with previous SERVQUAL research (Parasuraman et al., 1988) and because the industry is very interested in the effects of cultural differences on service quality perceptions. The bank that participated in the study is a major international bank with a large share of the Hong Kong immigrant market in the study city. Hong Kong immigrants were selected as representatives of Chinese culture because they form a very large component of the new Chinese immigrant community in the city in which the research was conducted with over 10,000 new Hong Kong immigrants annually (1992-1996) (BCSTATS, 1996). Their attractiveness as a potential market is also highlighted by their economic status. At the time of immigration, over 60 percent declared themselves entrepreneurs, investors or self-employed skilled workers and another 21 percent were self-sufficient retired individuals (data for British Columbia, 1994, Citizenship and Immigration Canada).

While some might argue that Hong Kong immigrants are among the most Westernized Chinese, they are none the less culturally distinct from long-time Canadians and represent a relatively conservative sample with which to test cultural sensitivity between East and West. Canada and Hong Kong represent virtually opposite ends of the Confucian Dynamism Scale of Hofstede and Bond (1988), and they differ markedly on all but the Masculinity/ Femininity dimension (Hofstede 1983). Given that traditional Chinese values have survived both time and revolution, we would not expect these values to quickly disappear after immigration to a new country – especially one such as Canada where multiculturalism is established, accepted and even encouraged. The existence of large, vibrant Chinese communities in many cities provides support for immigrant cultures.

Cross-cultural research often suffers from confounding of culture, sample characteristics and research conditions (Nasif et al., 1991). For some research questions all of these effects are relevant, however, in order to assess the stability of a measure, we want to control non-cultural factors as much as possible. By selecting respondents from both the host and immigrant cultures who bank at the same branch, we are able to obtain equivalent samples, equivalent data collection conditions as well as control the banking, political and economic conditions they experience. Research conducted in different countries (even if we use subsidiaries of the same parent bank) confounds the differences in scale usage due to culture with differences in scale results due to differences in the actual service environment. Since the major purpose of the research is to examine the differences between two distinct groups of customers as defined by their culture, confounding variables such as differences between service provided or data collection conditions are controlled. The degree of control provided by a 'within' country cross-cultural research is a major advantage, which in this case we believe balances out the disadvantage of using recent immigrants (many of whom are not yet Canadian citizens).

Customers were intercepted in the branch after completing their transactions and were qualified on the bases of race, ancestry and length of residence in Canada. The long-term sample were residents of Canada for more than ten years and of European ancestry. The Hong Kong sample were of Chinese ancestry and residents of Canada for the previous five years or less.

Instrument Construct Domain

We examined the adequacy of the SERVQUAL items to reflect Chinese cultural values relevant to service quality. Chinese cultural values are largely based upon interpersonal relationships with a long-term time orientation (Yau, 1988), therefore we focussed on the relationship items in particular. Most of the items in the original SERVQUAL assurance and empathy dimensions are related to relationships – understanding and knowing the customer, courtesy, trust, personal attention.

Nine items were added to reflect important Chinese values. The principle of *guanxi* or the doing of favours to build a relationship was reflected in two items that asked *whether the bank was flexible in order to gain continued support* and *whether staff offered professional suggestions.* The concept of face includes a concern for privacy in financial matters, therefore we added two items concerning *guarantee of confidentiality for banking records* and *facilities that assure privacy.* An item that asked for an evaluation of whether the bank was *committed to developing a long-term relationship* addressed the long-term time orientation value. *Reputation*, which was in the original conceptualization of SERVQUAL (Parasuraman, 1985), was included again to also address the long-term orientation. To represent strong group or collective values we included items on *friendly service, the ability to choose a familiar service provider* and *whether employees know customers by name.*

In addition several items were not clear during pretesting with Canadians of either origin. The SERVQUAL items that asked whether you feel safe, and whether you can trust the employees of the firm were found to be very ambiguous. The first item was revised to focus on *safety/security of investments* because personal safety in the main branch of a Canadian bank is simply not a cause for concern. Trust was defined with respect to *trust with personal information* and whether they *trusted the bank to keep its promises*, because Canadians feel they can trust their banks generally. In the context of banking, the item concerning having the customer's best interests at heart was clarified by providing an explanation of how one's interests might be protected by *providing information about appropriate financial options.* *Effective problem solving* replaced the original item, sympathy and reassurance in problem solving. The item concerning modern-looking equipment was modified by substituting *user friendly equipment.* The visually appealing facilities item was also dropped given the use of the main branch, which is an impressive facility.

The items were reviewed by bank staff and an English version was pre-tested on 15 MBA students of Canadian and Chinese origin and minor wording changes were made to improve understanding.

Item Equivalence

The Chinese version of the questionnaire was created after the English version was pre-tested. The translation was performed by a professional translator and then back-translated into English by another translator. Neither translator was otherwise involved in the research.

The Questionnaire

Following Cronin and Taylor (1992) and others (e.g. Parasuraman et al., 1994), we used only performance perceptions instead of a difference measure of service quality, to reduce statistical and data collection difficulties. Respondents provided evaluations of 29 service quality items and seven additional items of interest to the bank, using ten-point Likert scales anchored by 'Strongly Disagree' and Strongly Agree'. Following Parasuraman et al. (1991) all items were positively worded to reduce possible confusion among respondents and subsequent method bias.

In order to test the nomological validity of the scales, we expanded upon the single item scales of overall service quality of Cronin and Taylor (1992), Dabholkar et al. (1996) and Babakus and Boller (1992), with four items assessing overall quality and satisfaction.

Results

Respondents

During the two week period of data collection, 220 respondents were intercepted, resulting in 203 useable surveys: 105 from long-term Canadians and 98 from Hong Kong immigrants. Respondents were surveyed using the language they were most comfortable with. Slightly more of the Hong Kong immigrant sample was male, 58% compared to 46% for the long-term Canadians. The long-term Canadians were more likely to have some post-secondary education or training (75% Canadian; 64% Hong Kong).[1] The distribution of year of arrival in Canada for the newcomers was skewed toward the more recent arrivals with 45% having arrived that year or the year prior and the rest in the three years previous to that. The average number of years in Canada was less than two years.

In terms of banking products used, the Hong Kong Canadian customers had more extensive banking requirements, reflected by the greater number of accounts and services used. A larger proportion of Hong Kong-Canadian customers made use of the bank's credit card (51.5% for Hong Kong immigrants, 38.3% for long-time Canadians) safety deposit boxes (51.5%; 23.4%), mortgages (32.0%; 19.6%), guaranteed investment certificates (32.0%, 15.0%) and term deposits (30.1%, 1.9%). A greater proportion of long-term Canadians used the bank's loan services (9.7% Hong Kong immigrants; 24.3% long-term Canadians), Registered Retirement Savings Plan (15.5%, 29%), and mutual fund (8.7%, 14.0%) services.

Discriminant Validity – Between Groups

In this case, we tested the ability of the scale to discriminate between two groups that we expected to differ, rather than two constructs. Based on Hofstede's cultural dimensions, Canadian and Hong Kong cultures are quite different on 'Power Distance', 'Individualism' and 'Confucian Dynamism', moderately different on 'Uncertainty Avoidance', but fairly similar on 'Masculinity' (Hofstede, 1983;

---

[1] Income data was not collected because the bank's experience with customer surveys suggested considerable reluctance to provide this information. Non-response and bias are high for new Asian immigrants who are more sensitive to providing this kind of personal information.

Hofstede and Bond, 1988). Therefore, we expect the groups to differ on evaluations of service quality. If the scale were missing relevant dimensions that could distinguish the two groups, they might appear more similar than they actually are.

A Manova analysis was conducted to determine if the scale items together and individually differed between the two cultural groups. The 29 item scale was significantly different between the two groups (Pillais and Hotellings F sig.=.00), and univariate F tests were significantly different between groups for 14 of 29 items (α=.10). Table 7.1 presents the univariate results.

Table 7.1a   MANOVA Tests and Means for Service Quality Items for Canadian and Hong Kong Samples

Item	Canadian sample mean	Hong Kong sample mean	Univariate F value
Long term relationships	7.87	7.44	2.21
Good reputation	9.02	9.01	0.00
Good product knowledge	7.86	7.01	9.21**
Employees willing to help	9.19	8.35	23.66**
Employees well dressed and neat	9.38	8.76	15.41**
Convenient branch locations	8.46	7.89	3.87*
Performs services at promised time	8.37	7.92	3.41*
Friendly service	9.37	8.59	21.49**
Employees know me by name	4.38	4.17	0.26
Employees offer professional financial suggestions	5.82	6.09	0.72
Flexible as possible to gain my support	7.44	7.05	1.60
Choose to deal with familiar staff	6.82	6.48	1.03
Understands my needs	6.88	6.82	0.04
Performs transactions accurately	8.59	6.82	34.19**
Responds to requests promptly	8.56	7.52	17.76**
Protects interests by keeping me informed	6.69	6.62	0.04
Trust employees with personal information	8.42	7.96	3.14*
Employees consistently courteous	9.2	8.35	21.62**
Deposits and investments secured	8.91	8.79	0.45
Solves problems effectively	7.7	7.28	2.31

Confidentiality of records guaranteed	8.52	8.33	0.72
Convenient operating hours	8.47	7.80	5.55**
Dependable service	9.04	8.44	9.84**
Fills requests at promised time	8.22	7.45	7.78**
Short wait to be served	8.29	7.01	18.25**
Easy get hold of appropriate staff	8.08	7.40	5.97**
Facilities assure privacy	8.64	7.90	10.59**
Facilities are user friendly	9.02	8.07	24.56**
Faith in bank to keep service promises	8.70	8.36	2.4
Hotellings T^2	.470		2.81**

Items measured on 10-point scale ranging from 1=Strongly Disagree to 10=Strongly Agree
*p<.10 **p<.05.

Table 7.1b   MANOVA Tests and Means for Outcome Evaluation Items for Canadian and Hong Kong Samples

Item	Canadian sample mean	Hong Kong sample mean	Univariate F value
Service quality compared to other banks	8.23	7.78	5.46**
Satisfaction compared to other banks	8.35	7.70	8.73**
Planning to continue with the Bank	8.76	8.57	.73
Will you recommend the Bank to your friends	8.45	7.97	2.99*
Hotellings T^2	.056		2.78**

Items measured on 10-point scale ranging from 1=least positive to 10=most positive.
*p<.10 **p<.05.

Consistency of Internal Structure of the Scale

The SERVQUAL scale was designed as a multi-factor scale, with ten dimensions in the original conceptualization that was subsequently reduced to five (Parasuraman et al., 1988). Replications have found mixed support for a consistent factor structure across applications (Babakus and Boller, 1992; Carman, 1990; Parasuraman et al. 1994; Dabholkar et al.,1996). On this basis and, given that our study included nine new items to encompass the Asian culture, we used exploratory factor analysis on the long-term Canadian respondent data to build a second order factor model. Confirmatory factor analysis tested whether a measurement model derived from these respondents would be appropriate for our Hong Kong immigrant respondents. To reduce the skewness in the data we mean centered the data for each group (Sharma, 1996). Because of linear dependencies among the service quality items, four items were dropped for the structural equation analyses (*convenient locations, fills requests at promised time, good product knowledge* and *can choose to deal with familiar staff*). These four items represented different dimensions and because the scale was designed with multiple indicators, their loss did not leave any important gaps in the construct.

A six factor structure was selected on the basis of the eigenvalue greater than one criterion, and the interpretability of the factors. Together the six factors explained 62.6% of the variance among the items. This factor structure formed the basis of the measurement model, with service quality as a second-order construct that determined the six first-order dimensions (Figure 7.1). A comparison of these factors to the original SERVQUAL factors and the factor loadings are found in Table II. The measurement model component of the structural model was run as a separate confirmatory factor analysis using the EQS program under elliptical distributional assumptions[2] (Anderson and Gerbing, 1988). This confirmatory analysis formed the basis of comparison for the more important test of interest – a confirmatory analysis of the appropriateness of the long-term Canadian structure for the Hong Kong immigrant respondents.

The long-term Canadian measurement model met all preliminary fit criteria (Bagozzi and Yi, 1988) but the overall fit of the measurement model was not good, as judged by the chi-square value (χ^2 = 439, df.=269, p<.001) and the comparative fit index which was somewhat less than the desired value of .90 (CFI=.83) (Bagozzi and Yi, 1988; Anderson and Gerbing, 1988). However, all the items were significant, there were no anomolies in the model, and the standardized residuals were small (average value= .07, maximum=.30). Dimension reliabilities ranged from .57 to .90, which is consistent with results of Carman (1990), and Parasuraman et al. (1991), among others, although the average variance extracted for the service quality factors was low, ranging from 40 to 53 percent (Table 7.2). However, the issue is not so much goodness of fit of this particular model, whose lack of fit is consistent with much of the literature (Dabholkar et al., 1996), but whether or not a measurement model derived in one culture will be generalizable to another.

---

[2] Elliptical theory assumptions are robust to violations of normality where skewness is not extreme (Bentler, 1992).

We therefore conducted a two-sample confirmatory test to evaluate the applicability of the long-term Canadian measurement model for the Hong Kong immigrant sample. A multi-sample Lagrange Multiplier (LM) Test for equality of factor loadings and second order factor relationships rejected univariate equality of parameters between the two samples for 14 of the 24 constrained parameters and rejected multivariate equality for 6 parameters (see Table 7.2).[3] The χ^2 test of the difference between constrained and unconstrained models rejects equality of the factorial structure overall (Bentler, 1992; Mullen, 1995). In addition, the comparative fit index decreased for the structural model from .80 for the Canadian data to .76 for both samples. It should be noted that both groups suffered equally from small sample sizes for the confirmatory analyses, although each approaches the minimum recommended size (Hair, Anderson, Tatham, and Black, 1994, p.637).

After determining that the long-term Canadian structure was not confirmed for the Hong Kong immigrant sample, we conducted an exploratory factor analysis of the Hong Kong sample. A five factor structure explained 65.1% of the variation in the 25 items (Table 7.2). A comparison of the confirmatory factor analyses using the structural model shows that the confirmatory fit index for the Hong Kong sample increases to .85 from .81 with the unique Hong Kong measurement structure (Figure 7.2). Interestingly, the reliabilities of the factors are all greater than .70, which is better than the long-term Canadian sample and the Comparative Fit Index for the structural model is also higher than for the long-term Canadian model, although once again the average variance explained for the factors is low (38 to 61 percent).

---

[3] The number of constraints is less than the number of items because some factor loadings were fixed to set the scale of the factor (Bentler, 1992).

Table 7.2   Standardized Factor Loadings, Lagrange Multiplier tests for Parameter Equality

Long Term Canadian Factors

Immigrant Factors   **Factor Loadings**

ITEM (Original SERVQUAL factors)	F1	F2	F3	F4	F5	F6
Tangibles						
Employees well dressed and neat	-----	0.53	-----	-----	-----	-----
Facilities are user friendly	-----	0.54	-----	-----	-----	-----
Convenient branch locations[a]	-----	-----	-----	-----	-----	-----
Convenient operating hours	-----	-----	0.62	-----	-----	-----
Reliability						
Performs services at promised time	-----	-----	-----	-----	-----	0.60
Performs transactions accurately	-----	-----	-----	-----	-----	0.59
Fills requests at promised time[a]	-----	-----	-----	-----	-----	-----
Solves problems effectively	0.68	-----	-----	-----	-----	-----
Dependable service	0.66	-----	-----	-----	-----	-----
Responsiveness						
Employees willing to help	-----	0.77	-----	-----	-----	-----
Responds to requests promptly	-----	-----	-----	-----	-----	0.75
Short wait to be served	-----	-----	0.64	-----	-----	-----
Easy get hold of appropriate staff	0.68	-----	-----	-----	-----	-----
Assurance						
Good product knowledge[a]	-----	-----	-----	-----	----	-----
Employees consistently courteous	-----	0.64	-----	-----	-----	-----
Faith in bank to keep service promises	0.75	-----	-----	-----	-----	-----
Trust employees with personal information	-----	-----	-----	0.77	-----	-----

Deposits and investments secured	-----	-----	-----	0.70	-----	-----
Empathy						
Understands my needs	0.74	-----	-----	-----	-----	-----
Protects interests by keeping me informed	-----	-----	-----	-----	0.77	-----
New Asian Culture Items						
Long term relationships	0.78	-----	-----	-----	-----	-----
Good reputation	0.62	-----	-----	-----	-----	-----
Friendly service	-----	0.82	-----	-----	-----	-----
Employees know me by name	-----	-----	-----	-----	0.54	-----
Employees offer professional suggestions	-----	-----	-----	-----	0.58	-----
Flexible as possible to gain my support	0.84	-----	-----	-----	-----	-----
Choose to deal with familiar staff[a]	-----	-----	-----	-----	-----	-----
Confidentiality of records guaranteed	-----	-----	-----	0.79	-----	-----
Facilities assure privacy	-----	-----	-----	0.65	-----	-----
Factor Reliabilities (Cronbach's alpha)	.90	.80	.57	.82	.67	.68
Variance Explained (%)	52	45	40	53	41	42

Hong Kong

Immigrant Factors   **Factor Loadings**

ITEM (Original SERVQUAL factors)	F1	F2	F3	F4	F5	LM test[a]
Tangibles						
Employees well dressed and neat	0.56	-----	-----	-----	-----	1.00
Facilities are user friendly	-----	-----	-----	0.60	-----	-----
Convenient branch locations[a]	-----	-----	-----	-----	-----	-----
Convenient operating hours	-----	-----	-----	0.54	-----	-----
Reliability						
Performs services at promised time	-----	-----	-----	0.74	-----	-----
Performs transactions accurately	-----	0.67	-----	-----	-----	0.83
Fills requests at promised time[a]	-----	-----	-----	-----	-----	-----
Solves problems effectively	-----	-----	-----	-----	0.76	2.73
Dependable service	-----	-----	-----	0.83	-----	15.27*
Responsiveness						
Employees willing to help	0.75	-----	-----	-----	-----	-----
Responds to requests promptly	0.72	-----	-----	-----	-----	1.96
Short wait to be served	-----	-----	-----	0.66	-----	5.85*
Easy get hold of appropriate staff	-----	-----	-----	0.74	-----	4.87*
Assurance						
Good product knowledge[a]	-----	-----	-----	-----	-----	-----
Employees consistently courteous	0.84	-----	-----	-----	-----	3.02
Faith in bank to keep service promises	-----	-----	-----	0.82	-----	0.44
Trust employees with personal information	-----	-----	0.84	-----	-----	-----
Deposits and investments secured	0.60	-----	-----	-----	-----	3.90*

Empathy

Understands my needs	-----	-----	0.57	-----	-----	3.21
Protects interests by keeping me informed	-----	-----	0.64	-----	-----	3.26

New Asian Culture Items

Long term relationships	-----	0.6	-----	-----	-----	-----
Good reputation	0.59	-----	-----	-----	-----	0.02
Friendly service	0.85	-----	-----	-----	-----	3.26
Employees know me by name	-----	0.48	-----	-----	-----	-----
Employees offer professional suggestions	-----	0.71	-----	-----	-----	0.85
Flexible as possible to gain my support	-----	-----	-----	-----	0.80	4.36*
Choose to deal with familiar staff[a]	-----	-----	-----	-----	-----	-----
Confidentiality of records guaranteed	-----	-----	0.83	-----	-----	1.38
Facilities assure privacy	-----	-----	0.40	0.49	-----	3.85*
Factor Reliabilities (Cronbach's alpha)	.87	.71	.80	.87	.76	
Variance Explained (%)	50	38	46	47	61	

Items measured on 10-point scale ranging from 1=Strongly Disagree to 10=Strongly Agree.
a: not included in structural model or confirmatory factor analyses due to linear dependencies.
b: indicates no test statistic because parameter fixed in structural model for identification.
* p<.05.

Figure 7.1   Long-Term Canadian Structural Model of Service Quality

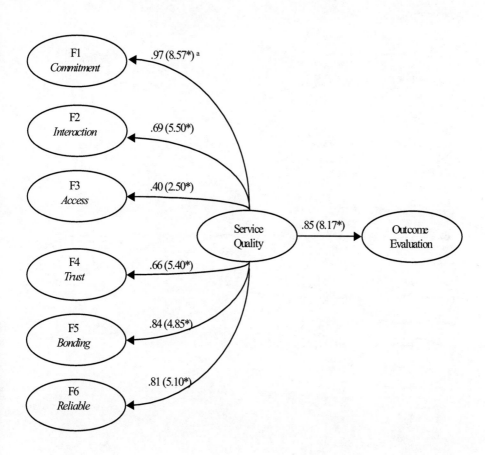

Comparative Fit Index=.81
[a] standardized coefficients (t values)
* p<.05

Figure 7.2   Hong Kong Structural Model of Service Quality

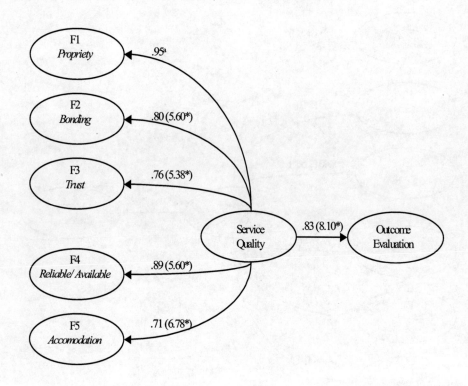

Comparative Fit Index= .85
[a] standardized coefficients (t values)
* p<.05

Discriminant Validity – Between Original and Extended Scales

For each final model, Canadian and Hong Kong Canadian, a Wald test was conducted to determine whether the nine items that were added to the scale contributed significantly beyond the original SERVQUAL items (Bentler, 1992). For both samples, these items individually and together provide significant univariate and multivariate increments to the fit of the model. Therefore, we conclude that there were gaps in the domain of the original SERVQUAL scale.

Concurrent Nomological Validity

In order to assess the concurrent validity of the service quality measure we related the second order *Service Quality* measurement model to a related concept that represented an overall outcome evaluation (Figure 7.1). As mentioned earlier, we used a multi-item measure for the dependent variable, which included *overall service quality, satisfaction with service quality, planning to continue relationship with the Bank,* and *whether respondents would recommend the Bank to a friend.*

The four outcome evaluations were also mean centered and factor analyzed. They formed a single factor for each group, although the loadings for the two groups differed. The Hong Kong immigrants' outcome factor was dominated by satisfaction with services while the Canadian long-term residents had a more balanced structure. The single factor explained 77% of the variance among the items for the long-term Canadians and 75% for the Hong Kong Canadians. The reliability of the four items as measured by Cronbach's alpha was .90 for both groups.

The *Outcome Evaluation* factor was included in the structural model as a dependent variable to be predicted by the second order *Service Quality* factor. Given that the Canadian measurement model was rejected for the Hong Kong sample, it is not surprising that the LM test also rejected equality between the groups for the parameter relating *Service Quality* to *Outcome Evaluation.* For the Canadian sample, the *Service Quality* factor explained 72% of the variability in the *Outcome Evaluation* factor – the Hong Kong sample 5-factor model did almost as well, with *Service Quality* explaining 69% of the *Outcome Evaluation.*

Discussion

We have seen that differences in culture are linked to service quality perceptions and how service quality is measured in cross-cultural or multicultural environments. The original SERVQUAL instrument has evolved since its conceptualization and the purpose of our work is to continue that evolution across cultures. Just as some customization of SERVQUAL items and dimensions are required for different service settings (Carman, 1990; Finn and Lamb, 1991; Dabholkar et al., 1996), we have found the same to be true for services in the same industry experienced by different cultures. Both our pre-test interviews and quantitative data suggest that additional scale development is required before firms can apply SERVQUAL in multicultural contexts. This research represents the first cross-cultural assessment and adaptation of SERVQUAL.

The Servqual scale as originally proposed, fails to recognize important Confucian values such as long-term time orientation, group interdependence and reciprocity, in particular. The addition of several new items helps to address this concern for the Hong Kong immigrant sample, and surprisingly, the items also play an important role in the service quality relationship for our long-term Canadian respondents. Perhaps, these relationship elements, while most closely associated with Confucian societies are not unique to them.

With respect to the properties of the revised scale, the good news is that the revised instrument itself is not a problem – the items themselves are all statistically significant in contributing to a measure of service quality for both groups. However, the dimensional structure is not stable across cultures, preventing the construction of a single set of sum scores for the subdimensions that can be directly compared between groups. The Hong Kong respondents do not define *Trust,* for example, in the same way as the Canadian respondents. This complicates any analysis of performance between branches with different customer cultural mixes. One cannot use the subdimensions from the original SERVQUAL work or those derived from one culture in the other.

The Canadian and Hong Kong factor structures differ in several interesting ways. The first factor for the Canadian sample is *Commitment* – which includes items dealing with the ability of the bank to understand customers' needs and address them through a long-term relationship. On the other hand, the first factor for the Hong Kong sample is *Propriety* – that aspect of the relationship that deals with how employees relate to customers as well as the reputation of the bank and whether deposits are secured, i.e., whether things are in their proper place. Both groups have a *Trust* dimension, however it is broader for the Hong Kong respondents. In addition to the Canadian items that relate to security of investments and confidentiality, the Hong Kong factor also includes understanding needs and protecting interests. The *Reliable/Available* actor for the Hong Kong sample combines all items related to ease of doing business: convenience, access, reliability and responsiveness, that are found in four separate factors for the Canadians. Problem solving and flexibility are seen as a unique dimension by Hong Kong immigrant respondents – they are not in the same factor for the Canadians. The *Bonding* dimension is also somewhat broader for the Hong Kong respondents compared to the Canadians. The Hong Kong *Bonding* factor includes long-term commitment and accuracy in addition to the personal involvement items.

Finally, the revised scale performed fairly well in terms of its ability to predict service quality related attitudes for both cultures. The general lack of fit of the structural model in both cultures, as measured by the Chi-Square values, while consistent with previous results (Finn and Lamb, 1991; Babakus and Boller, 1992; Cronin and Taylor, 1992; Dabholkar, Thorpe and Rentz, 1996), may be explained in part by the relatively small sample size. Hair et al (1994) note that the Chi-square test is not very sensitive for samples of this size (p. 651). It should be noted however, that the Comparative Fit Index measures were .848 for the Hong Kong

Canadian model and .808 for the Canadian model which is somewhat below the desired level of .90.

The other key limitations of the research other than those already mentioned include adaptation of the SERVQUAL scale rather than an exact replication. This is a limitation shared by other evaluations of SERVQUAL such as Carman (1990), and Dabholkar et al. (1996). To expect a scale for service quality to apply uniformly across industries may be overly ambitious given the personalized nature of service itself. Finally, we have used recent immigrants rather than foreign residents to represent Hong Kong culture in order to gain control over non-cultural confounding factors. This tends to make our tests between cultures somewhat conservative and we would expect to see even greater differences if we were able to conduct the study in each home country.

Of course the ideal course of action to completely capture Chinese values would be to follow the lead of Hofstede and Bond (1988) and attempt to have a team of Chinese researchers replicate the process used by Parasuraman, Zeithaml and Berry in their various studies and develop a completely 'made in China' (or Hong Kong or Singapore etc.) service quality measurement instrument which could be compared with the original for overlap and distinctiveness. Our study represents a collaberation in Canada by researchers of Canadian and Hong Kong origin, which is a small step in what we believe is the right direction.

The implications for managers brings us back to the discussions we had in early phases of the research with the managers and staff of branches with predominantly recent immigrant customers who believed that the bank's national customer service quality survey was stacked against them. They tended to do poorly on certain aspects of customer service quality surveys compared to all other branches across the country, but managers felt the results did not reflect their actual performance. In addition, they believed that the survey included elements that were unimportant to their customers, and failed to include components which were important. The issue is not only whether mean scores are different, but also the relationship between those scores and customer loyalty. We found with our Hong Kong Canadian respondents that even though their average service quality evaluations were lower than the Long Term Canadians, there were no significant differences in whether they planned to continue with the bank (Table 7.1b). Our results provide some solace for these branch employees and present some additional challenges and directions for anyone trying to evaluate quality of service in multicultural conditions.

References

Anderson, J.C. and Gerbing, D.W. (1988), 'Structural Equation Modeling in Practice: A Review and Recommended Two-Step Approach', *Psychological Bulletin*, Vol. 108 No. 3, pp. 411-423.

Athos, A.G. and Coffey, R.E. (1968), *Behavior in Organizations: A Multidimensional View*, Prentice Hall, Inc., Englewood Cliffs, NJ.

Babakus, E. and Boller, G.W. (1992), 'An Empirical Assessment of the SERVQUAL Scale', *Journal of Business Research*, Vol. 24, pp. 253-268.

Bagozzi, R.P. and Yi, Y. (1988), 'On the Evaluation of Structural Equation Models', *Journal of the Academy of Marketing Science*, Vol. 16, Spring, pp. 74-94.

Bentler, P.M. (1992), *EQS: Structural Equations Program Manual*, BMDP Statistical Software Inc., Los Angeles.

Churchill, G.A. Jr. (1979), 'A Paradigm for Developing Better Measures of Marketing Constructs', *Journal of Marketing Research*, Vol. 16, February, pp. 64-73.

Cronin, J.J. and Taylor, S.A. (1992), 'Measuring Service Quality: A Reexamination and Extension', *Journal of Marketing*, Vol. 56, July, pp. 55-68.

Dabholkar, P.A., Thorpe, D.I. and Rentz, J.O. (1996), 'A Measure of Service Quality for Retail Stores: Scale Development and Validation', *Journal of the Academy of Marketing Science*, Vol. 24, Winter, pp. 3-16.

Davis, H.J., Douglas, S.P. and Silk, A.J. (1981), 'Measure Unreliability: A Hidden Threat to Cross-National Marketing Research?', *Journal of Marketing*, Vol. 45, Spring, pp. 98-109.

Douglas, S.P. and Craig, C.S. (1983), *International Marketing Research*, Prentice Hall, Inc., Englewood Cliffs, NJ.

Durvasula, S.J., Andrews, C., Lysonski, S. and Netemeyer, R.G. (1993), 'Assessing the Cross-national Applicability of Consumer Behavior Models: A Model of Attitude toward Advertising in General', *Journal of Consumer Research*, Vol. 19, March, pp. 626-636.

Finn, D.W. and Lamb, C.W. Jr. (1991), 'An Evaluation of the SERVQUAL Scales in a Retail Setting', in Holmes, R.H. and Solomon, M.R. (Eds), *Advances in Consumer Research*, Vol. 18, pp. 483-490.

Hair, J. F. Jr., Anderson, R. E., Tatham, R. L., and Black, W.C. (1995), *Multivariate Analysis: with Readings*, 4th edition, Prentice Hall, Englewood Cliffs, NJ.

Hofstede, G. (1983), 'National Cultures in Four Dimensions', *International Studies of Management and Organization*, Vol. 13 No. 1-2, pp. 46-74.

____ and Bond, M. (1988), 'The Confucius Connection: From Cultural Roots to Economic Growth', *Organizational Dynamics*, Spring, pp. 5-21.

Hui, C.H. and Triandis, H.C. (1985), 'Measurement in Cross-Cultural Psychology: A Review and Comparison of Strategies', *Journal of Cross-Cultural Psychology*,Vol. 16, June, pp. 131-152.

Jain, S.C. (1993), *International Marketing Management*, 4th edition, Wadsworth, Belmont, California.

Johnston, J.H. (1987), 'Values, Culture and the Effective School', *NASSP Bulletin*, March, pp. 79-88.

Mullen, M. (1995), 'Diagnosing Measurement Equivalence in Cross-National Research', *Journal of International Business Studies*, Vol. 26 Third Quarter, pp. 573-596.

Nasif, E.G., Al-Daeaj, H., Ebrahimi, B. and Thibodeaux, M.S. (1991), 'Methodological Problems in Cross-Cultural Research: An Updated Review', *Management International Review,* Vol. 31 No. 1, pp. 79-91.

Netemeyer, R.G., Durvasula, S. and Lichtenstein, D. (1991), 'A Cross-National Assessment of the Reliability and Validity of the CETSCALE', *Journal of Marketing Research*, Vol. 28, August, pp. 320-327.

Ng, R. (1996), *Customers from Afar: Your Key to Serving Chinese Customers*, S.U.C.C.E.S.S. Publication, Vancouver, BC.

Parameswaran, R., and Yaprak, A. (1987), 'A Cross-National Comparison of Consumer Research Measures', *Journal of International Business Studies*, Vol. 18, No. 1, pp. 35-49.

Parasuraman, A., Berry, L.L. and Zeithaml, V.A. (1991), 'Refinement and Reassessment of the SERVQUAL Scale', *Journal of Retailing*, Vol. 67, No. 4, Winter, pp. 420-450.

____, (1986), *SERVQUAL: A Multiple-Item Scale for Measuring Customer Perceptions of Service Quality*, Marketing Science Institute Report #86-108, Marketing Science Institute, Cambridge, MA.

____, (1988), 'SERVQUAL: A Multiple-Item Scale for Measuring Consumer Perceptions of Service Quality', *Journal of Retailing*, Vol. 64, No. 1, Spring, pp. 12-40.

____, (1994), 'Alternative Scales for Measuring Service Quality: A Comparative Assessment Based on Psychometric and Diagnostic Criteria', *Journal of Retailing*, Vol. 70, No. 3, pp. 193-199.

Peter, P.J., Churchill, G.A. Jr. and Brown, T.J. (1993), 'Caution in the Use of Difference Scores in Consumer Research', *Journal of Consumer Research,* Vol.19, No.4, pp. 655-662.

Rokeach, M. (1968), *Beliefs, Attitudes and Values: A Theory of Organization and Change,* Jossey-Bass, San Francisco, CA.

Singh, J. (1995), 'Measurement Issues in Cross-National Research', *Journal of International Business Studies*, Vol. 26, Third Quarter, pp. 597-619.

Tung, R.L. (1982), *Chinese Industrial Society After Mao*, Lexington Books, Lexington, MA.

____ (1991), 'Handshakes Across the Sea: Cross-Cultural Negotiating for Business Success', *Organizational Dynamics*, Vol. 19, No. 3, pp. 30-40.

Yau, O.H.M. (1988), 'Chinese Cultural Values: Their Dimensions and Marketing Implications', *European Journal of Marketing*, Vol. 22 No. 5, pp. 44-57.

Zaichkowsky, J.L., and Sood, J.H. (1989), 'A Global Look at Consumer Involvement and Use of Products', *International Management Review*, Vol. 6 No. 1, pp. 20-34.

Zhaml, V.A., Berry, L.L. and Parasuraman, A. (1991), *The Nature and Determinants of Customer Expectations of Service,* Marketing Science Institute Report No. 91-113, Marketing Science Institute, Cambridge, MA.

Chapter 8

Direct Marketing of Shopping Centers: The Influence of Ethnic Background on Intention to Respond

Victoria A. Seitz

Introduction

Shopping Centers today face fierce competition, not only from freestanding stores and discount houses, but from neighboring Centers as well. Shilingburg (1994, p. 82) noted that after years of 'constant building, the landscape became saturated with shopping malls.' As a result, marketing efforts among malls have become more aggressive with advertising in mass and direct media outlets. As marketing directors continually play one upmanship with other Centers in obtaining patronage, challenges will continue to be forthcoming.

One major challenge is the growing ethnic diversity of the U.S. market, particularly the Asian and Hispanic markets, which are growing by leaps and bounds. One of the primary reasons why these markets have been overlooked is simply because marketers don't know how to communicate to these audiences. Although information on ethnic groups' purchasing behavior is available, there is limited research regarding their shopping center patronage motives. Specifically, in marketing shopping centers, only research regarding their shopping behavior has been observed (Herche & Balasubramanian, 1994).

But given the immense competition among shopping malls, how can marketers effectively advertise to various ethnic groups? Direct marketing has been one of the avenues that has experience success in reaching Anglo Americans, but is this a viable strategy for Hispanics, Asians or Blacks? Hence, the purpose of the study was to determine the influence of ethnic background regarding direct marketing strategies and their influence in shopping mall patronage. Specifically, the study sought to:

1. Determine ethnic background of shopping mall patrons in two Southern California Malls.
2. Determine attitudes toward direct marketing among Anglo-Americans, Hispanics, Asians and Blacks.
3. Determine shopping mall patronage motives among Anglo Americans,

Hispanics, Asians, and Blacks.

4. Determine the relationship between ethnic background and attitudes towards direct Marketing.
5. Determine the relationship between ethnic background and intention to respond to direct mail promotions of shopping malls.
6. Determine the relationship between attitudes toward direct marketing and salience of shopping mall patronage motives.

Relevant Literature

The retail market is saturated hence competition is stiff. One avenue for sales growth is targeting to ethnic markets. Projections for the year 2000 estimate that one of every three Americans will be of ethnic origin (Wilson, 1992). In fact, the three leading U.S. minority segments - Asians, Hispanics, and African Americans, currently make up approximately a $300 billion dollar market (Holliday, 1993). In particular, the Asian and Hispanic markets are growing by leaps and bounds. According to Santoro (1991), the Hispanic market is 25 million strong and growing six and a half times faster than the general market. The Asian marketing is also a rapidly growing group of highly educated individuals. In California, their population approximates 13 percent of the state's population or 4.5 million people (Fost, 1990). However, even given these startling statistics, marketers have, in general, skimped or ignored altogether marketing to these groups. One of the primary reasons why these markets have not been tapped is simply because marketers don't know how to communicate to these audiences. National companies such as AT&T, Sears and others have been the leaders in targeting ethnic groups. As well, Coca-Cola budgeted $10 million dollars to market their products to the Hispanic market along with Maxwell House (Stern, 1984). Regarding mall marketing only a limited number have attempted to target emerging ethnic groups. Cherry Creek Mall in Denver translated an existing advertising campaign into Spanish and Japanese due to a good percentage of these ethnic groups that were present in their target market (Antuana, 1994).

The Black community comprises 7.4 percent of the U.S. population or 29.3 million consumers, according to the 1990 Census ('The Changing Faces', 1992). As noted by Chain Store Age Executive ('The Changing Faces', 1992), the African American population has remained stable compared to growing Hispanic and Asian populations. However, as time has progressed, Blacks have moved up the socioeconomic ladder in America and represent an annual disposable income of $300 billion dollars (Kern-Foxworth, 1991). Given this, companies such as Cadillac have begun to view the African American as a viable target market. In fact, in 1994, Cadillac launched an ad campaign directed specifically to African Americans. This campaign was supported by sensitivity training to all employees at dealerships in several markets (Miller, 1994). Moreover, regarding their shopping orientations, Herche and Balasubramanian (1994) found that Blacks were more distinctive in their shopping patterns and tended to shop from within their ethnic group.

Marketers have often assumed that in America, 'one does as Americans do' when it comes to marketing to ethnic groups. However, given the growth of ethnic groups, new arrivals into the U.S. can chose to assimilate into the American lifestyle or continue to live as they did in their own country. Assimilation or acculturation is defined as the process of acquiring the customs of an alternate society. In a previous study Seitz (1998), found that Blacks were the most acculturated next to whites, followed by Hispanics. Asians were the least acculturated of the groups investigated. Therefore, the question remains how to reach growing ethnic groups as they begin their new lives in the U.S. Will they adapt the purchasing behaviors found in American culture or will they continue to follow the practices inherent in their culture?

Regarding direct response purchasing, Hispanics and Asians are receptive to this buying method. In fact, both Columbia House and Sears Roebuck & Co. rolled out campaigns to the Hispanic market in 1993. Moreover, Sears tapped into the Asian market with advertising and promotions directed at this group ('Sears Targets Asians,' 1994). AT&T found that direct mail pieces written in Spanish gained higher responses from Hispanics than when written in English. Moreover, other phone companies such as MCI and Sprint have achieve success in direct mail efforts directed to Hispanics because this group has relatives in distant places (Abel, 1993). But how successful are direct marketing strategies in promoting shopping mall patronage?

This study focuses on the concerns of marketers and advertisers regarding the influence of ethnic background on intention to respond to direct mail promotions of shopping malls. Given the above, the following hypotheses were tested:

H1: Individuals of different ethnic backgrounds will differ significantly regarding their attitudes toward direct marketing.

H2: Individuals of different ethnic backgrounds will differ significantly regarding their intention to respond to direct mail promotions of shopping malls.

H3: Individuals of different ethnic backgrounds will differ significantly regarding their shopping mall patronage motives.

H4: There will be a significant positive correlation between attitudes toward direct marketing and intention to respond to direct mail promotions of shopping malls.

H5: There will be a significant positive correlation between attitudes toward direct marketing and salience of shopping center motives.

Methodology

Sample

The population consisted of Anglo-Americans, Hispanics, Blacks and Asians living in Southern California. Patrons of two area malls were intercepted and asked to participate in a survey. Surveys were conducted Friday through Sunday at the beginning and middle of the month of April 1996. A total of 519 individuals participated in the study and completed the surveys.

Instrument

A self administered questionnaire was developed to assess the following information: 1) ethnic background; 2) attitudes toward direct marketing; 3) shopping mall patronage motives; 4) intention to respond to direct mail promotions of a shopping mall; and 5) demographic information. To measure ethnic background a single question regarding what the respondent's ethnic background was incorporated into the survey.

To measure attitudes toward direct marketing, the instrument developed by Akhter and Durvasula (1991) was used. This instrument examined general attitudes toward direct marketing, catalogs, and ordering by mail. Items were measured using a five point modified Likert scale ranging from strongly agree (5) to strongly disagree (1). To measure shopping mall patronage motives the instrument developed by Bellenger, Robertson, and Greenberg (1977) was used. The instrument included a list of 20 shopping center features, which respondents rated in terms of importance in the selection of a shopping center. Ratings were measured on a five point modified Likert scale ranging from very unimportant (1) to very important (5).

To measure intention to respond to a direct mail promotion of a shopping mall a modified version of the instrument developed by Dillon, Madden and Firtle (1990) was used. Two questions, one measuring the likelihood of responding to a direct mailer of an upcoming promotion and, two, the likelihood of responding to a direct mailer regarding a product purchase were employed. Respondents rated their likelihood of responding via a seven point modified Likert scale from 'very likely' (7) to 'very unlikely' (1). Demographic information solicited were based on the literature reviewed and included age, education, marital status, number of children living at home, income, employment status as well as number of years residing in the U.S.

Method of Analysis

To accomplish the stated objectives and to test the proposed hypotheses, measures of central tendency, Multivariate Analysis of Variance (MANOVA), Univariate Analysis of Variance (ANOVA) and Pearson's Correlational Analyses was used. To determine reliability of the instruments, Cronbach's Alpha analysis was used. To reduce the number of factors in the attitudes towards direct marketing instrument and to further define the underlying dimensions in the scale, factor analysis with varimax rotation was employed. The final factors were subsequently employed in further analysis and testing of the hypotheses.

Results

A total of 519 respondents completed the self-administered questionnaire. Most respondents (57 %) were between the ages of 25 to 54, were married (46.8%) had no or one child living at home (67.3%) had some college education (40.6%) and were employed full time (50.7%). Most respondents (27.4%) were in such occupations that included business people, merchants, engineers, secretaries as well as nurses. Moreover, the majority of the respondents (22.7%) reported annual family incomes between $20,000 and $35,000 and owned their own home (51.3%). Finally, the majority of respondents were White (43%), followed by Hispanics (21.2%), Blacks (20.6%) and Asians (5.4%).

Regarding attitudes towards direct marketing the majority of the respondents (approximately 30 %) neither agreed nor disagreed with the majority of statements in the scale; however, regarding the ease of placing orders 42.9 percent agreed with this statement. As well, 37.1 percent of the respondents agreed that catalogs made products look more attractive than they actually are. Approximately 32 percent of the respondents reported that catalogs do not provide enough information to compare different brands or judge the color of the item adequately (36.5%). Thirty seven percent of the respondents agreed that catalogs do not assure that consumers will like the products when they receive them and that ordering by mail delays delivery time. Moreover, approximately 36 percent of respondents reported that catalog shopping was a convenient form of buying but found the method impersonal (31.4%) and difficult (31.5%).

Regarding salience of selected shopping patronage motives, the majority of respondents considered security (62.8%), atmosphere (55.1%), cleanliness (64.7%), courtesy of personnel (64%), high quality of merchandise (53.9%), availability of parking (50.9%), store hours (44.7%), variety of stores (60.7%), and low prices (49.9%) to be most important. Convenience to home (75.5%), easy accessibility (81.5%), variety of department store (68.7%), availability of new fashions (70.3%), having restaurants (61.8%) and an enclosed mall (63.1%) were considered as important or very important.

Regarding the likelihood that respondents would respond to a direct mail promotion of an event at a mall or visit a mall to purchase an item advertised in a direct mailer, approximately 45 percent of respondents indicated neither likely nor unlikely. The mean response for both questions ranged from 4.2 to 4.5. Given that the scale ranged from 7 for very likely to 1 for very unlikely, respondents tended to lean toward the positive and would consider responding to such a direct response vehicle.

Cronbach's Alpha reliability testing was conducted to determine the reliability of the instruments used in the survey. Regarding the attitudes toward direct marketing scale, results showed reliability coefficient of .64 after one item was deleted. For the salience of shopping patronage motives scale, the Cronbach Alpha reliability coefficient was .85. As a result both scales were deemed reliable.

As a means to reduce the number of items in each scale, factor analysis with varimax rotation was employed. For items to be included in the factors a minimum level of 4.0 was used. For the attitudes toward direct marketing scale, varimax rotation reduced the number of items to four factors. The first factor included items highlighting the negative aspects of ordering by mail and catalog. Factor 2 included items illustrating the positive aspects of what direct marketers do. Factor 3 included items that highlighted the positive aspects of catalog shopping. Factor 4 included items that summarized the negative aspects of what direct marketers do. These four factors explained approximately 45 percent of the variance.

Regarding the shopping patronage motives scale, results of varimax rotation produced three factors that explained approximately 56 percent of the variance. The first factor included 11 items that reflected the most important attributes to shoppers when considering which shopping center to patronize. The second factor included four items and summarized the secondary factors that respondents consider in determining mall patronage. Finally, the third factor reflected items that were not as important to consumers in their patronage decision of shopping centers.

Testing the Hypotheses

H1: Individuals of different ethnic race will differ significantly regarding their attitudes toward direct marketing. Results of Multivariate Analysis of Variance yielded significant differences regarding this relationship at the $p < .05$ (DF, 20, F = 1.80). Univariate analysis of variance showed that Factor 2, the positive aspects of direct marketers, determined significance at the $p < .001$ level. Blacks (M = 13.95) and Hispanics (M = 13.52) were more positive regarding various aspects of direct marketers than Whites or Asians. Hypotheses 2-4 were not significant at the $p < .05$ level.

H5: There will be a significant positive correlation between attitudes toward direct marketing and salience of shopping mall patronage motives. Results of Pearson's Correlational Analysis revealed significant positive relationships at the p. $< .05$ level for Factors 1 and 2 of the direct marketing scale and Factor 1 and 2 of the Shopping Center Patronage scale. For Factor 1, of the attitudes of the direct marketing scale, which pointed out the negative aspects of ordering by mail and catalogs, as negativity increased, the importance of shopping center motives increased for both primary and secondary motives. However, for Factor 2, when positive aspects of direct marketers increase, so did the importance of the primary shopping mall patronage motives.

Conclusions and Discussion

Findings from this study are limited to the population and the sample surveyed. Results showed that ethnic background does not have a strong influence in intention to respond to direct mailers of shopping malls, or towards the importance of shopping center patronage motives. However, ethnic background played a significant role regarding attitudes toward direct marketing. Blacks and Hispanics regarded the aspects of what direct marketers do in a more positive light than Whites and Asians. This may be due to limited experience with direct marketing vehicles. Whites may have lower opinions of direct marketing due to perhaps greater experience with direct marketers and thus more opinionated regarding what they do. The low mean value among Asians coincides with previous research that suggests that Asians assimilate into mainstream American culture to a lesser degree than other ethnic groups (Seitz, 1998). Given, that shopping via direct marketing vehicles is a part of American culture, Asians would probably not participate in this buying method given their reluctance to assimilate into this culture.

Also found was that a significant positive relationship existed between salience of shopping mall patronage motives and attitudes toward direct marketing. This finding is supported by earlier research by Reynolds (1974) and others that found that those who shopped via catalogs and other direct marketing vehicles were also avid store shoppers that enjoyed the shopping experience. However, regarding the negative aspects of direct marketing, (Factor 1) the more that respondents agreed with these statements the more likely they were to place importance on shopping mall patronage attributes (Factors 1 and 2). This may be due to individual's present enjoyment and satisfaction with shopping at malls in relation to former or current experiences shopping via direct marketing methods.

A majority of respondents neither disagreed nor agreed regarding their attitudes towards direct marketing. This may have been due to their limited experience in shopping via direct marketing methods. However, since this was not investigated such conclusions cannot be drawn for this study. Given their limited attitudes toward direct marketing, this may have affected their responses towards questions concerning their likelihood of responding to direct mailers of shopping mall events or items that can be purchased at a mall. Although, most respondents were more positive than negative about their likelihood, the response was not strong one way or another. This may be due to the influence of product on shopping behavior. Although this was not investigated, individuals patronize different types of outlets or employ different shopping methods depending on the type of product to be purchased which may have affected response.

Implications

There are several implications of the study's findings. First, although the findings did not necessarily support direct mailers as a means of promoting an event or an item that can be purchased at the mall, this form of communication cannot be ruled out. Perhaps a newsletter or other no threatening direct mailers could be used rather than a straight advertisement of an item to be purchased. It is apparent that in this investigation that respondents were limited in their opinions and attitudes toward direct marketing; hence, mall marketers should consider their role in educating the public regarding various direct methods available to consumers for purchasing merchandise. Newsletters could include information about new store openings, new personnel, human interest stories as well as notices of upcoming events or items that are available for purchase for a special price. Research findings suggest that respondents considered security, courtesy of personnel, quality merchandise, pleasant atmosphere, variety of stores, the number of large department stores, convenience to home, store hours and such as very important in their mall patronage decisions. These reasons should be emphasized in all communication forms such as in advertisements and publicity materials.

Also, findings showed that as negative aspects of direct marketers rose so did the importance of shopping center patronage motives. Given this, it is still important that direct marketers work with consumers in making their purchase a satisfactory one. Although, most Americans have shopped via catalogs and other direct marketing vehicles, a bad experience can lead individuals away from this convenient form of shopping to others including shopping malls. As well, if a mall pursues direct response advertising in their marketing efforts, they would benefit by working with stores to make sure that a direct marketing transaction is a satisfactory one since a negative experience could jeopardize the mall's image and, hence, patronage.

Moreover, as the Internet becomes a common communication vehicle for consumers, manufacturers and service providers, shopping malls will want to take advantage of communicating to their target market via this advertising tool. However, mall marketers should use caution when approaching marketing their mall on the Internet since poor communication and advertising can affect the mall's image. However, if web sites are developed appropriately, malls can expand their trading area indefinitely. In addition, when producing a homepage on the World Wide Web, the graphics should invite viewers to further navigate the site, so several hyperlinks should be present. Furthermore, the web site should be updated constantly and promoted through traditional media to encourage repeat visits and click thrus. Mall marketers can familiarize Internet users with stores in the mall as well as update them on special events, sales and other upcoming activities. The homepage may develop interest among Internet users to physically visit the mall. In the future as consumers become more confident with buying on the Internet, mall marketers can work with stores to offer specials that are only available through the homepage site.

Finally, given the growing multiethnicity in the United States, marketers may fare better by adapting the principles of global advertising and marketing. As found by Sommers and Kernan (1967) some products lend themselves to a globalized strategy while others a more localized approach. By understanding the target market, marketers can adapt current direct marketing strategies to selected ethnic groups with only minor changes such as the copy written in the targeted market's language. However, if directing a campaign to less acculturated groups then a more localized approach would be need. For example, changes in catalog development, product and price changes and changes in promotional strategies may stimulate direct mail purchases.

Seitz and Johar (1993) found that some types of products lend themselves to globalized campaigns while others profit from more localized approaches. They found that clothing products benefited by a localized approach while perfumes a globalized approach. Clothing is seen as a personal reflection of oneself and of their culture, which can vary widely even within the U.S. Perfumes on the other hand, require little copy to sell the product and are primarily image driven suggesting that a globalized approach may enhance purchases. In addition, brands such as Levi's and Coca-Cola, well known throughout the world, could incorporate a more globalized campaign to ethnic groups here in the U.S. with much success. Other product categories such as cosmetics, although well known throughout the world, may require copy changes to explain features and benefits. With these types of product the copy may be translated and perhaps given different emphasis depending on the need of the target market. However, marketers should avoid direct translations since such action may communicate the wrong message.

Direct marketing methods, such as the Internet is growing in popularity overseas as well as cable television. Individuals that utilized these vehicles will find it easy to adapt into the American culture. However, such technological advances are in their infancy overseas and hence, ethnic groups living in the U.S., and depending on their length of stay, will have take more time to adapt to media and purchasing vehicles here. In the meantime, marketers would fare well to adapt the principles of globalized and localized campaign strategies marketing to ethnic groups in the U.S.

Future Research

This study entailed a mall intercept encompassing two area malls in Southern California. Future research may look to including more malls and perhaps surveying shoppers in other states to gain a true reflection of the impact of ethnic background on intention to respond to direct marketing materials.

Additionally, this study only looked at general attitudes toward direct marking. Future research should examine intention to respond to direct mailers of specific products and/or services produced by shopping malls to determine if differences exist among ethnic groups. A problem that occurs over and over in research of this nature is that some may respond to direct mailers for some products but not for others. Moreover, in surveying general attitudes without specifying a product, such attitudes may not be strong considering that no product has been identified and respondents may feel one way about one product and another about another item, resulting in an a somewhat indifferent response. Hence, future research should entail both general attitudes and identification of specific products.

Finally, future research should look at the relationship between past direct marketing experience and likelihood of responding to direct marketing vehicles for a shopping mall. Perhaps, a better understanding of this relationship can help define the differences and similarities regarding ethnic background and intention to respond to direct marketing efforts.

References

Abel, Judy (1993), 'Marketing to Hispanics,' *Direct*, 5(1), 36-39.

Akhter, Syed H. and Srinivas Durvasula (1991), 'Consumers' Attitudes Toward Direct Marketing and Purchase Intentions,' *Journal of Direct Marketing*, 5(3), 48-56.

Antuana, Ingrid Rizo (March 24, 1994), 'Cherry Creek Mall Goes Western New Ads Contrast Cowboy Tradition with Denver Today,' *The Denver Post*, C-01.

Bellenger, Danny N., Dan H. Robertson, and Barnett A. Greenberg (1977), 'Shopping Center Patronage Motives,' *Journal of Retailing*, 53(2), 30-38.

Dillon, William R., Thomas J. Madden and Neil H. Firtle (1990), *Marketing Research in a Marketing Environment*, Homewood, IL: Richard Irwin, Inc..

Fost, Dan (1990), 'California's Asian Market,' *American Demographics*, 12(10), 34-37.

Herche, Joel and Siva Balasubramanian (1994), Ethnicity and Shopping Behavior,' *Journal of Shopping Center Research*, 1(1), 65-80

Holliday, Karen (1993), 'Reaching Ethnic Markets,' *Bank Marketing*, 25(2), 35-37.

Kern-Foxworth, Marilyn (1991), 'Black, Brown, Red and Yellow Markets Equal Green Power,' *Public Relations Quarterly*, spring 27-30.

Miller, Cyndee (May 23, 1994), 'Cadillac Promo Targets African Americans,' *Marketing News*, 28, p. 12.

Reynolds, F. D. (1974), 'Analysis of Catalog Buying Behavior,' *Journal of Marketing*, 38 (July), 47-51.

Santoro, Elaine (October 1991), 'Hispanics Are Hot,' *Direct Marketing*, 28-30.

'Sears Targets Asians,' (October 10, 1994), *Advertising Age*, 16.

Seitz, Victoria and J.S. (Vic) Johar (1993), 'Relative Positioning of Self Image Projective Products Across Europe: A Content Analysis of Print Advertising.' *World Marketing Congress*, VII, 340-345.

Seitz, Victoria A. (1998), 'Acculturation and Direct Purchasing Behavior Among Whites, Blacks, Hispanics and Asians of Self Image Projective Products,' *Journal of Consumer Marketing*, 15(1), 23-31.

Shilingburg, Donald (1994), 'Entertainment Drives Retail,' *Architectural Record*, August, 82-85.

Sommers, M. and J.B. Kernan (1967), 'Why Products Flourish Here and Fizzle There,' *Columbia Journal of World Business*, March/April, pp. 89-97.

Stern, Aimee L. (July 1984), 'One Language, Four Cultures,' *Marketing Communications*, 45-50, 52-53, 55.

'The Changing Faces of California,' (May 1992), *Chain Store Age Executive*, 53-55.

Wilson, Roberta (1992), 'Beyond Black: Color Cosmetics For Other Ethnic Groups,' *Drug & Cosmetic Industry*, 151(5), 26-30.

Chapter 9

A Family Level Measure of Acculturation for Chinese Immigrants

Michel Laroche
Zhiyong Yang
Chankon Kim
Claudia Chan

Introduction

Acculturation refers to changes in cultural attitudes, values, and behaviors that take place as a result of continuous direct or indirect contacts of groups having different cultures (Broom and Selznick 1963). Consecutive waves of ethnic groups arriving in North America over the last century have adopted some values and behaviors of the mainstream culture (Silverstein and Chen 1999). In a particular cohort of immigrant families, the acculturation process is typically intensified in succeeding generations by their prolonged and direct contacts with the predominant North American culture (Redfield, Linton and Herskovits 1936).

The family is crucial in examining acculturation and its consequences because parenting practices and family relationships have much impact on intergenerational relationships (Silverstein and Chen 1999), children's purchase influence (Corfman 1991), cultural transmission (Phalet and Schönpflug 2001), and acculturation. All past studies related to family members' acculturation assessment (e.g., Tang and Dion 1999) have revealed a lack of convergence in multiple reports because gender, age and education levels have significant impacts on individuals' adaptation processes. This will cause a serious threat to the validity of family studies when using multiple respondents in depicting the relative level of acculturation. According to Kim and Lee (1997), multiple respondent data are of central significance in evaluating the qualities of family measures. Therefore, it is necessary to develop a valid and reliable family triadic acculturation scale using multiple respondents, multiple-item data. Family triadic reports enable researchers to not only examine the systematic and random measurement errors, as well as the construct of interest (Bagozzi, Yi and Phillips 1991), but also to correct for potential bias in estimating structural relationships among constructs (Cote and Buckley 1988). Despite the importance of family as a socialization agent (Moschis 1978), there has been a relative dearth of research that examines the acculturation patterns of immigrant families in North America. And no research has been found to investigate the proposed family triadic measures of acculturation. This paucity is somewhat surprising given that a large proportion of immigrant families comprise many foreign-born children whose mainstream and heritage cultures differ significantly.

Even worse, an examination of the extant literature reveals muddled thinking (Keefe and Padilla 1987) and a lack of coherence (Kim 1988) on the definition of acculturation, causing some apprehension concerning the validity of past research (Nguyen et al. 1999). This phenomenon is mainly due to the lack of consensus on the conceptual representation of the immigrant adaptation process as well as a multiplicity of operational approaches to key concepts characterizing the different facets of this process (Kim, Laroche and Tomiuk 2001). As a result, the examination of the relationship between acculturation and adjustment reveals divergent and often contradictory findings (Nguyen et al. 1999). This lack of theoretical coherence and integration of key aspects of immigrant ethnic change is further augmented by the diversity of construct measurement attempts. Much diversity has been found in measurement approaches of acculturation in terms of subjective vs. objective indices, single-item vs. multi-item scales, nominal vs. continuous measurement, and unipolar vs. bipolar dimensions (Kim, Laroche and Tomiuk 2001).

The purpose of this chapter is twofold: (1) to provide a conceptual framework for Chinese acculturation and (2) to develop a family level Chinese acculturation measure with acceptable validity and reliability.

Background

The consequences of migration are enormous. In line with Ryder, Alden and Paulhus (2001), when an immigrant moves to a new environment, many aspects of self-identity are modified to accommodate information about and experiences within the mainstream culture. Such changes may be observed in various categories such as attitudes, behaviors, values, and a sense of cultural identity (Ryder, Alden and Paulhus 2001). At a fundamental level, then, acculturation has an important impact on shaping family lifestyles (Tang and Dion 1999), psychological well-being of individual family members (e.g., Jayasuriya, Sang and Fielding 1992), and family consumption behavior (Webster 1992).

Of various explanations of what is meant by 'acculturation', two schools of thought can be found in the psychology literature. One is very broad and used interchangeably with assimilation, adaptation and ethnic change. Specifically, attached to the unidimensional approach of immigrant adaptation process, acculturation is considered as a linear bipolar process by which acculturating individuals are relinquishing the attitudes, values and behaviors of their heritage culture while simultaneously acquiring those of the mainstream culture (Gordon 1964). This definition confounds acquisition of mainstream cultural traits with loss of heritage cultural traits (Kim, Laroche and Tomiuk 2001). From a theoretical viewpoint, this unidimensional perspective fails to consider alternatives to assimilation, such as integrated or bicultural identities (Dion and Dion 1996).

The other definition relies on a bidimensional perspective and characterizes acculturation in a narrower way. Here, proponents of the 2-D approach maintain that when heritage and mainstream cultural identities are seen as being relatively independent of one another, the immigrant adaptation process can be more completely understood (Berry 1997). Congruent with this point of view, recent studies of various ethnic groups in the United States and Canada have found that the adaptation process does not necessarily cause the loss of one's original ethnic identity (Lambert, Mermigis and Taylor 1986). A primary reason for this may be the countries multicultural policies. According to Berry (1991), countries with official multicultural policies and public acceptance of ethnic cultures and identities allow for higher degrees of culture maintenance across generations of immigrants. Therefore, there should be two dimensions underlying the immigrant adaptation process: 1) *acculturation* refers to the learning of the traits of the mainstream society, and 2) *ethnic identification* represents maintenance of the original ethnic identity (Laroche et al. 1996).

The Suinn-Lew Asian Self-Identity Acculturation Scale (SL-ASLA; Suinn et al. 1987), under the assumption that acculturation is unidimentional and ranges from 'low acculturation' (i.e., Asian identification), through 'bicultural' identification at a midpoint, to 'high acculturation' (i.e., North American identification), is the most widely used measure of acculturation among Asian North Americans. SL-ASLA has yielded increasing attention (Iwamasa 1996); however, it has been increasingly criticized because it does not measure a range of acculturation behaviors and situations (Iwamasa 1996), or distinguish bicultural individuals who strongly identify with both cultures from the immigrants who have difficulty fitting into mainstream and heritage cultures (Barry 2001).

Derived from the bidimensional perspective to immigrant adaptation process, a growing group of researchers (e.g., Laroche et al. 1996) have taken a different approach by measuring the two dimensions (i.e., acculturation and ethnic identity) separately. Acculturation, as a part of immigration adaptation process, has been widely believed to be multidimensional in recent research (see Rogler et al. 1991 for a review of acculturation measures), implying that the adaptation process is likely to occur at different rates in different sociocultural spheres. The various indicators of acculturation have been classified into such categories as behavioral, attitudinal, linguistic, psychological, and socioeconomic (Olmedo, Martinez and Martinez 1978).

As in some early studies of family research, conclusions are drawn based solely on the self-reported responses of just one family member, usually the mother or wife (Atkin 1978). Fathers are included in recent studies because of the recognition of their important roles in the child rearing process and their significance as members of the family system. Besides, in immigrant families, fathers are more likely to be exposed, through their workplace, to values held by other groups in the new country. Researchers (e.g., Hearst 1985) find that their shift towards the new cultural values might not be shared by their wives. Moreover, younger members of immigrant families are found to be more likely than their elders to adopt the values and behavior of the predominant culture (Piere,

Clark and Kaufman 1978). Therefore, it will be not surprising to see frequent disagreements among family members when assessing acculturation levels.

Statistically, such observed discrepancies are believed to be caused by both systematic errors, such as reporting bias (Davis and Rigaux 1974), and random errors, especially those associated with a lack of communication among family members, and ambiguities in measurement items (Olson 1969). A methodology that combines the measure purification approach, confirmatory factor analyses (CFA), multitrait-multimethod (MTMM) data analysis, and the correlated uniqueness (CU) model enables researchers to evaluate and/or diminish these measurement errors by using multiple-informant, multiple-item data in the scale development and validation process.

Methodology

The Sample

The family data used in this study were collected through the cooperation of a Chinese language school and a Chinese church located in a Northeastern metropolitan area. Initially, 300 sets of questionnaires were distributed to the teachers of the school with the consent of their principal and supervisor. Additionally, 35 sets were distributed in a church. Out of the 335 sets of questionnaires distributed, a total of 108 family triadic sets were returned. 13 sets with missing variables were further deleted to keep the data authentic and complete, yielding a sample size of 95 family triads, which accounted for 28.4% of the total families that had been contacted initially.

Measures   The questionnaire contained 22 randomly arranged subjective acculturation measures covering three underlying dimensions: E-C Identification and Attachment (3 items), English Language Use (9 items), and E-C Social Interaction (10 items). Responses to each item were made on 5-point scales, which ranged from 1=disagree strongly to 5=agree strongly (see Table 9.1).

The average age of the children in the sample was 15.2 years, ranging from 13 to 19. Male children accounted for 41.3% and female 58.7%. The children had resided in North America for an average of 6.3 years. About 60.6% of the fathers and 71.6% mothers of the mothers were in the 41-50 age group. The average years of marriage for the parents were 20 years. The number of years resided in North America was 11.4 years for the mothers and 12.6 years for the fathers, respectively. 38.5% of the fathers and 29.3% of the mothers had completed above high school level. 85.3% of the fathers and 82.6% of the mothers felt most comfortable speaking Chinese. The mean household income, as reported by both the fathers and mothers, was about US$20,000-$30,000.

Analysis and Results

Measure Purification

A measure purification process (Bohrnstedt 1983) as in an individual-level measurement analysis was first performed to reduce systematic measurement errors. The purification process for the 22 items designed to assess acculturation involves two tasks: 1) to elicit a reliable item composite for each dimension of acculturation, and 2) to obtain a similar factor pattern across the three subgroups (i.e., fathers, mothers, and children). This process calls for exhaustive efforts in an iterative procedure involving exploratory factor analyses (EFA) and CFA. The final purification step yielded 9 reliable items with three factors (see Table 9.1), whose pattern was highly similar across the three subgroups. All the three extracted factors showed strong reliabilities, with all Cronbach's alphas above 0.70. The three-factor structure obtained from the purification process was confirmed with first-order CFA analyses for all subsamples. Estimation displayed equally desirable goodness of fit statistics for the three groups, as indicated by $\chi^2(24)=30.4$, p=.17, and CFI=0.99 for the fathers' data, $\chi^2(25)=24.7$, p=.48, and CFI=1.00 for the mothers' data, and $\chi^2(24)=26.6$, p=.32, and CFI=0.99 for the children's data, respectively.

Structural Equivalence Test: Multisample CFA

The three-factor measurement model was further subjected to a more rigorous test of structural equivalence across the three subsamples. Specifically, measurement-level constraints (i.e., configural invariance, metric invariance, factor covariance invariance, and error variance invariance) were introduced to test their equality simultaneously in the seven models shown in Table 9.2 by a set of multisample confirmatory factor analyses using covariance matrices (Byrne, 1994).

Given that Model 1 was the least restrictive among the seven, Models 2-7 which contained different sets of constraints were nested in Model 1, the baseline model. As indicated in Table 9.2, Model 2, 3, and 5 were not significantly different from the baseline: $\chi_d^2(12)=18.65$, p=.10, $\chi_d^2(6)=4.65$, p=.59, $\chi_d^2(18)=21.55$, p=.25.

Table 9.1   Results of the Measure Purification Process

Factors/Measures[a]	Loadings[d]			Cronbach α[d]		
	FA	MA	CA	FA	MA	CA
E-C Identification and Attachment				.80	.82	.78
I consider myself to be Canadian	.901	.920	.875			
I would like to be known as 'Canadian'	.901	.908	.874			
I feel very attached to all aspects of the English-Canadian culture						
English Language Use				.89	.91	.81
I speak English to my children[b]	.877	.871	.904			
I speak English to my spouse[c]	.887	.916	.668			
I speak English at family gatherings	.825	.896	.875			
The newspaper / magazines I read are mostly in English						
The movies / video tapes I see are mostly in English						
In general, I speak English to family members						
I speak English when I am angry						
I use English when talking about a personal or emotional problem with family members						
I speak English with most of my friends						
E-C Social Interaction				.87	.87	.85
Most of the people at the places I go to have fun and relax are English-Canadians	.798	.786	.809			
Of all the people I come in contact with on a day to day basis most are English-Canadians	.846	.875	.865			
Socially, I feel at ease with English-Canadians	.819	.841	.649			
I get together with English-Canadians very often	.804	.812	.878			
Most of my friends are English-Canadian						
I participate in activities of an English-Canadian church or association						
My closest friends are English-Canadian						

Most of the people who visit me are English-Canadian						
Most people I visit are English-Canadian						
I am very comfortable dealing with English-Canadian						

a.   These scales were measured on a 5-point Likert-type scale (disagree strongly to agree strongly).
b.   In children's questionnaire, this item was changed to 'I speak English to my parents'.
c.   In children's questionnaire, this item was changed to 'I speak English to my brothers & sisters'.
d.   FA=Fathers' Assessments; MA=Mothers' Assessments; CA=Children's Assessments. The items with factor loadings were remained after the measure purification process.

Additional model comparisons presented no significant χ^2 difference between Model 2 and Model 5 (χ_d^2 (6)=2.9, p=.82), or between Model 3 and Model 5 (χ_d^2 (12)=16.9, p=.15). Model 5, which hypothesized both metric invariance and factor covariance invariance, best represented the common measurement properties for the three groups. These results of the multisample CFA analyses indicate that these 9 acculturation items had at least the same factor patterns, factor structure, and factor covariances across three subsamples.

Construct Validation of the Triadic Measures: MTMM Analysis

The most popular procedure for the assessment of construct validity of multiple-responses, multiple-item data is the MTMM model (Campbell and Fiske 1959). The three dimensions of acculturation correspond to 'traits', while the independent responses of fathers, mothers, and children on the measures of acculturation correspond to 'methods'. Responses of individual family members on each of the three multiple-item acculturation measures were averaged so that each trait had three indicators: the fathers', mothers', and children's assessments.

Convergent validity refers to the extent to which the three methods of the same trait are statistically significantly correlated (Campbell and Fiske 1959). It was tested, based on Widaman's (1995) paradigm, by comparing a model in which traits were specified with one in which they were not. Based on our analysis, the $\Delta\chi^2$ between these two models was highly significant (χ_d^2 (11)=46.4, p<.00), thus supporting the convergent validity of the proposed acculturation measure.

Table 9.2   Results of Multisample CFA

Models	Goodness-of-Fit Indices			
	χ^2	df	p-value	CFI
M1: Configural Invariance	81.65	73	.23	.99
M2: Λ(fathers)= Λ(mothers)= Λ(children)	100.30	85	.12	.99
M3: Φ(fathers)= Φ(mothers)= Φ(children)	86.30	79	.27	.99
M4: Θ(fathers)= Θ(mothers)= Θ(children)	171.07	89	.00	.94
M5: Λ(fathers)= Λ(mothers)= Λ(children) Φ(fathers)= Φ(mothers)= Φ(children)	103.20	91	.18	.99
M6: Λ(fathers)= Λ(mothers)= Λ(children) Θ(fathers)= Θ(mothers)= Θ(children)	186.90	101	.00	.93
M7: Λ(fathers)= Λ(mothers)= Λ(children) Φ(fathers)= Φ(mothers)= Φ(children) Θ(fathers)= Θ(mothers)= Θ(children)	189.30	107	.00	.94

Model Comparisons	Difference in		
	χ^2	df	p-value
M2 vs. M1	18.65	12	.10
M3 vs. M1	4.65	6	.59
M5 vs. M1	21.55	18	.25

Discriminant validity, represented by the extent of the correlations among the independent measures of different traits, is typically assessed in terms of both traits and methods (Byrne 1994). Based on Byrne's (1994) method, evidence of discriminant validity among traits can be supported if a model in which traits correlate freely is significantly different from one in which they are perfectly correlated, while proof of discriminant validity related to method effects can be established by a significant difference between a model in which method factors are freely correlated and one in which the method factor correlations are specified as unity. Results showed strong support for discriminant validity for both methods and traits by the significant $\Delta\chi^2$ values in these two pairs, indicated by χ_d^2 (4)=21.9, p=.00, and χ_d^2 (1)=16.7, p=.00, respectively.

A more precise evidence of construct validity, according to Byrne (1994), is provided by the factor loadings and factor correlations of the hypothesized model (see Figure 9.1). Results revealed that all but two trait loadings were significant, showing strong evidence of convergent validity.

Figure 9.1   The Hypothesized MTMM Model of Acculturation

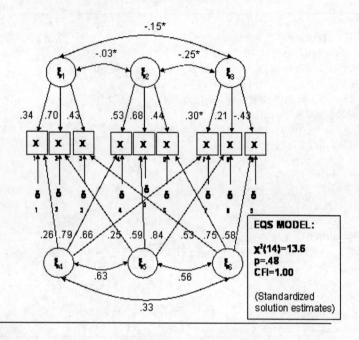

Notes:
ξ_1 = Trait 1 (E-C Identification and Attachment); ξ_2 = Trait 2 (English Language Use At Home); ξ_3 = Trait 3 (E-C Social Interaction). ξ_4 = Method 1 (Fathers' assessments); ξ_5 = Method 2 (Mothers' assessments); ξ_6 = Method 3 (Children's assessments).
x_1, x_2, x_3 = Fathers', mothers', and children's assessments of E-C Identification and Attachment.
x_4, x_5, x_6 = Fathers', mothers', and children's assessments of English Language Use At Home.
x_7, x_8, x_9 = Fathers', mothers', and children's assessments of E-C Social Interaction.
* Not statistically significant at .05 level.

Moreover, the correlations among traits were all not statistically significant (p>.05); therefore, discriminant validity among traits were satisfactorily supported. Of the three method correlations, we estimated a nested model in which the intermethod correlations were set simultaneously to unity. The χ^2 difference was then tested between this nested model and our hypothesized model. The difference was highly significant ($\chi_d^2(1)=16.7$, p=.00), providing a strong support that the methods were discriminant of each other.

Correlated Uniqueness (CU) Model

A possible ill-solution might exist in the MTMM analysis as all three correlations among traits in the hypothesized model were found to be insignificant. Conceptually, insignificance of all inter-trait correlations is a strong evidence of discriminant validity; however, such findings may be questionable since the three traits represent the same construct. This problem called for an alternative model specification, which could supply extra evidence to substantiate the validity of our proposed scale. To this end, the CU model was applied to examine our multiple-informant, multiple-item data since it included method effects as correlations among error terms.

Estimation of the CU model generated an excellent fit: $\chi^2(15)=19.0$, p=.21, and CFI=0.98. All but one factor loadings were significant (t>1.96), ranging from .37 to .95. Accordingly, convergent validity for our multiple-respondent measures was supported. Moreover, the average amount of trait variance (42%) was much higher than that found in the MTMM results (23%), showing a more favorable degree of convergence. Estimates revealed that two out of three of the uniqueness correlations for the fathers' assessments were significant (.27 and .53, respectively), while three correlations (.34, .40, and .42, respectively) for the children's were found significant. Therefore, method effects in both fathers' and children's assessments were in a moderate level. No significant uniqueness correlation was generated by the mothers' assessments, indicating that method effects in the mothers' data were negligible.

As estimated, the inter-trait correlation between the dimensions of English Language Use and E-C Social Interaction was statistically significant (.58, t>2.0). As the 95% confidence intervals (computed as: parameter estimate ± 1.96*[std. error]) for this value was [.41, .75], which did not include unity, we concluded that the traits were indeed separate and distinct.

Summary and Conclusion

The present research fills a void in family studies by the development and validation of an empirical family triadic self-report instrument, which examines the acculturation levels of Chinese immigrant families in North America. Different from the SL-ASIA, our family-level scale conceptualizes acculturation as a part of the immigrant adaptation process with multidimensional measures, which enable researchers to assess attitudes and behaviors in a variety of situations.

Unlike previous studies, the present research developed and validated an acculturation measure through multiple-respondent, multiple-item data from fathers, mothers, and children triads. The use of multiple respondents as multiple methods required a strict measure purification process, in which both internal consistency and intergroup agreement had to be taken into account. Of the 22 initial items, this process produced 9 items that measured three distinct facets of acculturation.

The test of construct validity entailed applying CFA to MTMM matrix data, regarding three dimensions of acculturation as 'traits', and the average scores from different respondents on the multiple-item measures as 'methods'. Since the MTMM generated an improper estimate, we performed the CU model, another CFA including the remedial measure. Although the underlying assumptions of the CU and MTMM models were different, the analyses of these two models yielded consistent evidence of the convergent and discriminant validity of the triadic measures. Therefore, our family-level scale can be asserted as a reliable measure in assessing the relative acculturation levels incorporating views of all family members for Chinese immigrant families.

Several potential limitations to this study should be noted. First of all, the sample size of 95 family triads is less than optimal for CFA analyses. A cross-validation study with a larger sample is needed. However, given difficulties in recruiting adequate families from this population, and the theoretical coherence of the three dimensions, our proposed scale may be theoretically and practically useful in family studies. Another issue is about acculturation measurement. Media consumption embedded in the category of English Language Use in the questionnaire of our study neither showed up as a distinct dimension of acculturation nor revealed significant loadings in factor analyses. This finding was surprising since media exposure has been found to relate significantly to immigrants' acculturation of the new social norms (Lee and Tse 1994). According to Douglas and Macquin (1977), the differences in lifestyles of consumers from different countries may lead to different effectiveness for different media. Given the distinctness of Chinese ethnic groups, further studies should extend media exposure measures to the exposure of TV and radio programs to investigate its role in acculturation assessment for family triads.

Overall, as an exploratory research, the results were encouraging. Although further studies are required with a larger sample and revised measures of mass communication, initial findings propose that the family-level acculturation scale may exhibit satisfactory validity and reliability, and shows promise as a useful tool for researchers working with Chinese immigrant families.

References

Atkin, C.K. (1978). Observation of parent-child interaction in supermarket decision making. *Journal of Marketing*, 42, 41-45.
Bagozzi, R.P., Yi, Y., & Phillips, L.W. (1991). Assessing construct validity in organizational research. *Administrative Science Quarterly*, 36, 421-58.
Barry, D.T. (2001). Development of a new scale for measuring acculturation: The East Asian Acculturation Measure (EAAM). *Journal of Immigration Health*, 3 (4), 193-

197.

Berry, J.W. (1991). Understanding and managing multiculturalism: Some possible implications of research in Canada. *Psychology and Development Societies*, 3, 17-49.

Berry, J.W. (1997). Immigration, acculturation, and adaptation. *Applied psychology: An international review*, 46, 5-68.

Bohrnstedt, G.W. (1983). Measurement. In *Handbook of survey research*, Rossi, P., Wright, J., & Anderson, A. (Eds.) New York: Academic Press, 69-121.

Broom, L. & Selznick, P. (1963). *Sociology*, New York: Harper and Row, p.84.

Byrne, B.M. (1994). *Structural Equation Modeling With EQS and EQS/Windows*. Thousand Oaks, CA: Sage Publications.

Campbell, D.T., & Fiske, D. W. (1959). Convergent and discriminant validation by the Multitrait-Multimethod Matrix. *Psychological Bulletin*, 56, 81-105.

Corfman, Kim P. (1991). Perceptions of relative influence: Formation and measurement. *Journal of Marketing Research*, 28 (May), 125-136.

Cote, J.A. & Buckley, M.R. (1988). Measurement error and theory testing in consumer research: An illustration of the importance of construct validation. *Journal of Consumer Research*, 14 (March), 579-582.

Davis, H.L., & Rigeaux, B.P. (1974). Perception of marital roles in decision processes. *Journal of Consumer Research*, 1, 51-62.

Dion, K.L., & Dion, K.K. (1996). Chinese adaptation to foreign cultures. In M. H. Bond (Ed.), *The handbook of Chinese psychology* (pp. 457-478). Hong Kong: Oxford University Press.

Douglas, S.P., & Macquin, A. (1977). The Use of Notions of Sociocultural Trends or Lifestyle Analysis in Media Selection (Working Paper).

Gordon, M.M. (1964). *Assimilation in American life*. New York: Oxford University Press.

Hearst, S. (1985). *The Psychology of Interpersonal Relations*, New York: Wiley.

Iwamasa, G.Y. (1996). Acculturation of Asian American university students. *Assessment*, 1, 99-102.

Jayasuriya, D.L., Sang, D.L., & Fielding, A. (1992). *Ethnicity, immigration and mental illness: A critical review of Australian research*. Canberra: Australian Government Publishing Service.

Kim, C., & Lee, H. (1997). Development of family triadic measures for children's purchase influence. *Journal of Marketing Research*, XXXIV (August), 307-321.

Kim, C., Laroche, M., & Tomiuk, M.A. (2001). A measure of acculturation for Italian Canadians: Scale development and construct validation. *International Journal of Intercultural Relations*, 25, 607-637.

Kim, Y.Y. (1988). *Communication and cross-cultural adaptation: An integrative theory*. Clevedon Avon, England: Multilingual Matters.

Lambert, W.E., Mermigis, L., & Taylor, D.M. (1986). Greek Canadians' attitudes towards own group and other ethnic groups: A test of the multiculturalism hypothesis. *Canadian Journal of Behavioral Science*, 18 (1), 35-51.

Laroche, M., Kim, C., Hui, M.K., & Joy, A. (1996). An empirical study of multidimensional ethnic change: The case of French Canadians in Quebec. *Journal of Cross-Cultural Psychology*, 27 (1), 114-131.

Lee, W., & Tse, D.K. (1994). Changing Media Consumption in a New Home: Acculturation Patterns Among Hong-Kong Immigrants to Canada. *Journal of Advertising*, 23(1), 57-70.

Moschis, G.P. (1978). *Consumer Socialization: A life-cycle perspective*. Lexington Books: D. C. Health and Company/Lexington, Massachusetts/Toronto.

Nguyen, H.H., Messe, L.A. & Stollak, G E. (1999). Toward a more complex understanding of acculturation and adjustment: Cultural involvements and psychosocial functioning in Vietnamese youth. *Journal of Cross-Cultural Psychology*, 30, 5-31.

Olmedo, E.L., Martinez, Jr., J.L., & Martinez, S. (1978). Measure of acculturation for Chicano adolescents. *Psychological Reports*, 42, 159-170.

Olson, D.H. (1969). The measurement of family power by self-report and behavioral methods. *Journal of Marriage and the Family*, 31 (August), 545-50.

Phalet, K., & Schönpflug, U. (2001). Intergenerational transmission of collectivism and achievement values in two acculturation contexts. *Journal of Cross-Cultural Psychology*, 32 (2), 186-201.

Redfield, R., Linton, R., & Herskovits, M. T. (1936). Memorandum for the study of acculturation. *American Anthropologist*, 38, 149-152.

Rogler, L.H., Cortes, D.E., & Malgady, R.G. (1991). Acculturation and mental health status among Hispanics: Convergence and new direction for research. *American Psychologist*, 46, 585-597.

Ryder, A.G., Alden, L.E., & Paulhus, D.L. (2001). Is acculturation unidimensional or bidimensional? A head-to-head comparison in the prediction of personality, self-identity, and adjustment. *Journal of Personality and Social Psychology*, 79 (1), 49-65.

Silverstein, M., & Chen, X. (1999). The impact of acculturation in Mexican American families on the quality of adult grandchild-grandparent relationships. *Journal of Marriage and Family*, 61 (1), 188-198.

Suinn, R.M., Rickard-Figueroa, K., Lew, S., & Vigil, P. (1987). The Suinn-Lew Asian Self-Identity Acculturation Scale: An initial report. *Educational and Psychological Measurement*, 47, 401-407.

Tang, T.N., & Dion, K.L. (1999). Gender and acculturation in relation to traditionalism: Perceptions of self and parents among Chinese students. *Sex Roles*, 41 (1/2), 17-29.

Webster, C. (1992). The effects of Hispanic subcultural identification on information search behavior. *Journal of Advertising Research*, 32 (5), 54-62.

Widaman, K.F. (1985). Hierarchically nested covariance structure models for Multitrait-Multimethod data. *Applied Psychological Measurement*, 9 (March), 1-26.

PART IV:

ETHNIC CONSUMER BEHAVIORS

Chapter 10

Psycho-Cultural Profile of Asian Immigrants: Implications for Marketing Initiatives

Bina Raval
Dinkar Raval

Introduction

The American population has become multicultural and ethnically more diverse since the liberalization of the U.S. immigration policy in the late 1960s (Lee, 1995; Locke, 1992). The Census Bureau projects that this diversity will persist as we enter the 21st century. These demographic changes will require marketers to be culturally sensitive in designing and developing marketing initiatives to satisfy the needs of existing and newly emerging ethnic groups (Rossman, 1994, Harris & Moran, 1996).

Asian-Americans one of the newly emerging ethnic groups is rapidly growing in number. Recent statistics show that this group grew almost 110 % between 1980-1990 with only a 53% growth in the Hispanic and *13%* in the African-American communities for the same period (Rossman, 1994). Their number could grow an additional 40% by the year 2000 (Shao, 1991).

Asian-Americans have made significant contributions to the U.S. economy since their arrival. They gained national attention because of their outstanding achievements and accomplishments. The contemporary impression of Asian-Americans is that they are successful and the group that has 'made it' in the American society (Sue & Sue, 1990). Their professional and economic success is generally attributed to their ability to rapidly assimilate into America's 'melting pot.' Consequently, the Asian-American's ethnic identity and cultural uniqueness; which sets them apart from the mainstream culture, is seldom recognized. Recent market studies support this view. These studies show that though Asian-Americans are similar to the members of the majority culture in some ways, many differences exist between the two groups that cannot be ignored (Steere, 1995). The characteristics that set the Asian-American and mainstream American groups apart are a result of differences in their cultural upbringing (Sue & Sue, 1990).

The role of culture therefore is critical in the development of behaviors. It distinguishes members of a society or group by influencing how they think and act

(Rossman, 1994). A study investigating how and why people of different cultures behave differently suggests that the cultural environment conditions the behaviors of individuals within a society. Different groups create their own culture or 'social environment' to develop and survive, and then pass on these behaviors to the next generation (Harris & Moran, 1979). Individuals within a group context subconsciously learn and accept what their culture teaches. There is a general acceptance that culture also influences individuals or groups information processing strategies, cognitive structures, attitudes and habits (Triandis, 1987; Rossman, 1994; Harris & Moran, 1996).

So the impact of culture and its influence on an individual or group's behavior is powerful. It not only motivates and shapes behaviors but also influences an individual's thinking and decision making process in the marketplace (Harris & Moran, 1979). In international trade, understanding cultural differences is considered important to overcome trade barriers between business partners. U.S. multinationals use culturally-driven criteria in making business decisions and promoting products and services in an overseas market. However, implementing culturally-driven criteria at the national level has not been vigorously adopted by U.S. marketers. They either perceive that the Asian-Americans within the U.S. are assimilating into the mainstream American culture and/or are considered as too small a market segment to require special attention (Aponte, Rivers & Wohl 1995; Rossman, 1994). What U.S. marketers at the national level generally overlook is that since the Civil Rights movement, the pressure for ethnic groups to blend into the American mainstream is on the decline (Locke, 1992). The existing and newly emerging ethnic groups including Asian-Americans take pride in maintaining their cultural identity (Abbot, 1970; Sue, 1973 Sue & Sue, 1990).

Therefore, understanding culturally conditioned behaviors of Asian Americans, which sets them apart from the mainstream culture are essential for businesses who wish to cater to the needs of Asian-Americans within the U.S. The purpose of this paper, therefore, is to conceptually identify psycho-cultural characteristics that distinguish Asian Americans from their American counterparts. An understanding of these characteristics is essential for marketing initiatives to reach this rapidly growing ethnic market.

Cultural Distinctions Between Asian-Americans

The cultural characteristics in this chapter refer to 'universal' sets of psycho-cultural behaviors that distinguish Asian-Americans from Americans. Although the Asian-Americans in the U.S. are from diverse backgrounds (e.g., Chinese, Filipinos, Japanese, Koreans, Vietnamese, Asian-Indians, and others), they have some common cultural characteristics that bind them together as a group (Rossman, 1994). Asian-Americans represent behavior characteristics associated with 'high context' cultures that emphasize the importance of group norms and expectations. By comparison the American culture is called a 'low context' culture. Members of 'low context' cultures are more individualistic and less likely to succumb to group norms or influences (Hall, 1976; Rossman, 1994).

Members of 'high context' cultures differ from members of 'low context' cultures in many different ways. Studies on differences between 'high and low context' groups suggest that the two groups differ on such dimensions, as; family structure, family involvement; style of communication, value orientation, traditions and customs (Rossman, 1994; Sue & Sue, 1990; Tsui & Schultz, 1985). While the Asian-American family structure is extended and hierarchical, the American family is nuclear and nonhierarchical. The roles of members within Asian-American families are often age and gender specific whereas American families are egalitarian and not age bound. Members of 'high context' or 'collective cultures' are also conscious of status and respond to norms, roles and dictates established by members who are a part of the 'in-group' such as the family and community as opposed to the 'out-group' (Triandis, 1987). Americans are independent minded and not status or role conscious. They do not place emphasis on the importance of adhering to norms of 'in-group' members and therefore exhibit characteristics that differ from Asian-Americans (Triandis, 1987). As a group Asian-Americans are enterprising and prefer to live in self-contained communities or enclaves (Rossman, 1994; Sue & Sue, 1990). There are no firm statistics available regarding how many Asian-Americans reside in enclaves in the U.S. However, there are enclaves such as; Chinatown, Manila town, Japan town, India town, that suggests that many Asian-Americans prefer to live in communities of their own (Sue & Sue, 1990). As Asian-Americans grow up in their 'collective' cultural environment, it influences the development of traits and behaviors that separate or differentiate them from Americans who are raised in a 'low context' or individualistic culture.

Asian-Americans, thus, are a different market segment. U.S. marketers, who are members of the majority culture, must understand the characteristics that bind Asian-Americans together and also those that separate them from the majority in the American society. These 'universal' characteristics however, should not be used to stereotype them, but they should serve as broad guidelines to reach the larger segment of the Asian-American community. Marketers must bear in mind that individual differences can and do exist within this community depending on factors such as the level of education, place and number of years of residence in the U.S., and differences in personality styles.

Psycho-Cultural Profile of Asian-Americans

The psycho-cultural characteristics in a nutshell are culturally-conditioned behaviors. While culturally-conditioned behaviors of Asian-Americans and their implications in cross-cultural counseling have received considerable attention, their implications for marketing initiatives are still in the formative stages. The psycho-cultural characteristics of Asian-Americans and their implications from a marketing perspective can therefore be conceptually described as follows:

Family Structure

A: Extended & Hierarchical Structure　As members of a 'collective' culture, Asian-Americans prefer to live in extended as opposed to nuclear families (Blakely, 1984). Although many Asian-Americans may start as a nuclear family, they eventually invite other family members to join them in the U.S. and form an extended family (Rossman, 1994). The extended family may include grandparents, parents, uncles, aunts and even cousins (Raval, 1981). They may live under the same roof or close to each other. For Asian-Americans the family is important. The importance of the family is explained by the concepts of filial piety or dharma (Shon & Ja, 1982; Sue & Sue, 1990: Raval, 1988). According to these concepts Asian-Americans are expected to cultivate the values of utmost respect, obedience and obligation to one's parents or family. The family structure is hierarchical i.e. the oldest member in the family is revered and respected (Raval, 1988). Therefore it is not unusual to see elderly members participating in important decisions in Asian-American families. In the absence of a family member a new Asian immigrant is likely to seek opinion of a member who is experienced and respected within his or her ethnic community. The immigrant often involves the experienced member to be the spokes-person in major purchasing decisions. Therefore, Asian-Americans are less likely to make individual/ independent business and/or career decisions. They may even avoid such decisions at all cost to the extent of losing a desirable opportunity or prospect if they do not reach an amiable consensus within the family.

B: Age-grading　Another distinguishing characteristic among Asian-Americans is the role assigned to members within a family. The oldest person in the family is considered the head and expected to assume responsibility for maintaining the well being of its members. As head of the family, the individual plays an authoritarian role and makes decisions for the unit or the family (Sue & Sue, 1990). Those younger in age play the role of being good listeners and followers though they may be better educated and better qualified in making such decisions. The younger member's opinion is likely to be ignored by the head of the family. Any outward defiance by a younger member, e.g., a younger brother or a child within the family can lead to him/her being chastised before other members of the family. A younger member in an Asian-American family has limited opportunity to exercise or participate in major decisions (Lee, 1995).

C: Role Differentiation　Another feature of a collective culture is the role it assigns to males and females. Not only are gender roles dichotomous in the Asian-American families, but they vest more power in males as opposed to females. Asian woman under the Confucius' teachings are given an inferior status in the family (Chu & Sue, 1984) and socialized to assume a submissive role (Homma-True, 1990). Therefore, even professional Asian women often can refrain from making final decision regarding purchases until they have conferred with their male counterparts.

Communication Style

A: Controlled, Restrained & Vertical   Research in verbal and nonverbal communication suggests that cultural factors influence communication styles (Sue & Sue, 1990). While Americans value verbal and emotional openness in expression of ideas and opinions, Asian-Americans value control and restraint in verbal expression (Lee, 1995). Moreover, the Asian-Americans pattern of communication is vertical, i.e., flowing from those who are higher in status to those who are lower. In business transactions Asian-Americans are likely to refrain from sharing their views openly regarding whether they like or dislike products that are being offered.' They also root their communication style in the physical context or in the person while less emphasis is placed on the explicitness with which content is delivered. The tone and emphasis with which a verbal message is presented are important rather than the content of the message. Americans, on the contrary place emphasis on explicit delivery of a message that is methodical and direct. Asian- Americans use subtle statements, and implicit messages in communication whereas Americans place emphasis on the actual content and look for a direct answer (Sue & Sue, 1990).

B: Gestures   Asian-Americans also differ in the meaning they associate to gestures, facial expressions and type of body language they use in conversation. While a failure to look someone in the eye may infer a lack of interest in what is being said according to American standards, by Asian standards, looking at someone face-to-face may imply a sign of disrespect particularly if that person is in a position of authority (Sue & Sue, 1990).

Specific Values

Values are questions that affect all people of all cultures. How people answer value oriented questions depends on their cultural orientation. People from 'high and low context' cultures differ from one another in their perception of time, social relations, and their relationship with nature (Ibrahim, 1985).

A: Time   Asian-Americans place considerable emphasis on learning from their history while planning for the future. By contrast, Americans are more future oriented and focused on working for better tomorrow (Sue, & Sue, 1990). Asian-Americans in comparison to Americans are likely to be cautious and moderate risk takers. While Americans perceive time as monochromic and are sensitive to maintaining their schedules and appointments to the minute, Asian-Americans overall are casual and do not attach too much significance to timetables or schedules.

B: Social Relations   Asian-Americans perceive relationships in vertical order with some individuals playing the role of a leader and others that of a follower (Sue, 1990). They are status conscious in expressing the relationship (Lee, 1995). They prefer to be addressed by their title, degrees and/or by any other indication of status

(Harris & Moran. 1996). Americans on the other hand express closeness of relationship more by informal expression such as; addressing individuals by their first names (Sue & Sue. 1990; Harris & Moran. 1996). Asian-Americans perceive relationships in long-term context. They take time to develop close relations but once they form the relationship, it is long lasting. Americans tend to develop relationship instantly and consider themselves as the primary role players in controlling and shaping the relationships (Sue & Sue, 1990).

Traditions and Customs

Asian-Americans, to maintain their cultural heritage and ties with their native land, follow their customs and traditions. They also celebrate social and cultural events and religious ceremonies. This is considered as an important tool to continue their linkage with their culture. They transmit norms and values to the younger generation by exposing them to this process.

A: Pride in Ethnic Heritage Although Asian-Americans do attempt to assimilate into the mainstream American culture, they maintain pride in their cultural heritage and customs (Sue & Sue, 1990). Some of the ways they display their pride in their heritage is through their ethnic dress, food, marriage customs and traditional celebrations (social and religious). They depend on ethnic market and their relatives back home to give them the necessary ingredients to maintain their traditional lifestyle and ethnic identity.

B: Aesthetic Value Asian-Americans take pride in the art and culture that is exclusive to their country and culture. They make considerable investments in bring in art and cultural products from back home because of the lack of availability of these goods in the mainstream market. While some Asian-American art work has penetrated the mainstream market, many more items are still not available.

C: Entrepreneur Spirit Another characteristic that binds Asian-Americans together is their enterprising spirit (Rossman, 1994). Many Asian-Americans operate small family owned businesses ranging from managing motels to running groceries and Laundromat's. Their enterprising spirit has enabled them to venture into ethnic and nonethnic markets.

Marketing Implications

Though the Asian-American market is made up of many subgroups, an understanding of the universal psycho-cultural characteristics identified here may allow marketers to target the Asian-American market overall. U.S. marketers should therefore keep the psycho-cultural characteristics and their implications in focus for marketing initiatives. These initiatives can eventually become a part of marketing strategies.

Marketing literature identifies four major strategies. They are: market penetration, market development, product development and market diversification. The psycho-cultural profile of Asian-Americans can be a useful guide in designing strategies to reach this market.

Market Penetration

Market penetration implies selling more of the same products to the same segment of the market. Firms that supply products to the Asian-American market can increase their sale by recognizing the decision making process used by Asian families. Asian-American families decide jointly or in consultation with family members. Male members play a dominant part in the decision making process. U.S. marketers must provide time and space to Asian buyers to make a purchase decision.

Rather than presenting the product and or information to Asian-Americans individually the marketers should attempt to reach the whole family through direct mail, conventions and exhibits. An American sales person should not be surprised when Asian buyers bring their entire family including friends to purchase a product. A sales pitch focusing only on an individual will not be very effective but one that addresses or captures the attention of all members as a group is likely to enhance a product's saleability.

The U.S. marketers can also penetrate the Asian-American market by considering the dominant role played by males in major purchases. They can adjust their sales technique to recognize the male's dominant role in Asian families. The U.S. marketers must also understand the Asian-Americans need to maintain family harmony. They should also remember that Asian women prefer to involve their male counterparts in purchasing decisions.

Market Development

Market development strategy involves selling products to new markets. Asian-American segments of the economy offers U.S. marketers new opportunities to attract Asian-Americans to buy their products and services by specific approaches directed toward this market. One approach is to use an Asian-American sales person who is familiar with the members of the community or is known to them. Many insurance companies in the U.S. are using Asian-Americans as sales people to reach this market. These sales representatives have social network linkages, cultural identity and the basic knowledge of the expectations of their group. The Asian-American customers are likely to communicate more openly because their style of communication and gesture will be well understood by the salesperson. AT&T is successfully using this market development strategy by hiring Asian-Americans as telemarketers to reach this segment.

Product Development

The product development strategy refers to developing new products and selling them to existing customers. This strategy can also be applied to address Asian-American target market by appropriately using the psycho-cultural profile. The important elements of the profile that are relevant for this strategy are the Asian community's intense desire and motivation to maintain its cultural identity and heritage. New Products that satisfies these desires and motivations of this community can be designed and developed. Marketers can develop or modify products such as arts, crafts, furniture, rugs, jewelry, and costumes to meet the taste of the Asian-American market. Asian-Americans extended family and group orientation can also be a valuable criterion in designing and developing products that they can enjoy or share as a family, e.g., designing of homes, autos and recreational vehicles, life and health insurance policies etc.

Product Diversification

Product diversification strategy means developing new products for a new set of customers. The U.S. marketers who are not developing new products and selling them to the Asian-American segment can consider developing culture-specific products for this market. Currently small Asian-American traders who import products from their native countries are meeting this need. Gradually some U.S. marketers are recognizing the need to explore this segment of the market. Recently grocery stores such as Giant Food and other supermarkets are introducing Asian products and gourmet foods that cater to the Asian-American market.

Marketing Mix

Another useful marketing concept for marketing initiative is marketing mix strategy. Marketing mix is a 'tactical marketing tool' marketers use as a blend to influence the demand for their products and are popularly known as the four P's (Kotler & Armstrong, 1994). They are product, price promotion and place (distribution). Understanding the psycho-cultural characteristics of the Asian-Americans can be useful in developing promotion and distribution programs. Marketers can use Asian style of vertical communication in advertising. They can develop programs that focus on elders approving purchase of products by younger generation, e.g., grandfather directing or approving the purchasing of candies or cereals by grandchildren in a market environment. Advertising communication can also stress on the theme that projects extended family relationship, e.g., advertising copy showing presence of an extended family either enjoying the product together or recommending others to buy.

In face to face personal selling of products to Asian-Americans, the sales force can be trained to recognize the notion of respect for elders, giving due recognition to the status and title of individual customers. Since Asian-Americans are status conscious addressing them by their professional title, can generate a positive response from them. This can also strengthen the relationship between the salesperson and the Asian-American customer. Addressing an Asian-American by his or her first name gene rally connotes lack of respect and therefore should be avoided. Sales people should also be made aware that Asians often use control and restrain in communicating their response or reaction to a sales pitch. The sales person should not interpret their restrained response as a lack of interest in the product or conversation. Often hard sell techniques may not dwell well with Asian customers.

The U.S. marketer's distribution approach to reach Asian-American market must include an understanding of the importance of building long term relationships with Asian-American distribution networks. The Asian-American's enterprising spirit has resulted in their owning and controlling, wholesale and retail outlets in urban areas of U.S. They reach the Asian population efficiently and effectively. U.S. marketers can distribute their products through these networks.

Conclusion

It is important for U.S. marketers interested in capturing the Asian-American segment of the market to consider the psycho-cultural characteristics of the Asian-Americans. By keeping these characteristics in mind they will be able to take appropriate marketing initiatives as suggested to reach this market.

References

Abbot, K.. *Harmony and Individualism*, Oriental Cultural Press, Taipei. 1970.

Aponte, J. F., Rivers, Y. R. & Wohl, J. *Psychological Interventions and Cultural Diversity*, Needham Heights, Allyn & Bacon, MA. 1995.

Blakely, M., *American Talking: Listen How Some Hmong, Khmer, Laotian and Vietnamese View American Schools*. ERIC Document Reproduction Service No. ED 241 652. (1984).

Chu, J., & Sue, S.. Asian/Pacific Americans and Group Practice. *Ethnicity in Group Work Practice*, 7 (1984): 23-26.

Hall, E. T. *Beyond Culture*, Anchor Press, New York, 1976.

_____, *The Hidden Dimension*, Doubleday, Garden City, New York, 1969.

Harris, P. R. and Moran., *Managing Cultural Differences*, Gulf Publishing Co., Houston, Texas, 1979.

_____, *Managing Cultural Differences*, Gulf Publishing Co., Houston, Tx. 1996.

Homma-True, R. Psychotherapeutic Issues with Asian American Women. *Sex-Role*, 22, (1990): 477-486.

Ibrahim, F. A. Effective Cross-cultural Counseling and Psychotherapy: A Framework. *The Counseling Psychologist*, 13 (1985): 625-652.

Kotler, P., Armstrong, G., *Principles of Marketing,* Prentice-Hall, Englewood, N. J. 1994.

Lee, C.. *Counseling for Diversity*, Allyn and Bacon, Needham Heights, MA. 1995.

Locke, D. C. *Increasing Multicultural Understanding: A Comprehensive Model*, Sage Publications, Inc., Newbury Park, CA. 1992.

Raval, B. *Emotional and Social Development of East Indian Child in the U.S.A.*, A Paper Presented At the Studies in Third World Psychology Conference in Psychotherapy. Boston 1981.

Raval, B., *The Balanced Personality: An Exchange of Concepts Between Indian and U. S. For Use in Cross-Cultural Counseling*, Paper Presented at the Annual Conference on Cross-Cultural Counseling and Communication at the Hutchings Psychiatric Center. Syracuse, N.Y. 1988.

Rossman, M.L. *Multicultural Marketing*, American Management Association, Amacom, N.Y. 1994

Shao, Maria., Suddenly, Asian-Americans Are a Marketer's Dream, *Business Week, Industrial/Technology Edition*, Vol. 3218, (June 17, 1991): 54-55.

Shon, S.P. and Ja, D.Y. Asian Families, In *Ethnicity and Family Therapy*, Eds. McGoldrick, M., Pearce, 1. K.& J. Giordano, Guilford Press, N.Y. (1982): 208-228.

Steere, John, How Asian-Americans make purchasing decisions, Marketing News, Vol. 29, #16. (March 13, 1995): 9.

Sue, D. W., Ethnic Identity, The Impact of Two Cultures on Psychological Development of Asian Americans, in *Asian-American Perspectives*, Eds. Sue, S. & Wagner, N., Science Behavior Books, Palo Alto, CA. 1973.

Sue, D.W. and Sue, D. *Counseling the Culturally Different: Theory and Practice*, John Wiley & Sons, N. Y. 1990.

Tsui, P., and Schultz, G. L. Failure of Rapport: When Psychotherapeutic Engagement Fails in the Treatment of Asian clients. *American Journal of Orthopsychiatry*, 55 (1985): 561-569.

Triandis, H. Some Major Dimensions of Cultural Variation in Client Populations. In *Handbook of Cross Cultural Counseling and Therapy*, Paul Pedersen, ed. Praeger, N.Y. 1987, pp. 21-28.

Chapter 11

Consumer Behavior in East/West Cultures: Implications for Marketing a Consumer Durable

Patricia M. Anderson
Xiaohong He

Introduction

A problem facing international marketers is whether or not to use the same marketing mix for the same product in Eastern and Western markets where social and economic systems differ. Research about consumers in these markets can provide information for making this decision. However, it can be difficult to make direct comparisons between two extremely different cultures without considering cultural differences throughout the research. The contribution of this chapter is: a) to provide some basic information regarding an Eastern culture's norms and values of the Peoples' Republic of China (PRC) in comparison with a Western culture of the United States of America (USA); and b) to report a research done cooperatively by researchers of two countries. Results describing advertising-influence, price-influence and age segments in each country provide information for marketing similar recreational durables in what some call the world's richest market (USA) versus the world's largest market (PRC). One might expect greater East/West differences in marketing such durables compared with marketing less-expensive and more-perishable products.

Relevant Literature

P. R. China and USA Consumer Behavior

Relevant Western literature offers insights about Western consumer behavior for cameras and similar goods. A camera has the Richins (1994) 'private meaning' of enjoyment, defined as: provides pleasure, allows enjoyable activity (entertainment or relaxation); and 'public meaning' of a practical (as opposed to symbolic), instrumental possession. Of Holt's (1995) four consumption categories: experiencing, integrating, classifying, and playing with others including families and peers, goods like cameras fit best into 'playing.' Goods like cameras can be gifts to others and also self gifts (see Mick and deMoss, 1990). Giving products like cameras is probably related more to family agapic love than to romantic agapic love (Belk and Coon, 1993).

Consumers in different countries do not necessarily use the same product for the same purpose; a shortcoming of United States research is that it seldom considers research from other countries (Costa and Bamossy, 1995). Much cross-cultural marketing research with implications for different countries relies on foreign students in the United States (not consumers in their own countries), and also on English-language questionnaires (Samiee, 1994). Using the same instrument for all subjects can violate equivalence tests in cross-cultural studies (Green and White 1976).

Results of research about Western consumers do not necessarily predict behavior of Eastern consumers. Foreign marketers must consider 'guo qing,' i.e. in Chinese language the special situation in PRC (Yan, 1994). PRC now has an open door policy; foreign brands appeared in the Deng era (1978 to 1997), after the 1949-1976 Mao era (Xu 1990). After the 1989, Tienanmen-Square, incident; Westerners returned in 1992. PRC is adapting to Western consumer tendencies while trying to keep traditional values (Tse, Belk and Zhou, 1989). Foreign camera brands entered PRC in 1978; before 1978, six domestic brands were sold in stationery stores (Tu, 1990). In 1994, three PRC households in 100 bought a camera; PRC has about twelve million households (Lee, 1993).

East/West Consumers and Marketing Mix Influences

Camera benefits include: 1) the recreational experience of collecting, owning and sharing visual images in photographs, and 2) a consumer image associated with owning/using a particular camera brand. Western research about novice/expert preference formation suggests that memory and prior knowledge guide ad processing, evaluation and decisions about cameras (Sujan, 1985). The brand consideration set is the pool of brands from which choice is made (Brown and Wildt, 1992). Relationships between price and brand name are positive and statistically significant (Rao and Monroe, 1989). Western consumers are more responsive to price discounts for mature products (Sethuraman and Tellis, 1991).

Social self is a better predictor of Chinese consumption behavior than private self (Kindel, 1983). Brands are important in PRC for prestige reasons. In PRC, product loyalty seems related to age (Xu, 1990). At the time of this research, Chinese like to show wealth and social status not with expensive neighborhood or car as in the USA, but with modern electronics and appliances. Cameras are considered a luxury good in PRC; mean price is an average person's half-month salary.

Advertised consumption appeals differed by Eastern country (Tse, Belk and Zhou, 1989). Product performance was the modal appeal in PRC; pleasure, in Hong Kong; and image, in Taiwan. Magazine ads in PRC sent messages about product availability, performance and quality (Rice and Lu, 1988). Like ads, store displays send messages about products. In the West, the combination of price reductions (including coupons) and product display sold more merchandise than separate use of this marketing effort (Woodside and Waddle, 1975). Chinese want product information placed next to a product in a store; they tend to do comparison shopping in at least three stores, and like to window shop (Yan, 1994).

Hypotheses and Method

The literature review suggests that consumers tend to view a camera as a recreational (USA) or prestige (PRC) good, and that behavior is related to their different experiences and environments. In PRC, with rapid economic and social changes, multinational marketing effort is relatively new at the time of this research. For historic and cultural reasons mentioned in cited literature, consumer behavior related to cameras is expected to differ in USA versus PRC. Relevant literature suggests variables and hypotheses that describe advertising, price and age segments. Explanatory variables include the influence of product, price, place and promotion in the marketing mix; and consumer behavior and demographics. Important definitions are in Exhibit 1.

The socially conscious Chinese culture emphasizes mutual dependence and strong cultural and kinship ties. PRC mass media are more limited in competing with traditional word-of-mouth communication channels than are USA mass media. China has evolved from a planning economy; advertising is a phenomenon of the recent decade; thus Chinese rely less on advertising than do USA consumers in making a purchase decision. However, PRC ads help in brand recognition and make an impression in PRC consumers' minds. In a high-context culture like Chinese culture, the communication style is implicit. People look for what is *not* being said instead of what *is* said. When ads are implicit about selling, the traditional Chinese tend to think that something may be wrong with the product. They tend to rely more on family and friends to check whether their experience confirms the ad claims (Yan, 1994). Therefore, because of cultural and economic differences in the two countries:

H1: For PRC versus USA camera consumers, a different set of marketing-mix, behavioral and demographic variables, differentiates the advertising-influenced segment from the not-influenced segment.

Income levels in PRC are much lower (mean= $2,067/person/year) than those in USA (Lee, 1993). However, 4.3 million PRC households had an annual income of $3,750-$6,250 in 1994 ('Toward...', 1996), which is similar to mean annual USA household automotive costs of $4,021 ('Population' 1994). In 1994, median annual disposable income by county in the US ranged from $30,000 to $55,000. The USA's housing and healthcare is more expensive than in PRC.

The concept of 'face' or 'mian-zi' is very important in the Chinese culture. 'Face' is a reputation and prestige obtained through one's efforts or conduct, and is related to tangible and intangible personal success. In PRC, which evolved from a long feudal society, position in the hierarchy is demonstrated through the concept of 'face'. Price is related to this hierarchy. 'Expensive is good' tends to show how an individual succeeds economically in a fast-changing society. Therefore, price can embody a different message for the US and PRC consumers. For PRC consumers, price is related to country of origin; foreign brands are more expensive and prestigious than PRC brands due to quality and tariff. Price signals externalities like luxury and a socially well-off status, as PRC society rearranges its participants by economic rules instead of political orientation. Price represents an investment value due to higher inflation during price reform. Farther along in economic growth, USA camera consumers tend to be more motivated by practical needs for ease of use, need for gift, desired optional features, and response to price promotions. Because of the social versus practical difference in PRC versus USA consumers, and the difference in economic-growth stages and price levels:

H2: For PRC versus USA camera consumers, a different set of marketing-mix, behavioral and demographic variables, differentiates the price-influenced segment from the not-influenced segment.

Place-influence is not included in this research because it is mainly an institutional rather than cultural difference. Consumers in both countries buy different domestic but similar imported camera brands, mostly Japanese. Single-use cameras were not available in PRC at the time of this research, but they are important enough in the USA to include them in the US survey. A demographic segmentation that can differ in PRC versus USA is age segmentation, because the USA did not experience PRC's great change from the Mao to Deng regimes. The fast pace of economic progress has increased the range of income levels, and changed occupational structure and consumption patterns. A young, internationally-oriented, fashion-conscious consumer group, is forming with this fast economic change, coexists with traditional culture- oriented older generation. Young Chinese look for novelty and material progress. Fashion has more influence on young adults and women than on men, children and older people. Consumers, who are influenced by fashion, sacrifice buying for basic needs (food, clothing) to buy products (like cameras) that show money, wealth and power (Lin, 1985). Because of cultural, economic-related age-segment differences:

H3: For PRC versus USA camera consumers, a different set of marketing mix, behavioral and demographic variables differentiates the age 16-35 segment from the age over 35 segment.

USA and PRC colleagues planned the questionnaire. The bilingual, bicultural co-author in the United States translated culture and language; colleagues in PRC adapted and translated the questionnaire into Chinese and collected data. Even so, differences remained in questions, variables, and response categories as shown in Exhibit 1. Because crime makes house-to-house interviewing potentially dangerous for interviewer or respondent, the 1994 United States survey of a random sample in a northeast state was conducted by a professional telephone-polling facility. Because the PRC telephone system was somewhat unreliable at that time, self-administered surveys written in Chinese characters were distributed and collected in communities/neighborhoods in northeast PRC, Beijing and surrounding areas – a geographic entity about the size of the northeast US state. A community official distributed and collected questionnaires in apartment buildings that housed workers from several work units.

Results and Discussion

After deleting unusable questionnaires, there were 633 Chinese and 371 United States responses. Response rates were 90% in PRC, and 67% in USA. USA-respondent age distribution (66% over age 35) was similar to the population distribution in the state surveyed ('Population' 1994). PRC-respondent gender distribution was same as in Beijing population (48% females, Lee, 1993). Percent classified correctly in the discriminant analysis tests of H1 through H3 ranged from 64 (H3, PRC) to 80 (H2, PRC). Exhibit 2 shows strategies suggested by the top five variables in each discriminant analysis: those with the largest structure-matrix loadings, and also in the discriminant function.

Results support H1. A larger proportion of PRC camera consumers in the advertising-influence segment, rather than in the other segment, is influenced by product quality and brand name and has a slightly larger mean consideration set. PRC consumers *not* influenced by advertising are on the average older, and a larger proportion of these consumers say that they buy on 'impulse' (refer to the definition in Exhibit 1). USA consumers influenced by advertising give more durable cameras as gifts, use more single-use cameras, use cameras less frequently, and are older. Chinese influenced by advertising pay less on the average for cameras than those not influenced by advertising, but US respondents influenced by advertising pay more.

Results support H2. PRC camera consumers influenced by pricing pay less for cameras on the average than those not influenced by pricing; a larger proportion of them is interested in durability and quality, and a smaller proportion is influenced by brand name and appearance. USA consumers in the price-influence segment are more influenced than those in the other segment by: helpful salespersons, ease of camera use, and convenient store location. In both countries, those influenced by price pay less on the average than those not influenced by price.

Results support H3. Older Chinese and younger USA camera consumers live in the larger households. The younger PRC group is more influenced by fashion and advertising; a larger proportion is female and shops in department stores. The older USA consumers are more influenced by helpful salespersons and ease of use, shop in discount stores, and pay a higher mean price for cameras than do the younger USA consumers.

PRC advertising and price segments at present can be related to the product component of the marketing mix as in Rice and Lu (1988) and Tse, Belk and Zhou (1989). Differences in price-influence and age groups in USA and PRC are related to the position of camera as a luxury, status durable in PRC versus a practical, easy-to-use good in USA. The young, relatively wealthy, global segment in PRC represents a fast-moving economic and cultural transformation contrasting with older, traditional PRC segment. USA camera-consumer segments are related to marketing-mix components: ease-of-use product (H2, H3), price paid (H3), distribution – stores (H2, H3), and promotion (displays for H1, helpful salesperson for H2, H3), as in Woodside and Waddle (1975). Exhibit 2 summarizes the marketing strategy mix adaptation needed based on these results. However, marketers should continuously monitor developments in the changing PRC, and while the present conditions hold, focus on product in PRC, and emphasize promotion in USA. Cameras are included in a larger USA/PRC research project with three non-durable product types: fast food, soft drinks and cosmetics, surveyed separately. Cameras represent both the highest price level of these four product types, and an 'externally-consumed' durable. Fast food and soft drinks represent less expensive, 'internally-consumed' product types; cosmetics are consumed externally. Marketing-mix variables predominate in the top five variables explaining purchase frequency, and also the top five variables discriminating between the segment preferring 'fast' (delivery speed) and segment preferring 'food' (taste and nutrition) in USA and PRC; however, specific variables differ (Anderson and He, 1999). Although the world grows rapidly smaller in terms of transportation and communication, change is more rapid for some products and markets than for others. The focus on this camera research and on the fast food research just mentioned has been to study PRC and USA consumers of one product type.

The focus of a related set of research has been to study consumers of four product types in the PRC market, a large and rapidly growing market for Western goods. Environmental and cultural issues are important influences on PRC market segments for cameras and cosmetics. Important variables distinguishing the fashion-oriented younger PRC segment from the traditional older segment include retail patronage customs and marketing-mix components related to image and prestige (Anderson and He, 1997). PRC price and age segments can be defined for imported Western-type recreational durables like cameras and nondurables like cosmetics, fast food and soft drinks (Anderson and He, 1998). PRC (as opposed to Hong Kong, Taiwan, and other Chinese) consumer behavior with respect to the four products studied suggests a new model that integrates three types of influence different from that in the West: traditional Chinese cultural values, rapid development towards modernization, and socialist ideology. However, a dual trend emerges. The older PRC consumers are more traditional but a younger segment is becoming more like Western consumers. The relative importance of culture, ideology and economics depends on product type and economic-development stage (He and Anderson, 1999).

Limitations, Suggestions for Future Research

Results from this research are not generalizable beyond northeast USA and PRC, or beyond similar recreational consumer durables. Durables similar to the research product, cameras that use film, have a nondurable complement, like golf balls for golf clubs. Results can change as technology, global communications, marketing mix and environments change. In 1996, the same firms that marketed traditional durable cameras and single-use cameras, introduced the Advanced Photo Systems into the U.S. market following these surveys. At the time of this research, only the traditional cameras were available in Beijing area. Competition for technology that records experience in visual images will come from film-free cameras. The video camera is now a 'hot item' in PRC and its demand increased 28.9 percent within a year ('Toward...', 1996). On the one hand, the comparing of consumers in these countries is limited by their different environments and responses to these environments. On the other hand, marketers can better understand how to market in different cultures when research allows for cultural and environmental differences (see Costa and Bamossy, 1995; Green and White, 1976; Samiee, 1994).

Research strategies for similar types of recreational durables (Holt, 1995; Richins, 1994) need to consider cultural and economic differences in different countries. The same English words can have different meanings in different cultures. To communicate intelligently with bilingual, bicultural resources, it is essential to understand language and culture of a target market. Bicultural resources can work with native marketers in the target market to help multinational marketers understand why and how target consumers make buying decisions and the implications for marketing strategy.

References

Anderson, Patricia M., and Xiaohong He, Culture and the Fast-Food Marketing Mix in the People's Republic of China and the USA: Implications for Research and Marketing. *Journal of International Consumer Marketing* 11 (1) (1999): 77-95.

Anderson, Patricia M. and Xiaohong He, Environmental and Cultural Issues for PRC Market Segments. *The Journal of Contemporary Issues* 5 (2) (Fall 1997): 56-64.

Anderson, Patricia M. and Xiaohong He, Price-Influence and Age Segments of Beijing Consumers. *Journal of Consumer Marketing* 15 (2) (1998): 152-169.

Belk, Russell W., and Gregory S. Coon, Gift Giving as Agapic Love: An Alternative to the Exchange Paradigm Based on Dating Experiences. *Journal of Consumer Research* 20 (December 1993): 393-417.

Brown, Juanita J., and Albert R. Wildt, Consideration Set Measurement. *Journal of the Academy of Marketing Science* 20 (3) (1992): 235-243.

Costa, Janeen A. and Gary J. Bamossy. Eds, *Marketing in a Multicultural World*, Thousand Oaks, CA: Sage Publications. 1995.

Green, Robert T., and Philip D. White, Methodological Considerations in Cross-National Consumer Research. *Journal of International Business Studies* 7 (Fall-Winter 1976): 81-87.

He, Xiaohong and Patricia M. Anderson, The Influence of Traditional Values, Ideology, and Development on Consumer Behavior in the People's Republic of China, *The Journal of Marketing Management* 9 (1) (Spring 1999): 14-31.

Holt, Douglas B., How Consumers Consume: A Typology of Consumption Practices. *Journal of Consumer Research* 22 (June 1995): 1-16.

Kindel, Thomas I., A Partial Theory of Chinese consumer Behavior: Marketing Strategy Implications.' *Hong Kong Journal of Business Management* 1 (1983).

Lee, Hessler, *Profile of China Markets: Complete Market Data on Spending Patterns of 1.1 Billion Consumers in China.* British Columbia, Canada: Hercules Publishing House. 1993.

Lin, Pin-hsien, *Consumer Behavior.* Beijing: Electronics Industry Publisher. 1985.

Mick, David G., and DeMoss, Michelle, Self-Gifts: Phenomenological Insights from Four Contexts. *Journal of Consumer Research* 17 (December 1990): 322-332.

'Population.' *Sales and Marketing Management.* (August 30 1994): C-2.

Rao, Akshay, and Kent B. Monroe, The Effect of Price, Brand Name and Store Name on Buyers' Perceptions of Product Quality: An Integrative Review. *Journal of Marketing Research* 26 (August 1989): 351-357.

Rice, M. D., and Z. Lu, A Content Analysis of Chinese Magazine Ads. *Journal of Advertising* 17 (1998): 43-48.

Richins, Marsha, Valuing things: The Public and Private Meaning of Possessions. *Journal of Consumer Research* 21 (December 1994): 504-521.

Samiee, Saeed, Customer Evaluation of Products in a Global Market. *Journal of International Business Studies* 25 (No.3) (1994): 579-604.

Sethuraman, Raj, and Gerard J. Tellis, An Analysis of the Tradeoff Between Advertising and Price Discounting. *Journal of Marketing Research* 28 (May 1991): 160-174.

Sujan, Mita, Consumer Knowledge: Effects on Evaluation Strategies Mediating Consumer Judgements. *Journal of Consumer Research* 12 (June 1985): 31-46.

'Towards the Diversity of the Residents' Consumption Structure.' Peoples' Daily (February 2, 1998): 2.

Tse, David K., Russell W. Belk, and Nan Zhou, Becoming a Consumer Society: A Longitudinal and Cross- Cultural Content Analysis of Print Ads from Hong Kong, the People's Republic of China, and Taiwan. *Journal of Consumer Research* 15 (March 1998): 457-472.

Tu, Pao-tsai, *Overview of China's Market.* Beijing: Atomic Energy Publisher (1990).

Woodside, Arch G., and Gerald L. Waddle, Sales Effects of In-Store Advertising. *Journal of Advertising Research* 15 (June 1975): 29-33.

Xu Bai Yi. *Marketing to China.* Lincolnwood, IL: NTC Business Books. 1990

Yan, Rick, To Reach China's Consumers, Adapt to Guo Qing. *Harvard Business Review.* (September-October 1994): 66-74.

Exhibit 1

Operational Definitions of Important Camera Research Variables in H1-H3, PRC and USA*.

Frequency USA (H1): How often use a camera? Almost daily=360; once or twice a week=104; once or twice a month=24; a few times a year=8.

Shop for camera in: camera stores (H2-USA), department stores (H3-PRC).

Consideration set size (H1-PRC): Canon, Minolta, Nikon; PRC: Li Guang, Sea Gull; USA: Fuji, Kodak, Konica, Polaroid, other; =1 if checked; =0 otherwise; add the 1s.

Use a single-use camera: USA (H1): likelihood on 5-point scale where 5=very likely; 1=not at all.

Give durable-camera gift: USA (H1): likelihood to buy as gift for someone else; 5=very; 1=not at all.

Influences: PRC: ranking in groups of 4-6; recoded such that top two ranks=1 and other ranks=0. USA: 5 point scale where 5=a lot and 1=not at all. For USA discriminant analyses, dependent variables recoded to 4,5=1 and 1-3=0. PRC 'consideration factors': *Quality# (H1, H2-PRC), price#, brand name# (H1, H2-PRC), appearance (H2-PRC)#*; PRC 'channel of influence: *ad/promotion# (H2-PRC), display (H1-USA), impulse* (U.S. 'had in mind and display reminds;' P.R.C. 'go with your heart'--H1); *fashion* (used by socio-economic leaders, celebrities, athletes, movie stars--H3); PRC 'main concerns when using': *easy to use# (H2, H3 PRC), durability* (H2-PRC). USA: *helpful salesperson (H2, H3).*

Gender: 0=male; 1=female. (H3-PRC).
Age: (H1) PRC: under 18, 18-25, 26-35, 36-50, over 50; use midpoints. USA: year of birth; subtract from 1995. *Number in household*: (H3) for USA, actual number; for PRC: under 3, 3-5, over 5 (recoded to 1.5, 4, 6).
Price paid for camera: PRC, in reminbi: under 200, 200-500; 501=1000; over 1000. USA: price would pay today: under $30, $30-129; $130-249; $250-499; $500-1000; over $1000. Use midpoints of ranges. Note: exchange rate is about 8 reminbi for $1.
variable; hypothesis number given where significant.
Variables used in both countries' questionnaires.

Exhibit 2

Implications for International Camera Marketing Strategy, H1-H3, PRC and USA.

Segment	Peoples' Republic of China	United States of America
H1: Advertising Strategies		
Advertising	Build a quality image for the brand	Advertise durables as gifts and single use to user
Segments ads	Get into the consideration set	Coordinate displays with ads
H2: Price Strategies		
Price-influence segment	Quality, durability	Ease of use, helpful salesperson
Other segment	Brand name, appearance	Convenient store
H3: Age Strategies		
Younger (age 16-35)	Advertise fashion to men	Promote to/for family
Older (over age 35)	Store displays for women	Helpful employees, ease of use

PART V:

ORGANIZATIONAL CULTURES AND RELATIONSHIPS

Chapter 12

Service Management Effectiveness and Organizational Culture: A Modification of the Competing Values Model

Michele Paulin
Ronald J. Ferguson
Marielle Payaud

Introduction

The service management paradigm (Gummesson, 1994), or perspective (Grönroos, 1992; 1994), offers strategic insights for creating customer value and improved business performance. This perspective, which focuses more on the external than the internal performance of the firm, is a shift from the traditional manufacturing and bureaucratic management paradigms. Its origins can be traced back to the literature on relationship marketing, services marketing and service quality. Under the service management paradigm, the customer is a partner and value creation is a balance between human input and technology, between revenue and costs, and between customer perceived quality and productivity (Gummesson, 1994).

In a business-to-business context, service management effectiveness occurs when the client-company is highly satisfied, recognizes excellent service quality, intends to continue the relationship and is willing to recommend the service firm to other businesses. In order to have effective service management, a service firm needs to be client-oriented and develop the managerial processes and an organizational culture compatible with the creation of client-perceived value, the driver of longer-term profitability. Globalization and the emergence of regional trading blocks have been accompanied by deregulation in several service industries. However, many service firms have been slow to adapt their strategy, managerial processes and organizational cultures to a service management perspective.

Previous studies of the organizational cultures of commercial banks and their corporate clients leads one to suspect that a Market-type culture, as measured by the competing values model, is not compatible with the service management perspective (Paulin et al., 1998a; 1998b; Paulin et al., 1999). The objectives of this study were to: a) determine if the competing values model of organizational culture would be compatible with the service management perspective and b) if a modification of the competing values model of organizational culture, which included a fifth culture type (Service-type), would yield a significantly different profile of organizational culture.

Organizational Culture

Corporate culture is the set of common norms and values shared by people in an organization (Deshpandé and Webster, 1989). The corporate culture forms the basis of collaborative human behavior and makes human actions to some extent predictable and directed towards a set of commonly held purposes (Grönroos, 1990). Mintzberg and Quinn (1992) describes corporate culture as '...the way people are chosen, developed, nurtured and rewarded in the organization'. It has also been described as the organization's internal climate, which reflects the members' perceptions of the extent to which the organization is currently fulfilling their expectations (Schneider, 1986; Schneider and Bowen, 1995). Organizational culture exists on two levels, the visible and invisible. The visible aspects of culture encompass behavior patterns, the physical and social environment and the written and spoken language used by the group. The invisible level of culture relates to the group's values or the group's basic assumptions (Schein, 1991). The shared values consist of the goals and concerns that shape a group's sense of what 'ought' to be. Most authors in the service marketing and service management literature refer to the deeper and less visible level of culture.

Within the service management perspective, a Service-type culture has greater implications than paying 'lip service to client orientation'. The Service-type culture is not the same as a Market-type culture, which emphasizes a transactional sales, approach to services based on short-term profitability, market-share and opportunistic behaviors. Normann (1991) has identified a common pattern of culture and dominating ideas of 'new culture' companies that have adopted a service-oriented culture and matching management philosophies. Mostly, these companies are characterized by: (1) quality and excellence within the company and with clients, (2) a client orientation which means that every aspect of the interaction with a client is part of a long-term marketing process, (3) a long-term investment in people and social technology, (4) managing on a small scale with regards to factors vital to successful client relationships and, (5) a careful choice of market segments to mobilize resources and energy to achieve maximum excellence. Normann (1991) insists on the notion of social innovation which means that there is a willingness to 'mobilize and to focus human energy, for example, by creating new roles or new linkages, by bringing out the energy and productivity potential of the client, by inventive recruitment, effective communication, and by creative 'packaging' for the reproduction of knowledge and service systems' (Normann, 1991: 167). Initially, it was thought that the competing values model of organizational culture, as developed by Deshpandé, Webster and Farley (1993), would be adequate for the service management perspective. This competing values model categorizes organizational culture into four quadrants (Clan, Adhocracy, Market and Hierarchy) based on the organization's dominant attributes, leadership styles, bonding mechanisms and overall strategic emphasis. A Clan-type culture emphasizes tradition, loyalty and internal maintenance. An Adhocratic-type culture focuses on innovation, entrepreneurship and risk-taking. A Market-type culture emphasizes competitive advantage and market superiority and a Hierarchical-type culture is bureaucratic and concerned with predictable and smooth operations. Deshpandé, Webster and Farley (1993) suggested that, although organizations are a mixture of culture types, one type of culture seems to be dominant over time. Also, the best business performance would be achieved by an innovative, client-oriented firm with a Market-type culture. Conversely, a Hierarchical-type culture would be the least conducive to business performance.

Methodology

Organizational culture was assessed by interviews with one senior officer in each of 91 major companies in France. The respondents were either the company's president, vice-president or chief financial officer. The competing values model of organizational culture was modified in order to take into account a fifth type of culture (Service-type) which would be compatible with the service management perspective (Figure 12.1).

Two modifications were made. Firstly, a fifth area, the role of contact personnel, was added to the areas of dominant attributes, leadership styles, bonding mechanisms and overall strategic emphasis. In a service-oriented business, the contact person has a strategic boundary role in representing the organization when dealing with other businesses and individual clients (Grönroos, 1992; Normann, 1991). In the modified version, the role of contact personnel was defined as being loyal (Clan), taking initiative (Adhocracy), being competitive (Market), following orders (Hierarchy) and knowledge of clients (Service beliefs).

Secondly, a fifth question reflecting a client-oriented service management approach was added to each of the five above mentioned areas. Thus, instead of distributing the 100 hundred points among four categories of culture, the respondent was obliged to distribute the 100 points among five categories (Clan, Adhocracy, Market, Hierarchy and Service) for the questions related to the five areas of: shared, dominant organizational attributes, leadership styles, organizational bonding mechanisms, overall strategic emphasis and the role of contact personnel. Within the service management perspective, a Service-type culture would have: client service as the dominant organizational attribute, contact personnel with considerable knowledge of clients, a leadership style which reinforces the development of processes to create client-perceived value, a quest for client satisfaction as the glue bonding the members of the organization, and a strategic emphasis on profitability resulting from long-term client relationships.

**Figure 12.1   Modified Version of the Competing Values Model of
Organizational Culture**

Results

Original version of the competing value model: Bankers in Canada, Mexico and the United States classified their organizations as being primarily Market-type cultures (Table 12.1). However, there was no positive relationship between Market-type culture and service management effectiveness. Also, the more the bankers perceived their organization as being a Market-type culture, the less they felt that the bank was client-oriented and that the organizational culture supported their efforts to satisfy clients. Finally, when client-company executives in Mexico and the United States classed their own organizational cultures, it was found that companies with a predominantly Market-type culture rated the bank's service management effectiveness lower than companies with other cultures. This suggests that strong business-to-business relationships might be difficult to establish when both parties are primarily Market-type cultures. On the other hand, as would be predicted, a Hierarchical-type culture was found to be negatively related to the service management perspective. The more bankers classed their organizations as being Hierarchical-type cultures, the lower were their client companies assessment of effectiveness.

Table 12.1   Organizational Cultures of Commercial Banks (Means and Standard Deviation of Sum of Four Scores out of 100)

	Mexico (n = 75) Mean (SD)	Canada (n = 77) Mean (SD)	U.S.A. (n = 25) Mean (SD)
Clan	68 (26)	58 (31)	69 (26)
Adhocracy	100 (32)	101 (48)	71 (37)
Market	122 (39)	130 (39)	129 (45)
Hierarchy	104 (41)	110 (49)	130 (47)

Modified version of the competing value model: Based on the original version of the competing values model, it can be seen that the organizational cultures of the client companies in Mexico and the United States were different than the cultures of their banks (Comparing data in Tables 12.1 and 12.2). Whereas the three Mexican banks were primarily Market-type cultures, their clients were mainly Hierarchical-type companies. The culture of the United States bank was equally Hierarchical and Market whereas their client-companies were primarily Clan-type cultures. These differences in client-company cultures are due to both national characteristics and to the business sectors studied in each country.

The new category of Service-type culture was found to be the dominant culture in the sample of 91 companies in France. One-way ANOVA showed that the overall score for the Service-type culture was significantly higher than those of the other culture types. Also, the ANOVA were significantly greater for the Service-type culture than the other culture types on each of the five areas making up the overall score (dominant organizational attributes, the leadership styles, the organizational bonding mechanisms, the overall strategic emphasis and the role of contact personnel).

Table 12.2   Organizational Cultures of Client-Companies $^{\Psi}$

	Mexico n = 60 Mean (SD)	U.S.A. n = 39 Mean (SD)	France n = 91 Mean (SD)
Clan	84 (41)	128 (73)	51 (29)
Adhocracy	92 (30)	110 (43)	89 (34)
Market	91 (33)	96 (52)	124 (46)
Hierarchy	133 (39)	64 (37))	75 (36)
Service	-----	-----	161 (56)

Ψ Scores for Mexico and the United States are the Means and Standard Deviation of
        Sum of Four Scores out of 100. The scores for France are the Means and Standard
        Deviation of Sum of Five Scores out of 100.

Discussion and Conclusion

A Market-type culture, as measured by the competing values model of organizational culture, does not reflect a culture compatible with the creation of client-perceived value but rather a transactional approach where organizational effectiveness is measured by productivity attained through market mechanisms. The Deshpandé, Webster and Farley (1993) definition of organizational effectiveness or business performance is the company's relative profitability, size, market share and growth rate. Although the indicators of their Market-type culture reflect a firm's outward (external positioning) rather than an inward (internal maintenance) perspective, it is more a transactional sales approach rather than a relational approach to the market. A Market-type culture does not adequately reflect an organizational culture conducive to service management effectiveness and profitability related to long-term client relationships.

The application of the modified version of the competing values measure of organizational culture, in a fairly large sample of successful French companies doing business nationally and internationally, demonstrated the importance of a Service-type culture oriented towards organizational values that emphasize the client relationship. Also, the introduction of another important area, the role of the contact person, was shown to be coherent with the other areas in which organizational culture is manifest (dominant attributes, leadership styles, bonding mechanisms and strategic emphasis). People are necessary for relationships between the firm and its customers and between firms in a business-to-business context.

Furthermore, within a business-to-business relationship perspective, there is a clear indication that business clients with Market and Hierarchy-type cultures do not have the propensity or interest in developing long-term relationships partly because they are more concerned with short-term profitability and opportunity costs. In the present study in France, 14 of the 91 companies indicated that they were likely to switch banks. These 14 companies were significantly more Market-type cultures than the other 77 companies willing to maintain their banking relationships. Similarly, as mentioned previously, Mexican companies with a Market-type culture had lower assessments of the strength of their relationship with their banks.

Theoretical Implications

More research needs to be done with regards to nuancing the Service-type culture in different service settings. In particular, the Service-type culture should be validated by determining if companies with a strong Service-type culture actually achieve significantly higher service management effectiveness.

The cultural relativity of the operationalization of the theoretical constructs may have introduced some cultural biases into these international studies. In fact, the influence of culture on management is subtle (Triandis, 1983), invisible and most often not recognized by the researchers coming from within a particular culture. It could be that the competing values model of organizational may reflect more of an American market definition of organizational culture. Cultural values are rooted in the fundamental problems facing any human society and the ways in which different groups address these problems (Hofstede, 1983; 1994). However, in this study the introduction of a Service-type culture and adding the role of contact personnel was done following a thorough literature review and with the guidance of extensive international business experience. As pointed out by Boyacigiller and Adler (1991), cross cultural research requires working in contexts involving people with different backgrounds, culture and experiences.

References

Boyacigiller, Nakiye A., and Adler, Nancy J., The Parochial Dinosaur: Organisational Science in a Global Context, *A. of Man. Rev.*, 16 (2) (1991): 262-290.

Deshpandé, Rohit, and Webster, Frederick E., Jr., Organisational Culture and Marketing: Defining the Research Agenda, *Journal of Marketing*, 53 (January 1989): 3-15.

Deshpandé, Rohit, Farley, John U., and Webster, Frederick E. Jr., Corporate Culture, Customer Orientation, and Innovativeness in Japanese Firms: A Quadrad Analysis, *Journal of Marketing*, 57 (January 1993): 23-27.

_____, Christian, Relationship Approach to Marketing in Service Contexts: The Marketing and Organisational Behavior Interface, *Journal of Business Resources*, 20 (1990): 3-11.

_____, Christian, Service Management: A Management Focus for Service Competition, in *Managing Services: Marketing, Operations and Human Resources*, Christopher. H. Lovelock, 2nd ed., Prentice Hall, Englewood Cliffs, NJ. 1992, 9-16.

_____, Christian, From Scientific Management to Service Management: A Management Perspective for the Age of Service Competition, *International Journal of Serv. Ind. Man.*, 5 (1), (1994): 5-20.

Gummesson, Evert, Service Management: An Evaluation and the Future, *International Journal of Serv. Ind. Man.*, 5 (1), (1994): 77-96.

Hofstede, Goert, National Cultures in Four Dimensions: A Research-based Theory of Cultural Differences among Nations, *International Studies of Man. and Org.*, XIII (1-2), (1983): 46-74.

_____, Goert, Management Scientists are Human, *Man. Sc.*, 40 (1), (1994): 4-13.

Mintzberg, H. and Quinn, J.B., *The Strategy Process: Concepts and Contexts*, Prentice-Hall,: Englewood Cliffs, NJ. 1992.

Normann, R., *Service Management: Strategy and Leadership in Service Business.*, 2nd ed., John Wiley, Chichester, UK. 1991.

Paulin, Michèle, Perrien, Jean, and Ferguson, Ronald, Relational Contract Norms and the Effectiveness of Commercial Banking Relationships, *I. J. of Serv. Ind. Man.*, 8 (5) (1997): 435-452.

Paulin, Michèle, Perrien, Jean, and Ferguson, Ronald J., *Organizational Culture and Services Management in Canada, Mexico and the United States: An Empirical Study of Commercial Banking*, Proceeding of the Multicultural Marketing Conference, Jean-Charles Chebat and A. Ben Oumlil, ed., Montreal, Canada, (September 1998a): 191.

Paulin, Michèle, Perrien, Jean and Ferguson, Ronald J., *Organizational Culture in a Professional Business-to-Business Service Context: Implications for Business Performance and Long-Term Relationships in Mexican Commercial Banking*, Proceeding of the Multicultural Marketing Conference, Jean-Charles Chebat and A. Ben Oumlil, ed., Montreal, Canada, (September 1998b): 478.

Paulin, Michèle, Ferguson, Ronald J., and Alvarez Salazar, Ana-Maria, External Effectiveness of Service Management: A Study of Business-to-Business Relationships in Mexico, Canada and the United States, *I. J. of Serv. Ind. Man.*, (1999).

Schein, Edgar H., *Organizational Culture and Leadership.*, 2nd Ed., Jossey Bass, San Francisco, CAL. 1991.

Schneider, Benjamin, Note on Climate and Culture, In *Creativity in Services Marketing: What's New, What Works and What's Developing*, M. Venkatesan, D.M. Schmalensee and C. Marshall, eds., American Marketing Association, Chicago, IL, 1996, 63-67.

Schneider, B. and Bowen, D.E., *Winning the Service Game*, Harvard Business School Press, Boston, Mass. 1995.

Triandis, Harry C., Dimensions of Cultural Variations as Parameters of Organizational Theories, *I. Stud. of Man. and Org.*, 12 (4).

Chapter 13

Cross-Cultural Importer-Exporter Relationship Model

J.B. Ha

Introduction

The objective of this chapter is to extend the buyer-seller literature in the context of international channels. It focuses on the relationship between exporters and importers, and using behavioral factors, proposes a process by which exporter-importer relationships develop. The study specifically investigates the relationships between behavioral constructs such as trust, dependence, cooperation, satisfaction, and commitment in order to find out the way exporters and importers develop their long-term relationship and how these behavioral constructs play the role for deepening the relationships between parties so that they accomplish long-term, committed relationships. The study was conducted in the context of importers within Korea.

There are two different broad approaches to analyze the buyer-seller relationship phenomenon. One approach is to attempt to explain the relationship by economic factors as the main reason for the long-term relationship. This approach includes the Transaction Cost Analysis (TCA) and Agency Theory. Even though these economic factors can explain the buyer-seller relationship to some extent, they only partially explain the relationship phenomenon and typically do not address the other important part of the phenomenon which deals with the non-economic factors. Therefore, to explain the buyer-seller relationship phenomenon fully, it is necessary to consider both economic and behavioral factors together (Stern and Reve 1980).

Since the buyer-seller relationship based on economic factors has been researched intensively, studies based on non-economic factors need to be explored in depth, especially in the international setting. In the international setting, the importance of buyer-seller relationships has been well-recognized (e.g., Ford 1984; Katsikeas and Piercy 1992; Leonidou 1989). At the same time the limitations of the approaches based on economic factors have been repeatedly pointed out in the extant literature (e.g., Weitz and Jap 1995; Stern and Reve 1980). Therefore, this study extends the buyer-seller relationship into the international channel relationship by focusing on the relationship between exporters and importers from the perspective of Korean importers.

Previous generic buyer-seller relationship studies focusing on behavioral aspects found several factors that affect the long-term relationship development process (e.g., Dwyer, Schur, and Oh 1987; Wilson 1995). The Researchers such as Dwyer, Schur, and Oh (1987) defined the difference between discrete and relational exchange based on MacNeil's (1980) contractual relationship and developed the five phases of the relationship development process. These are awareness, exploration, expansion, commitment, and dissolution. Through these development process phases, the relationship is developed by several different factors. Different empirical studies concerning the buyer-seller relationship used different factors to investigate the links among these variables. Based on earlier research (e.g., Morgan and Hunt 1994; Ganesan 1994), some of the frequently mentioned variables in buyer-seller relationship studies are trust, dependence, satisfaction, cooperation, and commitment. The interrelationships among these variables in exporter-importer relationship contexts form the scope of this research study. As endogenous variables, trust plays an attitudinal construct role while dependence plays a structural construct role. These two endogenous variables lead to the exogenous variable, cooperation. The logic behind this causal relationship is that both the trusted and dependent relationships lead to more cooperative action in the relationship. Furthermore, this cooperative relationship leads to another exogenous variable-satisfaction. Finally, a more satisfied relationship culminates in the desired committed relationship. The results of this research should contribute to a better understanding of buyer-seller relationships in international settings involving exporters and importers from different cultures.

Exporter-Importer Relationships

Exporting is often an appropriate mode of entry into foreign markets, especially for the small to medium size companies. This is because of low risks, low resource commitment, and high flexibility of action (Young et al. 1989). Many firms begin their global expansion as exporters and later switch to another mode for serving a foreign market (Hill 1994). Growing liberalization, integration and competition in world economies after World War II have been contributed to firms' increasing engagement in exporting activities. The export trade has grown from approximately $40 billion in 1945 to more than $4.5 trillion in 1993 and this amount accounts for 20% of world GDP (World Bank 1995). Also, compared to other entry methods such as licensing, franchising, joint ventures, and direct investment where the relationships between parties is usually characterized by asymmetric dependence. This is due to the fact that the relationship between parties from these modes is based on a formal contract, and this contract defends specific dependence within the relationship. However, exporting represents symmetric interdependent relationships between parties fairly well because, unlike the other modes of entry, its relationship is based more on both parties' individual decisions from transaction to transaction. With these advantages, using the exporting mode of foreign entry to study relationships between international channels of distribution is very appropriate.

Limitations of Economic Theories on Exporter-Importer Relationships

Economic theories dealing with long-term channel relationships are not sufficient or robust enough to describe the channel members' relationship phenomenon because they narrowly focus on the limited economic rationale, consisting of the control and coordination actions affecting channel relationships (Weitz and Jap 1995). Furthermore, they are dealing with unilateral control rather than bilateral control (Hill 1994). In other words, the economic theories focus on only one party making decisions to maximize its profits or benefits rather than both parties working together to maximize the total profits or benefits produced by both of them. In contrast, relationship marketing (RM) is devoted to shaping the channel structure from the perspectives of both parties to enlarge profits or benefits. Among other perspectives of the RM (see Nevin 1995 for more details), the relational exchange concept is the one that was most influential when building a channel structure. Dwyer, Schurr, and Oh (1987) describes relational exchange as an exchange relationship that invests in the long-term, shares benefits and burdens, establishes mutual trust, and plans for future transactions. In short, both economic theories mainly focus on the economic aspects of channel structure and utilize unilateral control, whereas RM is concerned with behavioral aspects of channel structure and utilizes bilateral control. Since exporter-importer relationship is based on business transactions, we cannot disregard the economic factors influencing relationship building. However, the importance of non-economic factors to the long-term relationship building process is critical and cannot be ignored.

Among the economic theories explaining channel relationships, Transaction Cost Analysis (TCA) and Agency theory have been considered prominent in the export literature. Thus, these two theories are worth reviewing as examples to illustrate limitations for explaining the channel relationships in marketing in general and in international marketing in particular.

The major problem for applying agency theory in channel relationships is that the principal-agent structure implies the use of unilateral control by the principal, not bilateral control by both parties. While unilateral control explains that one firm makes decisions to maximize its profit, bilateral control explains two firms who work together to maximize the profit generated by the relationship, as well as their individual profits (Heide 1994). Since exporter-importer relationships in the international context can be described as bilateral control rather than unilateral control, the relationship approach is more appropriate because it focuses on the bilateral control aspect rather than the unilateral control aspect. Furthermore, since this theory defines the efficiency based on only maximizing the principal's benefit rather than both parties' mutual benefits, this is also not appropriate for the exporter-importer relationship study.

Along with the agency theory's limitation, TCA ignores interdependencies between the firms and takes the perspective of minimizing transaction costs incurred by a single firm, not the costs incurred by both firms in the transaction.

Another limitation for applying this theory to the study of the exporter-importer relationship is that asset specificity of TCA is not applicable to the E-I relationship. Asset specificity refers to the ability of one party to transfer skills, knowledge, and especially capital equipment to the other party in one particular relationship. Because of the nature of E-I relationships, along with the existence of distance gap as well as cultural gap between exporters and importers, asset specificity of TCA is not significantly effective to the E-I relationships.

Channel Relationship in the International Market

International Marketing Channel

Marketing channel study in the international market place becomes the most prominent channel research area. Even if the domestic business transaction is still considered to be important, most nations rely heavily on international business trade. Like other business disciplines, marketing has put a major effort into the international arena. However, most of the studies in international marketing are only in the first phase of the growing trend. Channel study in the international framework is not an exception; it has been large in terms of quantities, but it remains in the explorer stage. Most international channel studies emphasize a small number of developed countries, such as Japan, the United Kingdom, and Canada because of their convenience. Among them, Japan has been the most interesting country to study channels for scholars in the United States, because Japan has several fascinating features. First, its channel system is very different from that of North American countries. Secondly, with its growing economy, it is very important for the United States to study Japanese marketing channels to enter Japanese market. By the same argument, Korea would be a very worthwhile country to study international marketing channels.

While exploring channel study, Borin, Van Vranken, and Farris (1991) examined the existence of discrimination against foreign products in the Japanese distribution system. They collected data about a consumer product (shampoo) from 131 retail stores in Tokyo. These stores were divided into six different types; their study results indicated that foreign products receive fair treatment in Japan's distribution systems. Goldman (1992) evaluated the Japanese distribution systems performance by three different dimensions. They are productivity (sales/employee, gross margin etc.), effectiveness (quality of output, consumer satisfaction etc.), and equity (equal accessibility, fairness etc.). It was found that Japanese distribution system's productivity was relatively low, but it had high levels of effectiveness and equity. Goldman also examined, in his 1991 study, the overall Japanese distribution structure, and he indicated that the traditional nature of the Japanese distribution system is more closely related to the internal political economy rather than to the institutional structure. Therefore, modernization of the Japanese distribution system will be achieved only through a change in the internal political economy of the modern sector.

Along with exploring the study of Japanese distribution channel systems, different perceptions between Japanese firms and The United States firms have been studied by channel researchers. Johnson, Sakano, and Onzo (1990) surveyed Japanese distributors of the United States products and found that mediated influence inversely related to the control but did not increase conflict. Non-mediated influence inversely related to conflict but did not relate any way to the control. Japanese distributors reacted to control in the same way as western channel members in that control resolution increases conflict. Johnson et al. (1993) in their Japan-the United States power perception study found that the Japanese channel participants view and operationalize power differently than the United States channel participants. The Japanese do not view the power sources along the mediated vs. non-mediated dichotomy as in western cultures.

With its distinct international characteristics, parallel importing becomes one of the serious issues in the trading area. Weigand (1991) explained the parallel marketing (gray marketing) in channels. Parallel marketing occurs when products are re-imported from the producing country, being illegally returned back to the home market. This is caused by differences in exchange rates, monopolistic power, and opportunistic behavior of administered channel members. He suggested strategies for overcoming parallel marketing. Those strategies included second-currency price quotes, legal avenues, differentiate products, terminate channels, and product buy-backs. Palia and Keown (1991) measured the extent to which the United States exporters operating in the Asia-Pacific region experience parallel importing. According to their study, 40% of the United States surveyed exporters had experienced the parallel importing and 30% of them had been experiencing from other Asian importers to the United States exporters selling products at reduced prices. They found that the most frequently cited strategies to overcome this were price adjustments and thorough procedures for screening buyers.

Klein, Farzier, and Roth (1990) examined the reasons underlying firms' channel integration decisions in international markets. They found that asset specificity is shown to differentiate significantly between the use of market exchanges and hierarchical exchange, and there is a positive relationship between environmental volatility and the probability that a foreign sales subsidiary would be established by the firm. The study results indicate that strong support is found for the impact of production costs on channel choice (as channel volume for the firm's product line in the foreign market increased, the integration of the channel increased as well), the firm is more likely to use an integrated channel when it can distribute multiple product lines through the channel because of economies of scale; additionally, the channel volume and shared channel constructs have stronger relationships with the level of channel integration than do asset specificity and environmental volatility.

Klein and Roth (1993) examined factors leading to a firm's satisfaction with its marketing channels. Their study was based on two theories predictions – the discrepancy model and transaction cost analysis. The discrepancy model's basic idea is that prior expectations compared to actual performance result in an evaluation of satisfaction (Day 1984). They found that domestic performance and more experience in foreign markets enhances satisfaction and this result supports discrepancy model. The other theory stated that lower transaction costs enhance performance, leading to greater satisfaction. The study result indicated that the easier it is perceived to be to change channel and the more predictable the market, the more satisfied is the firm. However, the more difficult it is to monitor the channel, the lower the firm's satisfaction, however, channel structure has no effect on management satisfaction. These results also support transaction cost analysis.

Rosenbloom (1990) suggested three elements to motivate international channel partners. First, find out the needs and problems of channel partners; then offer support to the channel partners that is consistent with their needs and problems. Finally, build a continuing relationship. Rosenbloom and Larsen (1992) investigated foreign manufacturer's views of their United States industrial distributor partners. They noticed that United States distributors are held in high regard in terms of their capabilities for performing key marketing functions, but they held in low regard in terms of providing market information and advice and technical support functions.

Exporter-Importer Relationships

As early as the 1970s Kotler and Levy (1973) emphasized that marketing concerns are not only the seller's side, but also the buyer's side. They gave a warning to marketers who have focused on the marketing process primarily from the seller's perspective. In recent years, researchers have begun to pay attention to the importer's perspectives, their responses to export marketing practices, and to the exporter-importer relationship in general. Among many research tracks in importer decisions, several studies tried to identify the important determinants in a buying decision. An early study by Hakansson and Wootz (1975) studied the perceived risk in purchasing. They identified the decision variables as supplier characteristics, such as location, reputation, and size, as well as bid characteristics, such as price and quality. They surveyed forty-three purchasers in Swedish companies that involved international businesses and concluded that location of the supplier was a more important factor than the size of the supplier and price was more valued than quality. Unlike the Hakansson and Wootz study, White's (1979) purchasing managers study in England, France, Italy, and West Germany showed that quality was the most important variable. This was followed secondly by market characteristic variables and thirdly, price factor. Ghymn (1983) examined the relative importance of variables that influence the decision process of the United States importers when they import goods from developed and developing countries. Through multiple discriminant analysis, he grouped fifteen variables into product-oriented variables and service-oriented variables. The service-oriented variables received the higher mean score than the product-oriented variables. He found that while the timely delivery variable received the highest overall importance scores, the United States importers regarded the product brand name and style more important when they were importing from developed countries. However, the price was considered the most important variable when importing from developing countries.

Yavas et al. (1987) studied Saudi Arabian purchasing agents' reaction to exporter practices from the United States, Japan, England, and Taiwan. They found that a significant country of origin effect drives the Saudi Arabian purchasing agent's importer behavior. They also noted that the Saudi Arabian importer, for example, considered price to be an important factor with goods from Taiwan, while quality was viewed as relatively insignificant. However, the Saudi Arabian importers considered quality as the most important factor for a United States product, while price was the least important factor for them.

Kraft and Chung (1992) compared the practices of Japanese and the United States exporters by Korean importers' evaluation to both countries' exporters. They evaluated Korean importers' perceptions of key variables such as product characteristics, reputation, and negotiation style for both groups of exporters. They found that the Japanese were rated more favorably on almost all of the dimensions measured.

Ghymn and Jacobs (1993) followed up Ghymn's (1983) initial study with a comparative effort which focused on the influences for Japanese import managers. Although both the Japanese and the United States managers viewed the variables of interest as important, several important differences between the groups were noticed. Japanese importers considered product specific elements, such as product quality and product safety, much more important than the United States importers did. The United States importers, on the other hand, viewed service-oriented elements, such as timely delivery and dependability, as more significant than the Japanese importers.

As specific factors to be perceived for individual countries, Ghymn et al. (1993) found that the product quality, price, and timely delivery were considered most important factors by both Thailand and Chinese managers. In a similar study for the Taiwanese importers, Rao, Jou, and Ford (1995) found that the factors such as communications, dependable long-term supply, price adjustments, timely delivery, and quality levels were recognized as important variables for Taiwanese importers. In measuring the satisfaction with export marketing practices, they found that satisfaction ratings are far below those of importance ratings across all the export marketing practices and for all the triad countries. Among triad countries, the United States obtained the least satisfaction level, according to their study results.

In the same line of research, Katsikeas and Al-Khalifa (1993) explored the forces that stimulated Bahraini importers to trade with U.K. exporters. They found that non-economic considerations, such as effective communication and after-sale support were quite important to these importers.

As another track of research in exporter-importer relationship, researchers have investigated the dyadic relationships between firms from different countries. Leonidou (1989) investigated the nature of the power structure in the exporter-importer dyad involving exporters from a developing country and importers of a developed country. These studies concluded that importers generally exercise a higher degree of power over the exporters.

Llanes, Otago, and Melgar (1993) studied the antecedents of underlying exporter-importer relationships in the case of developed countries' importers and developing countries' exporters. They analyzed data by using factor analysis and found four antecedents, each from developing countries' importers (Philippines) and developed countries' importers (the United States, Europe, etc.). Four antecedents underlying foreign buyers' perceptions of Filipino exporters are aggressiveness, adaptability, time-orientation and trustworthiness, and the four antecedents of Filipino exporters' perceptions towards foreign buyers are buyer's market mentality, buyer's support, and working relations and practices.

Moor (1991) studied the dyadic relationship status of U.K. exporting manufacturers and their west German agents and distributors. The research examined the previously studied four phases of the supplier-distributor dyadic relationship model by Ford and Rosson (1982). This model includes the new, growing, troubled, and static or inert state of dyadic relationships. Firms would move overtime from being in the new through final state inert. He evaluated these four states by four dimensions (performance, experience, uncertainty, satisfaction) and found that the new state can be subdivided to completely new, added new, and replacing new state. Additionally, the study results indicated that most firms move from the new to the growing state; however, once in the growing state, firms may eventually move into one of the remaining three categories of troubled, static and decline.

The relationship between export channel structure and manufacturer evaluation of export middleman was measured (Bello, Urban, and Verhage 1991). They found that manufacturers' performance evaluation of export middleman is most favorable in contractual channel and single-indirect channels but least favorable in conventional channels and dual-direct channels. Dependence evaluation is also found to be affected by economic structure but is highest in single-indirect channels and lowest in dual-direct channels.

Katsikeas and Piercy (1991) examined the conflict between a developing country's (Greece) exporters and a developed country's (U.K.) importers; they found that even if there exists some degree of conflict between parties and different perceptions of conflict, this conflict is low-level and is even a healthy sign for the relationship.

Wortzel, Wortzel and Deng (1988) found that neophyte exporters from a developing country such as the People's Republic of China are influenced by their home country business environment and culture in when dealing with the United States importers. Other empirical research confirmed that buying firms in developed countries often are willing, and prefer, to engage in long-term relationships with supplying firms (Hakansson and Wootz 1975).

In a more recent study, Egan and Mody (1992) found that cultivating the buyer-seller links is essential for export development. They reduce the United States buyers' most important elements when choosing suppliers to these three: price, quality, and delivery. They found that the United States buyers want the long-term relationship because of following reasons: (1) cost reduction for not searching a new partner (switching cost), (2) reducing various business uncertainties by learning each other's demands and capabilities, (3) having efficient relationships when both are working together for the same problem, (4) cutting the production cost by suppliers' collaborating with buyers' product design and contributing the needed manufacturing technology.

Proposed Exporter-Importer Relationship Model

Drawing on the literature one can propose three stages in the exporter-importer relationship process as depicted in Table 13.1.

Table 13.1 Exporter-Importer Relationship Process

Relational Variables	Stage 1: Casual Relationship	Stage 2: On-going Relationship	Stage 3: Committed Relationship
Trust	none or very little	somewhat	very much
Dependence	none or very little total dependence	- somewhat total dependence - asymmetric dependence	- very much total dependence - toward symmetric dependence
Cooperation	very little cooperative action	somewhat cooperative actions	very many cooperative actions
Satisfaction	different satisfaction level for each transaction	somewhat satisfied with partner	overall satisfied with partner
Commitment	None	intention for commitment	strong commitment

One more important factor in exporter-importer relationship development relates to the result of the relationship. It could be classified as tangible or intangible results from the relationship. Tangible relationship results can be the economical or financial benefits from that relationship. On the other hand, intangible relationship results can be the satisfaction from the relationship in the form of friendship, human interaction, etc. Especially in the E-I relationship context, intangible benefits can be derived from the relationship because of culture and value differences between the two parties. For example, both parties have a chance to learn the other's culture and value these experiences, which becomes an asset for successful future business relationships with people of different cultures and values. This, then, becomes one more step toward a globalized organization.

As mentioned above, a different exporter-importer relationship status can be determined by the strength of the relationships and this strength is developed by several different non-economic factors. Since the exporter-importer relationship is one form of buyer-seller relationship, one can use the generic buyer-seller studies as the framework for the exporter-importer relationship research proposed here. Different empirical studies in the buyer-seller relationship used different non-economic factors to investigate the links among those variables. However, one can extract important variables based on previous buyer-seller research studies. Some of the frequently mentioned variables in the buyer-seller relationship studies are: trust, dependence, satisfaction, cooperation, and commitment. Based on the behavioral variables the following Exporter-Importer relationship model is proposed.

Unlike the two economic theories (i.e., Agency theory and TCA), relationship marketing concept views relational exchanges between channel members as working partnerships (Anderson and Narus 1990) centered on norms of sharing and commitment (Figure 13.1).

Figure 13.1 Exporter-Importer Relationship Model

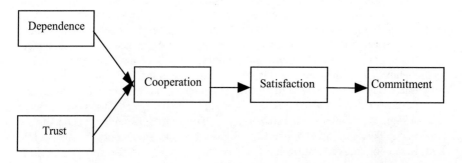

Based on trust (Achrol 1991) compared with other alternatives, partnerships are believed to derive greater benefits, such as product profitability, customer satisfaction, product performance and commitment through the relationship in relationship marketing (Morgan and Hunt 1994). It is also suggested that multinational companies facing a dynamic international marketing environment are likely to compete more effectively if they are a trusted cooperator rather than a hostile competitor (Morgan and Hunt 1994). Especially in the exporter-importer relationship context, the partnership approach is more important than other forms of buyer-seller relationships because of the nature of the relationship which is based on contractual agreement, as well as built-in difficulties of export-import business relationship from economic, cultural, legal, and marketing infra structural gaps between the exporter and importer countries. The above ingredients of the exporter-importer relationship development process are imbedded in the model proposed in the figure above. Although several empirical studies in buyer-seller relationships found the relationship between behavioral constructs (e.g. Anderson and Weitz 1989, 1992; Anderson and Narus 1990; Ganesan 1994; Heide and John 1988, 1990; Morgan and Hunt 1994), these relationships between behavioral constructs describe the relationship as only one stage phenomenon rather than an incremental process. However, as mentioned earlier, the buyer-seller relationship building develops through different stages (Dwyer, Schurr, and Oh 1987). In order to achieve the ultimate objective of the exporter-importer relationship, which is commitment, the relationship has to be developed through stages of the relationship development process. However, stages of relationship development depend not only on time but also on the strength of the relationship. Even if the relationship belongs to any of the stages of development, the relationship requires the strength steps to reach the objective variable of commitment. As can be seen in Table 1, the exporter-importer relationship development is achieved through the relationship strength steps.

Conclusions

The main purpose of this chapter is to extend the buyer-seller literature in the context of the international channel. It focuses on the relationship between exporters and importers. Using behavioral factors, it proposes a relationship model and the interrelationships among these behavioral factors, such as dependence, trust, cooperation, satisfaction and commitment in the exporter-importer relationship. The exporter-importer relationship develops its primary objective-committed relationship- by utilizing several behavioral factors. First of all, a trusted relationship between the exporter and importer leads to a cooperative relationship, as well as a satisfactory relationship. Secondly, a dependent relationship between the exporter and importer leads to a cooperative relationship. Thirdly, a cooperative relationship between the exporter and the importer leads to both satisfactory and committed relationships. Finally, a satisfactory relationship between the exporter and the importer leads to the committed relationship that is the ultimate goal for the exporter-importer relationship.

References

Achrol, Ravi (1991), 'Evolution of the Marketing Organization: New Forms for Turbulent Environments,' *Journal of Marketing*, 55(4), 77-93.

Alderson, E. (1965), *Dynamic Marketing Behavior*, Homewood, Illinois: Richard D. Irwin, Inc.

Anderson, Erin and Barton Weitz (1992), 'The Use of Pledges to Build and Sustain Commitment in Distribution Channels,' *Journal of Marketing Research*, 29(Feb.), 18-34.

Bello, Daniel C., David J. Urban, and Bronislaw J. Verhage (1991), 'Evaluating Export Middleman in Alternative Channel Structures,' *International Marketing Review*, 8(5), 49-64.

Borin, Norm, Cynthia Van Vranken, and Paul W. Farris (1991), ' A Pilot Test of Discrimination in the Japanese Distribution System,' *Journal of Retailing*, 67(spring), 93-106.

Deutsch, Morton (1958), 'Trust and Suspicion,' *Journal of Conflict Resolution*, 2(4), 26-279.

Doney, Patricia M. and Joseph P. Cannon (1997), 'An Examination of the Nature of Trust in Buyer-Seller Relationships,' *Journal of Marketing*, 61(April), 35-51.

Dwyer, F. Robert, Paul H. Schurr, and Sejo Oh (1987), ' Developing Buyer-Seller Relationships,' *Journal of Marketing*, 51(2), 11-27.

El-Ansary, Adel and Louis W. Stern (1972), 'Power Measurement in the Distribution Channel,' *Journal of Marketing Research*, 9(1), 47-52.

Emerson, Richard (1962), 'Power-Dependence Relations, *American Sociological Review*, 27(Feb), 31-41.

Ford, I.D. and Rosson, P.J. (1982), 'The Relationship between Export Manufacturers and Their Overseas Distributors,' In Czinkota, M.R. and Tesar, G. (Eds.), *Export Management: An International Context*, Praeger Publishers, New York, 257-275.

Ganesan, Shankar (1994), 'Determinants of Long-term Orientation in Buyer-Seller relationships,' *Journal of Marketing*, 58(2), 1-19.

Ghymn, Kyung-il (1983), 'The Relative Importance of Import Decision Variables,' *Journal of the Academy of Marketing Science*, 11(3), 304-312.

Ghymn, Kyung-il and Laurence W. Jacobs (1993), 'Import Purchasing Decision Behaviour: An Empirical Study of Japanese Import Managers,' *International Marketing Review*, 10(4), 4-14.

Ghymn, Kyung-il, B. Srinil, and P. Johnson (1993), 'Thailand Import Managers' Purchasing Behaviour,' *Journal of Asian Business*, 9(1), 1-12.

Hakansson, H. And B. Wootz (1975), 'Supplier Selection in an International Environment - An Experimental Study,' *Journal of Marketing Research*, 12(1), 46-51.

Heide, Jan B. (1994), 'Interorganizational Governance in Marketing Channels,' *Journal of Marketing*, 58(Jan.), 71-85.

Johnson, Jean L. et al. (1993), 'The Exercise of Interfirm Power and Its Repercussions in the United States-Japanese Channel Relationships,' *Journal of Marketing*, 57(Apr.), 1-10.

Katsikeas, Constantine S. And Al-Khalifa, Ali (1993), 'The Issue of importers Motivation in Manufacturer-Overseas Distributor Relationships: Implications for Exporters,' *Journal of Marketing Management*, 9(Jan.), 65-77.

Katsikeas, Constanine S. and Nigel F. Piercy (1991), 'The Relationship Between Exporters from a Developing Country and Importers Based in a Developed Country: Conflict Considerations,' *European Journal of Marketing*, 25(1), 6-25.

Klein, Saul and Victor J. Roth (1993), 'Satisfaction With International Marketing Channels,' *Journal of the Academy of Marketing Science*, 21(winter), 39-44.

Kotler, philip and S.J. Levy (1973), 'Buying is Marketing Too!' *Journal of Marketing*, 37(1), 45-49.

Kraft, Frederic B. and Kae H. Chung (1992), 'Korean Importer Perceptions of the United States and Japanese Industrial Goods Exporters,' *International Marketing Review*, 9(2), 59-73.

Kumar, Nirmalya, Lisa K. Scheer, and Jan-Benedict E. M. Steenkap (1995), 'The Effects of Perceived Interdependence on Dealer Attitudes,' *Journal of Marketing Research*, 32(August), 348-356.

Larzelere, Robert E. and Ted L. Huston (1980), 'The Dyadic Trust Scale: Toward Understanding Interpersonal Trust in Close Relationships,' *Journal of Marriage and the Family*, 42(August), 595-604.

Llanes, Viloeta A. and Isabel E. Melgar (1993), 'Antecedents of Export Channel Relationship between Exporters from a Developing Country and Foreign Importers,' *Multinational Business Review*, 1(1), 27-37.

Moore, Richard A. (1991), 'Relationship States in an International Marketing Channel,' *European Journal of Marketing*, 25(5), 47-59.

Moorman, Christine, Rohit Deshpande, and Gerald Zaltman (1993), 'Factors Affecting Trust in Market Research Relationships,' *Journal of Marketing*, 57(January), 81-101.

Morgan, Robert and Shelby D. Hunt (1994), 'The Commitment-Trust Theory of Relationship Marketing,' *Journal of Marketing*, 58(3), 20-38.

Nevin, John R. (1995), 'Relationship Marketing and Distribution Channels: Exploring Fundamental Issues,' *Journal of the Academy of Marketing Science*, 23(4), 327-334.

Palia, Aspy P. and Charles F. Keown (1991), 'Combating Parallel Importing: Views of US Exporters to the Asia-Pacific Region,' *International Marketing Review*, 8(1), 47-56.

Rao, C.P., Jacob H. Jou, and John B. Ford (1995), 'A Micro Level Investigation of Business Relationships between the USA and Taiwan,' *Marketing Educators and Researchers International Conference*, D. Horace Sogar and Ian Weber Eds. 402-416.

Rempel, John K., John G. Holmes, and Mark P. Zanna (1985), 'Trust in Close Relationships,' *Journal of Personality and Social Psychology*, 49(1), 95-112.

Rosenbloom, Bert and Trina L. Larsen (1992), 'How Foreign Firms View Their U.S. Distributors,' *Industrial Marketing Management*, 21(May), 93-101.

Rosenbloom, Bert (1990), 'Motivating Your International Channel Partner, *Business Horizons*, 33(Mar.-Apr.), 53-57.

Stern, Louis and Adel El-Ansary (1992), *Marketing Channels*. Englewood Cliffs, NJ: Prentice-Hall.

Stern, Louis, W., and Torger Reve (1980), 'Distribution Channels As Political Economies: A Framework for Comparative Analysis,' *Journal of Marketing*, 44(3), 52-64.

Weigand, Robert E. (1991), 'Parallel Import Channels-Options for Preserving Territorial Integrity,' *Columbia Journal of World Business*, 26(1), 53-60.

Weitz, Barton A. and Sandy D. Jap (1995), 'Relationship Marketing and Distribution Channels,' *Journal of the Academy of Marketing Science*, 23(4), 305-320.

World Bank (1995), *World tables*, Baltimore, Md: The Johns Hopkins University Press.

Worzel, H. Vernon, Lawrence H. Wortzel, and Shengliang Deng (1988), 'Do Neophyte Exporters Understand Importers?,' *Columbia Journal of World Business*, 23(4), 49-56.

Yavas, U., Cavusgil, S.T., and S. Tunclap (1987), 'Assessment of Selected Foreign Suppliers by Saudi Importers: Implications for Exporters,' *Journal of Business Research*, 15(3), 237-246.

Young, Stephen, James Hamill, Colin Wheeler and Richard Davies (1989), *International Market Entry and Development*, Englewood Cliffs, NJ: Prentice-Hall.

PART VI:

GLOBAL CONSUMER DIVERSITY

Chapter 14

The Marketing Challenge of Multiculturalism: An Exploratory Study

Sonny Nwankwo
Joseph Aiyeku
Alphonso Ogbuehi

Introduction

Multiculturalism has become a central discourse in the contemporary marketing literature as marketers struggle to cope with the increasing diversity of markets. The trend towards globalisation of business strategies (encapsulated in the cliché; *the world is a global village*) has led many marketing practitioners to view the marketplace monolithically. But the intensely competitive nature of modern business environments (and the attendant discontinuities) are constantly exposing the bankruptcies of conventional marketing paradigms. This is exacerbated by the growing explosion of immigrant populations across international borderlines and thus requiring that marketers must keep track of, and be ready to respond to the behavioural signals exhibited by consumers. Consequently, attention is now, more than ever, focused on multicultural marketing and the imperatives of developing successful marketing strategies to serve the needs of culturally diverse markets.

The need to focus on this aspect of marketing lies in that fact that many modern social institutions are characterised by a plurality of interests and consumers cannot be expected to share a common value system. Marketing activities takes place in social settings and must accordingly acknowledge the inherent diversity of cultures. Multicultural marketing thus offers a conceptual platform within which organisations can refine their strategies for coping with the heterogeneity of the marketing system. Paradoxically, many managers (and scholars) are well-entrenched in their functionalist (belief in universal shared values) rather than a structuralist (belief in fragment orientation) view of the nature of the society (Burrel and Morgan 1979). Consequently, many organisations lack an awareness of the basic factors that must embed an effective marketing plan in a multicultural context. This chapter highlights those critical issues that should underpin an effective multicultural marketing campaign. This will help to shed light on the dynamics of marketing in a contemporary world and thus illuminate how such an understanding can be of value to marketing practitioners who are attempting to deal with the implications of a diverse society. This chapter is accordingly a preliminary attempt at exploring the state of multicultural marketing in Britain.

Multiculturalism: The Construct

Until recently, studies in multiculturalism have encompassed political ethics (Gutman 1993), education research and curriculum development (Meacham 1996), communications analysis (Wilson and Gutierrez 1995), sociological analysis of organisations (Burrel and Morgan 1979), managing diversity programmes in complex organisations (Nemetz and Christensen 1997), and the wide area of cultural and anthropological research (Goldberg 1994). By way of definition, multiculturalism refers to the 'state of a society or the world containing many cultures that interact in some significant way with each other' (Gutman 1993, p.171); an environment designed for a combination of several distinct cultures (Nemetz and Christensen 1997). These definitions, while useful in shedding some light on the mobility and diversity of cultures, lacks the clarity necessary to fully describe the concept's complexities in contemporary society. It is this lack of proper understanding that has tended to complicate organisational approaches to multicultural marketing (Venkatesh 1995). Nemetz and Christensen (1997) argue that 'lack of a well-defined foundation of knowledge about multiculturalism has created situations whereby much of the information about multiculturalism comes in the form of rhetoric' (p.456).

Multiculturalism encompasses race, nationalism, gender and ethnicity. It has also been extended to include issues related to sexuality, philosophical episteme and political doctrines (Goldberg 1994). Goldberg (1994) goes on to argue that multiculturalism cannot be reductively defined although it can be phenomenologically described, that is, its conditions can be specified and characterised. Nevertheless, a useful framework has been provided by Nemetz and Christensen (1997), based on three dimensions (population variation, cultural variation and moral philosophy) for understanding the state of multiculturalism from the individual or societal perspective.

- Population variation: This ranges from 'separation' to 'integration', which lies respectively on both extremes of a spectrum and applied to explain the extent of a subgroup members' relationship with other subgroups.
- Cultural variation: This refers to the variety and concentration of values, behaviours, and attitude experienced and accepted by various subgroups within a society. Again, this ranges from cultural particularism (high context) to cultural homogenisation (low context).
- Moral philosophy: This dimension is embedded in the different approaches to moral philosophy. As in the other dimensions, the broad dichotomy focus on: relativism (i.e. accepts differences in moral codes and beliefs between groups within a complex community) and universalism (belief in a core of universal principles, i.e. doctrines of general application).

Beliefs about these three dimensions can be combined to define an individual's state of multiculturalism. This is an important starting point for a multicultural marketer because it helps in the assessment of (individuals') strategic orientation. For example, because the multicultural approach to marketing involves unlearning past (stereotypical) behaviours in order to keep abreast with the changing times, the above dimensions usefully tests the 'mind-set setting' of marketers. Clearly, it is a helpful conceptual frame, which might allow marketers to avoid unwittingly becoming entrapped in parochialism and cultural tokenism as they deal with the realities of today's markets.

Ethnic Marketing in Britain

'Ethnic marketing' is a term widely used to refer to the study of marketing within ethnic minorities contexts (Venkatesh 1995). Although there is a fundamental difference between ethnic marketing and multicultural marketing, the two terms are often used interchangeably (Nwankwo, Aiyeku and Ogbuehi 1997) – a position adopted in this chapter.

Efforts at marketing to ethnic minorities in Britain are currently at an embryonic stage. Very few companies have considered ethnic marketing in a manner evident in the USA (Hirschman 1981, Segal and Sosa 1983, O'Guinn and Meyer 1984, Rossman 1994, Stamps and Arnould 1996, Burton 1996). It is hard to find large British companies with a well-developed multicultural marketing plan. Consequently, there are inadequate strategic insights into the nature of the ethnic minority market. It is rather disturbing that in spite of the advances in marketing theory acknowledging the growing importance of 'diversity' issues in marketing (Brownlie et al 1994, Hunt 1994) and the attendant implications of such issues for the strategic development of modern organisations (Robinson and Dechant 1997, Chemer, Oskamp and Costanzo 1995), there exists a lacuna in the marketing literature in terms providing useful frameworks and/or empirical evidence which might help improve marketing practices in this important but hitherto neglected sector in Britain.

Recently, however, marketing practitioners in Britain have started to show a growing interest in ethnic marketing and this demonstrates how important this area has become (Dwek 1997). This burgeoning interest is in part a result of the profoundly changing multicultural landscape of Britain and the heightened awareness that many people from the ethnic minority population are more likely than those from the majority mainstream population to define themselves according to their ethnic identities (Nwankwo, Aiyeku and Ogbuehi 1997). Thus the prevalent idea in the USA that the 'melting pot' metaphor is being supplanted by the 'tossed salad' or 'cultural mosaic' metaphors (Venkatesh 1995) is, to a significant extent, also true of Britain's large cities such as Birmingham, Bradford, Leicester, London, Manchester, and Sheffield. With an estimated 5.5 per cent of the UK population, and annual spending power of £10bn, the size of ethnic minority populations is sufficiently large that they cannot be treated as marginal. In addition, because their consumption patterns may differ from the mainstream population, marketers should show a genuine desire to understand ethnic groups, their practices and buying/consumption behaviours.

Ethnic Minorities in Britain

'Ethnic minorities' refers to population groups that are small in number and by definition less than the majority mainstream population. As a theoretical construct, it has been euphemistically used as a substitute for several identifiers – race, religion, language group, a shared history and origin, nationality, etc. (Venkatesh 1995). In today's Britain, it is used to acknowledge the multicultural social setting by according a separate status to people belonging to differentiated ethnic groups. In everyday usage, it is associated with immigrant populations, a convenient umbrella category under which any 'population that is not White' could be placed (Jones 1993, Wilson and Gutierrez 1995). The term 'White' usually is applied to people of European ancestry (for a detailed discussion of ethnicity, nationalism and cultural identity, see Phinney (1996a), Costa and Bamossy (1995).

Britain experienced its first growth of ethnic minorities during the 18th and 19th centuries largely due to British conquests and colonial expansion in Africa, the Caribbean and Indian sub-continent. Over the last fifty years, the influx of people from countries that formerly comprised the British empire has resulted in a discernible trend towards a more visibly heterogeneous society. Today, ethnic minorities are estimated at around 3.3 million people, and growing. Available statistics indicate that the annual percentage growth rate of the ethnic minority population far out-strips that of the White population (Social Trend 27, 1997). For example, between 1981 and 1990, there was a 23 per cent increase in ethnic minority population compared to 1 per cent rise in the White population. Paradoxically, this fast growing market segment remains inadequately targeted by marketing strategists (see box 14.1).

Box 14. 1   Missing a Marketing Opportunity

- Much marketing alienates ethnic minorities.
- Ethnics have a fervent desire to be accepted, understood and integrated into British life.
- They miss nuances and references in UK advertising.
- They spend £10 billion a year, comprise 5.5 % of the UK population and nearly half were born in the UK, of whom 80% are under 25.
- The ethnic population will double in the next 50 years.
- In customer profile terms, they can be divided into: 'survivors' - often first generation who are inward-looking and less sophisticated, 'socially mobile' – who want to make the most of their opportunities, and 'sophisticates' – often second or third generation, who are younger and well-educated, ambitious and critical. However, all the three groups are united in wanting to be part of British life.

- Tokenism is rejected by ethnic minorities, who want to appear naturally within mainstream advertisements.
- The young are most attuned and comfortable with brand imagery, but they risk becoming alienated from brand images, as they grow older and retreat to their own cultural identity.
- Two-thirds of ethnic minority people ages 16-19 remain in full-time education, compared with just half of whites.
- 50 per cent of ethnic students are studying a science subject, compared with less than 40 per cent of whites.
- 34 per cent of ethnic minority people are from the professional/managerial classes, compared with 33 per cent of whites.
- 30 per cent of Indians between 19 and 35 are studying for a degree, compared with 13 per cent of whites.
- Indian families are most likely to own two or more cars.
- More Indian households than white households own telephones, washing machines, video recorders, microwaves and PCs.
- Black Africans are the most highly qualified group in society, with 27 per cent possessing post A-level qualifications.

Source: Building Business Bridges Report, cited by Dwek (1997).

The major ethnic groups are:

- Asians – this group mainly comprises Indians, Pakistanis and Bangladeshis. Together, they represent about 51% of the UK's ethnic minority population. Indians are the single largest ethnic group in Britain;
- Blacks – the second largest ethnic group which represents 28% of the ethnic minority population in Britain and;
- Others – this includes Chinese and Arabs.

Blacks and Asians from the Indian sub-continent together account for about 76% of the total ethnic minority population in Britain (see table 14.1).

Table 14.1   **Population by Ethnic Groups (%)**

Percentage	No. (000)	Ethnic Groups
14	477	Black Caribbean
8	281	Black Africa
3	117	Other Black
27	877	Indian
18	579	Pakistani
6	183	Bangladeshi
4	126	Chinese
5	161	Other Asian
15	506	Others*

* Includes those of mixed origin.
Source: Adapted from the Social Trend 27, 1997.

Methodology

In the process of gathering information for this chapter, we wrote to major advertising agencies in Britain soliciting information on how multicultural marketing concepts are being integrated in marketing promotions. The choice of advertising agencies as the starting point for our research was informed by the findings of an earlier study which revealed that much of what goes on in the realm of multicultural marketing in Britain largely revolves around marketing promotions, and in particular advertising (Nwankwo 1996).

Responses were very poor which required us to follow up with telephone interviews. This was extended to include senior marketing managers from a range of industries randomly selected from the Sheffield Business School (SBS) Corporate Membership database. The idea was to capture as much variety as possible with regard to organisational responsiveness to the increasingly heterogeneous marketplace. Interviewees were asked, in part, to comment on the state of multicultural marketing in Britain, their interest (or lack of it) in knowing more about marketing to ethnic minorities; to discuss things they like or do not like about multicultural marketing; to evaluate the perceived impact of multiculturalism on marketing practices; to describe what they would like marketing professionals to know about multicultural marketing; and to indicate whether they would change their marketing strategies to reflect multicultural realism if they could. Responses, although very poor, provided a good indication of how much respondents have thought about, and can articulate, the implications of marketing in multicultural contexts.

The statement below sums up the underlying problem and dearth of information in relation to multicultural marketing in Britain.

…You have chosen a difficult subject and you are right in thinking there is little published data which will help you. The research group Mintel were preparing a special report on exactly your subject but even they have given up (Ms Caroline Mills, Head of Information, GGT Advertising Limited).

Rethinking Marketing Segmentation

Until the 1990s, studies on ethnic minority marketing, especially in the USA, concentrated on assessing the market potential of subcultural groups as new market segments (Albonetti and Dominguez 1989, Bauer and Cunningham 1970, O'Guinn and Meyer 1984). As a result, the basic criteria for market segments often determined the direction of the study and the type of knowledge generated (Costa and Bamossy 1995). Implicitly, the conventional techniques of market segmentation were deemed adequate to capture the heterogeneity of the marketplace. Now, however, it is clear that traditional approaches to market segmentation can no longer accommodate adequately the diversities, complexities and peculiarities of the modern marketing system especially as new contexts, with all their attendant paradoxes, are focused.

Hoek et al. (1993) points out that segmentation often involves a number of assumptions and arbitrary decisions which renders the outcome unstable and insufficiently robust. What seems to emerge from the contemporary literature, therefore, is that the discontinuities of our time are increasingly exposing the bankruptcy of conventional marketing paradigms (Thomas 1994). Consequently, there is a growing interest in fleshing out the inadequacy of traditional approaches to market segmentation (Humby 1991, Mead 1993, Andreasen 1995, Datta 1996, Wright 1996). Wright (1996), for example, highlights and warns of the widespread and uncritical acceptance by the marketing community of some very dubious assumptions resulting from the application of the conventional segmentation techniques.

By and large, the ever-changing nature of the modern marketing environment, cut-throat competition in many consumer goods markets and the need to target consumers more effectively are driving marketers continually to review methods of segmenting markets in which they are interested. While socio-economic segmentation, for example, can still give a wide picture of the market place, marketing researchers are now exhorted to deploy other more meaningful methods of segmentation, such as those identified by Humby (1991), Mead (1993), and Mitchell (1995). As aptly observed by Mead (1993), the old socio-economic categories – on which so many vital marketing and advertising decisions have depended – are increasingly being replaced by other, more sophisticated segmenting techniques that try to probe consumer psyche, not just allocate social class.

However, one problem that may remain unsolved, even with the emerging multitudinous approaches, is that segmentation analysis may predominantly focus on marketing cues, which, in the context of multicultural marketing, could be misdirected and grossly inaccurate. A deeper understanding of the 'states of multiculturalism' (Nemetz and Christensen 1997) is important in order to help analysts appreciate the mundane factors that distinguish different ethnic groups and the effects on their buying behaviour. For example, a person's ethnic identification is important in that it may bind that person to a group as well as the lifestyles that arise from that background. Successfully identifying these new distinctions, in addition to other useful characterisations, increasingly looks like the key to finding new customers and retaining their loyalty. Marketing researchers have the potential to make important contributions to the development of knowledge in this area. Such research activities will reveal the potentials of multicultural marketing especially now that socio-cultural and demographic profile of Britain has vastly changed. From publicly available data (e.g. Social Trends, Labour Force Surveys) it is possible to construct a profile of Britain's ethnic minority population based on ethnic idiosyncrasies. Such a profile could provide the basis for comparison within (and between) different ethnic groups, and thus generate more useful variables for market segmentation purposes.

Although research in both Britain and USA reveals that ethnic minorities are potentially profitable market segments to enter (Segal and Sosa 1983, Lieblich 1988, Swenson 1990, Higgins 1995, Burton 1996, Dwek 1997), Fennel et al (1992) reminds us that it may be counter-productive to segment a market based on ethnic origin alone. Segmentation can only be successful where different consumption-related behaviours have been clearly identified and differ enough from the norm to motivate a change in an organisation's marketing efforts.

For organisations to target ethnic minorities in a coherent and co-ordinated manner, research should be conducted to substantiate the feasibility of ethnic groupings as viable market segments. It no longer makes sense to talk about ethnic minorities as a single group because of the growing differences within and between ethnic minority groups. For example, there may be a wide variation in the cultural norms and values maintained by members of an ethnic group consequent upon the differences in acculturation, generation of immigration, social class and regional influences. In addition, it may be difficult to assign individuals from mixed ethnic backgrounds to a single ethnic group and this has tended to blur the boundaries of ethnic groups. For these reasons, there is limited value in attempting to describe ethnic groups objectively in generalisations assumed to apply to all members of the group (Phinney 1996b). To be helpful, research on ethnic minorities should involve an emphasis on how groups' members themselves understand and interpret their own ethnicity and how these may change over time. Both conceptual and empirical writings acknowledge that 'ethnic identity is a dynamic construct that changes over time and context and varies across individuals' (Phinney 1996a, p.145). Clearly, this has implications for how people live their lives, interact with people from other groups, view society as a whole and, very importantly, for the practice of marketing.

Understanding the Ethno-Marketing Environment

Aspects of environmental analysis that might help in formulating an effective ethnic marketing strategy include demographics, life styles, culture, education and employment.

Demographics (age distribution) There are differences in age structures between most ethnic groups and the White population. For example, about 21 per cent of the White population is 60 years or over while the corresponding figure for all ethnic groups is less than 6 per cent (see table 14.2).

Table 14.2   Population by Age Structure

Population by Age	Under 16	16-29	30-44	45-59	Over 60
Black*	29.0	25.5	27.0	11.3	7.2
Indian	25.o	26.0	25.5	16.0	7.2
Pakistani/Bangladeshi	40.6	26.4	19.4	9.3	4.3
Others**	37.2	23.3	26.0	9.6	3.9
All ethnic groups	32.6	25.3	24.6	11.7	5.8
White	20.1	19.0	21.6	18.3	20.9

* Black includes African, Caribbean and other black people from non-mixed origin.
** Others include Chinese and other ethnic minority groups of non-mixed origin and those of mixed origin.
Source: *Social Trend*, 26, 1996.

From the above table, although age structure varies among the different ethnic groups in Great Britain, it is clear that the ethnic minority population has a younger age structure than the White population. For example, the under-30s represent nearly 7 in 10 of the Pakistani/Bangladeshi groups compared with just 4 in 10 of the White population. Government statistics also indicate that 8 in 10 members of the ethnic minority population aged under 25 were born in the UK compared with just over a fifth of those aged 25 and over. This, therefore, implies that the youth market in the ethnic minority population is sizeable and may be indicative of the next 'marketing battleground'. In the age bracket 0-29, the percentage share of the White population is nearly half of the ethnic minority population. It is not imponderable that ethnic minorities may show buying preferences that reflect their ethnic background and age. Products in the fashion, cosmetics and entertainment industries have a potentially high level of appeal to this age group.

Based on the rate of growth of ethnic minority populations, it now being suggested that the minority/majority divide may disappear in many of Britain's big cities in the foreseeable future. For example, it is predicted that ethnic population will double within the next 50 years and by the year 2011, ethnic minorities will make up the majority in half of the London boroughs (Dwek 1997).

Life style Many ethnic minority groups in Britain tend to have more dependent children in the households and larger average household size than the White population. Statistics show that households from the Asian community were the most likely to consist of six or more people (compared with two in the White population). Although data vary among the different ethnic groups, one common feature among them is the importance they place on the extended family. Black African-Caribbeans are known to have small household units as overall as the White population but they tend to subscribe to 'collectivism' in contrast with the 'individualism' of the White community orientation.

A recent phenomenon among the ethnic population is the steady upward movement in Britain's socio-economic hierarchy. The most prominent ethnic group, the Asians, and particularly the Indian community, have now overtaken Whites as the people most likely to have their own businesses and professional qualifications. A recent study shows that Indians have taken over from the Jewish community as the most upwardly-mobile group: they do well not by adopting British ways of doing things but by keeping their culture distinct within it (Maung, Carey and Swann, 1996). Theirs is a culture that embraces and reinforces the extended family system and this helps them to get ahead in business. One of the 300 Asian millionaires opined that 'having a large family means you can share the workload and the capital. It also means you can push business in your relatives' direction'. The multicultural marketer, therefore, has a lot to learn regarding the dynamics of buying decisions, the locus of power and authority to initiate, influence and/or execute marketing exchanges, and the wide area of behaviour referents in extended family contexts.

Education/employment: The government's Labour Force Survey shows that higher proportions of young people from Indian, Black African and African Asian, and Chinese origin stay in full-time education after 16 than their White counterparts, and are therefore, increasingly well-qualified in comparison. This is now being reflected in employment, with these groups substantially increasing their presence in the higher levels of the job market, particularly in professional areas such as accountancy, medicine, legal services and computer consultancy (see table 14.3).

A study by the Policy Studies Institute found that 'there is evidence of a strong dynamic among ethnic minority communities driving them to develop beyond the social and economic niche they filled for the first 20 years - a major shift from previous studies which generally found even well-qualified people from ethnic minority groups were more often confined to lower job levels than similarly qualified Whites' (Jones 1993). In essence, this means that marketers must begin to question some stereotypes and out-dated assumptions about consumers and markets. Old ideas must give way to new ones.

Table 14.3   Job Profile of Ethnic Groups in the UK (%)

	White	Indian	Black African	Black Caribbean	Chinese	Pakistani	Bangladeshi
Unskilled	8	5	8	10	3	8	9
Semi-skilled	15	16	16	20	7	20	30
Skilled	32	22	17	40	29	32	32
Clerical	11	17	19	13	20	12	13
Management	26	26	24	13	23	20	9
Professional	8	14	16	4	18	8	7

Source: Adapted from Maung, Carey and Swain (1996).

The Role of Culture in Marketing to Ethnic Minorities

Ethnic minorities exist within unique subcultures that require in-depth analysis. From a sociological perspective, cultures vary in their complexities and often characterised as either high-context or low-context (Hall 1960). Characteristics of high-context cultures include:

- information is implicit in the physical context or internalised within the people;
- there are strong bonds and increased involvement between people;
- higher distinctions between 'insiders' and 'outsiders' – the tendency to categorise individuals into either in-group (family, relatives, etc.) or out-group (friends, strangers, competitors, etc.) in the context of which membership forms the basis of social interactions;
- cultural patterns are long-lived and slow to change.

In low-context cultures, the following characteristics may be observed:

- information is contained in coded, explicitly transmitted messages;
- tangible bonds and decreased involvement between people;
- few distinctions made between insiders and outsiders;
- favours the rights of the individual over the rights of the society at large;
- implicit rejection of the extended families in favour of smaller, nuclear families.

Lee et al (1996) highlighted some of the areas where the Caucasian and ethnic population cultures differ. Also, the study conducted by Rabin (1994) revealed that many ethnic minority cultures are high-context when compared with the mainstream population. He argues that ethnic minorities may have a greater ability to send and receive messages through symbols and gestures, and more likely to define themselves in terms of ethnic identity than Whites.

This is not to say that there is a commonality of cultural values among Britain's ethnic minorities. Differences also exist within the ethnic minority population. However, a common feature among the ethnic groups is that they exhibit high-context cultures in contrast with the low-context features of the dominant culture. In multicultural marketing, culture matters (Pereira 1996, Yau 1988). For example, based on the Confucian and Buddhist philosophies among the Chinese, Yau (1988) argues that the notion of consumer satisfaction, dissatisfaction and complaint behaviour of Chinese would differ from a comparable observation in the West, noting that Chinese are more likely to blame their own fate when a product fails rather than attribute such blame to product failures. Understanding these important dimensions will greatly improve the practice of marketing in a multicultural context.

A Schema for Cultural Classification of Ethnic Minorities

Understandably, UK marketers face a dilemma in marketing to multicultural consumers. A vast majority believe that becoming 'multiculturally conscious' on one hand and avoiding the entrapment of a possible racial segregation on the other is a tough balancing act. While recognising the reality of today's multi-ethnic Britain, they often recourse to 'taken-for-granted' assumptions about consumers and markets. There have been problems arising from such a clumsy approach to marketing. A good example is the Homepride promotional fiasco in 1996 in which a Sikh family with a Liverpool accent was featured but, ironically, the male head of the family was not seen to be wearing the distinctive Sikh beard. For whatever reason – ignorance, tokenism, or parochialism – such marketing practices are likely to alienate a section of ethnic minorities particularly those who have a strong association with their native (ethnic) culture.

Understanding the ethno-cultural values is a necessary step to reaching the ethnic minority market. There is, therefore, a need to provide a schema for identifying ethnic subcultures in Britain. Ethnic minorities are varied in terms of their assimilation into the mainstream culture. The role of culture in understanding consumer behaviour cannot be over-emphasised. However, it might be preposterous to argue that people from a given ethnic group are likely to subscribe, prima facie, to the same cultural orientation. A framework for identifying variations even within a subculture is proffered below. It is based upon the *Acculturation Influence Group* (AIG) illustration by Segal and Sosa (1983), which espouses the notion that the key to identifying and understanding ethnic minority groups lies in the degree of acculturation. The framework has four broad classifications indicating the influence that the dominant culture exerts on the ethnic minority individual. The positioning within the framework is not based on age but on exposure and adaptation to the dominant Caucasian culture. The premise is that a person of Asian descent, for example, who has lived in Britain all his/her life, is likely to display a higher level of acculturation to the Caucasian culture than one who has only recently immigrated. The schema consists of the following:

Group One: Least Acculturated

- More at ease with items closely related to their own culture;
- Tend to live in close-knit family groups and ethnic dwelling areas;
- Low income and blue collar workers;
- Very limited knowledge of English language;
- Do not accept the dominant Caucasian culture as relevant to their lifestyle;
- Are not motivated to adjust to their new environment;
- Behaviour heavily influenced by native culture;
- Poorly educated (Western style);
- Dress mainly in their ethnic clothes.

Group Two: Moderately Acculturated

- Have a working knowledge of English language;
- Prefer to speak in their native language;
- Behavioural patterns are predominantly influenced by their subculture's values;
- Combine some characteristics of groups one and three.

Group Three: Most Acculturated

- Fluent in both English and their native tongue;
- At ease in a predominantly Caucasian environment;
- Live in areas not predominantly ethnic oriented;
- Their behavioural pattern are largely driven by the dominant culture;
- Have some pride in their ethnic background.

Group Four: Totally Acculturated:

- Fluent only in English;
- Have little knowledge of their ethnic culture;
- Likely to be born in the UK;
- View themselves as 'English' and have patriotic feelings towards England only;
- Ignorant and not motivated to understand their own ethnic background.

This schema may be useful to marketers in segmenting the ethnic minority population. Nevertheless, its main weaknesses is likely to manifest itself when attempting to work out the finer details regarding, for example, what statistical measurement to use in order to generate a reliable and sensible classification of individuals into one of the four clusters. Use of psychometric instruments may help alleviate this difficulty. Once classified, it becomes more meaningful to apply other segmentation parameters such as age, occupation, marital status, disposable income/consumer spending and employment.

Researching the Ethnic Minority Population

Ethnic research is not a recent phenomenon in the field of consumer behaviour (Engel, Blackwell and Kollat 1978, Hirschman 1981). Most of the earlier studies aimed to establish a relationship between ethnicity as an independent variable and consumption as a dependent variable. A major setback in multicultural marketing research is that often 'culture is implicitly considered to be a constant, and the interpretation and discussion of the studies' results tend to reflect the dominant norms, values, and processes of the researchers' origin' (Costa and Bamossy 1995, p.20). Venkatesh's (1995) criticism of these efforts lies in the problem of treating ethnicity:

...as an existential condition and the problems of the ethnic groups and their coping strategies seldom invoked ... The interpretive questions in these studies are necessarily limited because ethnicity is treated as a scientific construct leading to a reductionism of sorts, and ethnicity is regarded as just any other demographic variable, such as disposable income or household size. The problem with such a treatment is that ethnicity becomes a faceless variable in research...(pp.35-36).

Venkatesh goes on to suggest that ethnic research will be profoundly enriched if researchers attempt to go beyond the over-dependence on standard positivist research methods 'because the epistemological position of the researcher might become too rigid to capture the existential condition of the researched subjects in a meaningful way' (p.36). Furthermore, studies by Jain and Costa (1991), Joy and Dholakia (1991), and Mehta and Belk (1991) revealed the complexities in conducting ethno-marketing research by illustrating that issues relating to ethnicity are part of a cultural condition with attendant implications for the nature and consequences of consumption experience among different groups. For these reasons, it may not be useful to treat ethnicity as merely another variable but, rather, as a cluster of interrelated variables that accords an identity to a people. However, recent publications which apply ethnographic perspectives have shed more light on the underlying factors which shape consumption behaviour and, in addition, signalled the need to be more critically thoughtful before imposing theoretical frameworks and constructs from one culture to another. At a more practical level, researching ethnic minorities is complicated and poses a number of problems. These problems include:

(a) Obtaining reliable universe data It is often difficult to obtain reliable universe data because a significant proportion of immigrant populations in Britain are either not registered as bona fide residents (on account of immigration difficulties) and/or many of those who are entitled to vote are not on the electoral register. Although this situation has improved over the years, work by the Commission for Racial Equality (CRE) found that between 20 and 30% of ethnic groups were consistently unregistered. Therefore, identifying and sampling ethnic minorities using conventional methods may prove to be impractical and past attempts have revealed several methodological weaknesses (Watson 1992). To overcome this, it may be sensible to use a focused enumeration approach to select areas of high known ethnic concentration. Within these areas, broad quota controls can be set on sex and age as well as ethnic origin.

(b) Interviewing The process of interviewing presents another practical problem, especially in selecting who should interview respondents of ethnic origin. When the Centre for Disease Control and Prevention in USA tested public-service announcements about AIDS through focused groups, it found that single-race panels and multicultural panels reacted differently. The groups provided important insights on which creative strategies were most appropriate for targeted versus broad audience (Rabin 1994). Box14.2 below provides a further insight into this problem.

Box 14.2   Problems in Interviewing Ethnic Minorities

The Harris Research on unemployment among young West Indian males was very revealing. During the pilot phase, split samples were used – half of the sample were interviewed by White interviewers and the other half by interviewers from their own peer group. When asked what efforts they had been making to secure work, the White interviewers were told of the daily Jobcentre visits, interviews applied for, local job columns scoured and so on. The peer group interviewers were told that they did only what they had to do, to continue to draw benefit. The truth was probably somewhere between the extremes expressed but this clearly illustrates that bias certainly can be induced by unsuitable interviewers.

Source: Watson (1992).

We recently conducted a face-to-face survey among black consumers to gauge General Election opinions using a split sample, randomly divided between black and white interviewers. On sensitive issues a significantly different picture emerged between the black-interviewed sample and the white-interviewed sample. We further investigated the split sample, reversing the interviewing force. The earlier situation was confirmed. If it is accepted that kinship is a key element in respondent communication, one interviewing set is more genuine. It is our view that the black-interviewed sample provided a truer reflection because of belonging and common identity.

Source: Abi Adeniran - Director, Hothouse Marketing & PR, London.

(c) Language   Difficulties often arise as a result of language barriers. English is widely spoken by the Black population (Caribbean and African) but the largest ethnic group, Asians, presents a challenge.   Projects involving older Asians often require translation into one or more of the major Asian languages: Urdu, Punjabi, Bengali, Hindi, Gujarati or Chinese. Bilingualism is a critical success factor in the interviewing process. Marwaha of the Asian Publishing Ltd suggests the use of Gujarati while Dhillion (1993) proposes that marketing communications to Asians be conducted in Hindi. Hindi is the most widely spoken Asian language in Britain, while Punjabi and Urdu are similar variants of this language (Dhillion 1993). It is important to bear in mind that the use of local dialects may prove to be counter-productive if not well thought-through because of rivalries/animosities that may have historically existed in original home countries.

(d) Gender matching   Among many Asian groups, and principally Moslems, gender matching is crucially important in face-to-face communication. For example, in orthodox Moslem settings, it is generally unacceptable for females (especially the unmarried ones) to be interviewed by males. Conversely, conservative Moslem males may find it insulting to be confronted with a female interviewer.

(e) Ethnic matching Ethnic matching may be important in a group discussion – particularly if the subject-matter is ethnically sensitive. A particularly careful screening process is needed to get a balanced group with similar characteristics. 'There is no such thing as an 'Asian' group discussion. A group of three Hindus, two Sikhs, two Moslems and a Christian is asking for problems' (Watson 1992, p.341).

(f) Cultural barriers The high-context culture of many ethnic minority groups means that there are often 'protective walls' against being 'probed' or seen to be too 'revealing' to 'outsiders'. Consequently, postal surveys have been known to attract extremely low response rates, unless the issue is directly relevant to the focal ethnic group. Watson suggests that normal semantic agree-disagree scales may not produce credible results. Among older Asian respondents, for example, scales of five, seven, nine inevitably attracts the central, neutral response due to a desire not to cause any offence, so four point scales are more preferable.

Factors to Consider in Developing Ethno-marketing Mix

Both empirical and anecdotal evidence indicate a need for fundamental strategic adjustments in how UK marketers approach ethnic markets (see Box 14.2).

Box 14.3   The Rhetoric and Reality

Companies have been comparatively ignorant of the differences across racial groups in the UK. Perhaps naively ignorant, perhaps arrogant to assume that the view they engender with the populace at large is common across all racial groups (Julie Mellor – Diversity consultant).

The UK's ethnic minority communities are an increasingly large and important part of our society, but   statistic show that while they represent a major business potential, it is largely untapped (Robert Ayling – Chief executive, British Airways).

Some of the language and images highlighted by our report were found to be both confusing and confounding to some ethnic groups, and possibly insulting to most. We (UK companies) are all starting from a point of inadequacy on this subject (Graham Bann – Executive director, Race for Opportunity).

Marketwatch survey (telephone omnibus survey of more than 1000 adults):

Does advertising generally address Britain's ethnic minorities? 44% said yes, 37% said no, and 19% did not know.

Only 8% thought that ethnic groups should be specifically targeted, 85% thought they should be treated as an integral part of British society.

Recall of recent advertising campaigns thought to be 'ethnically sensitive' or 'ethnically insensitive': 95% had no views.

Source: Adapted from *Marketing Business*, March 1997.

All aspects of the marketing mix qualify for a thorough review. However, we have chosen to focus on selected elements of the marketing mix, with emphasis on promotion because of the reason earlier given.

Product: On a general level, ethnic minorities are known to exhibit a higher degree of brand loyalty than the White population. This was confirmed by a limited observation study carried out in the South Yorkshire area (Lindridge 1993). The study also revealed that ethnic minorities from the Indian subcontinent are more 'brand loyal' than any other ethnic group. The degree of brand loyalty appears to be higher among new immigrants. This attitude might be explained either by the varying levels of acculturation or as a way of dealing with possible post-purchase dissonance, hence the tendency to buy well known branded goods which they are familiar with. The implication is that marketers must work hard to induce brand switching. More positively, it means that customer retention and bonding is easier with ethnic minority groups.

Distribution In terms of geographical spread, ethnic groups tend to concentrate in urban areas. For example, data extracted from various issues of Employment Gazette show that 98 per cent of ethnic minorities live in England, 60 per cent of them in the South East. Whereas Black Caribbeans live predominantly in the South East and the West of England, this is not true of Asians. The Asian population has expanded across England as they have improved their socio-economic position. Nevertheless, they tend to live in observable clusters.

Distribution channels may be fragmented and expensive to operate, which obviously may have some impact on margins if not carefully worked out. Ethnic minority consumers operate a two-way shopping process involving purchasing basic goods from mainstream shops and ethnic products from specialty shops. It might not, therefore, be helpful to distribute goods targeted at ethnic consumers through large mainstream retail outlets. Market penetration through ethnic wholesalers may help overcome some of the problems of geographically diversified markets.

Promotion Ethnic minorities have in the past been presented in a stereotypical and unflattering manner in advertising (Wells, Burnett and Moriaty 1989, Stevenson

1991). Recent examples of advertisements which have caused offence among ethnic minorities include Ford motors (the erasure of black faces from the advertisement adapted for the Polish market); Persil fiasco in which a black and white-spotted dog was seen shaking off its black spots in a bid to demonstrate the effectiveness of the detergent, and the crass ignorance of multiculturalism revealed in the Vauxhall advertisement featuring babies, supposedly a reflection of the wider society, but ironically, not a single one of them had a black face.

According to Kathy Gilliard, a partner in a London-based advertising agency,

> ...offending potential ethnic customers could do more than just give a firm a bad name. It could cause serious bottom line damage as well ... You really need to be a student of a particular culture to know how to avoid stereotypes. There are some that are blatantly offensive and that anyone with some common sense can avoid ... Others, however, are less obvious to members of another culture. Without a knowledge of current trends and thinking in a particular culture, you might accidentally push one of those hot buttons.

Promotional campaigns needs to be creative in order to avoid being patronising or condescending to a stereotype (Swenson 1990). An effective marketing communication strategy should consider the following:

(a) Stereotypes   Ethnic stereotypes may reinforce obvious cultural differences and racist views. The significance of stereotypes is to be seen in the wider context on the debate concerning advertising (Stevenson 1991). Should advertising shape a society's values or merely reflect those values? If advertising influences a society's values and beliefs, then it is important to consider how people are presented in advertising campaigns.

Whether stereotypes are relevant in promotional campaigns may depends on the context. For example, the Metropolitan Police Force deliberately used the issue of stereotyping in their recruitment drive for ethnic minorities. One of their advertisements featured a Black Caribbean being chased by a policeman with the caption: *'Another example of police prejudice? Or another example of yours?'* A closer inspection of the advertisement revealed that the person being chased was a Black Caribbean policeman, out of uniform, chasing an unseen third party. This campaign relied on stereotype to present an effective message.

(b) Condescending   Understanding the culture of the target market, avoiding predictability in the message and the method of presentation will prevent marketing communication from being condescending. The Metropolitan Police advertisement avoided being condescending by carrying an honest message, which did not insult the individuals and did not trivialise the subject matter.

(c) Culture   Presentation of some ethnic groups in advertisements presents problems due to religious and cultural beliefs. The Muslim religion prescribes a strict dress code for women while some other Asian cultures may perceive the use of women to promote a product as derogatory. The 'Miss Asia United Kingdom' contest was cancelled due to Indian pressure groups perceiving the event to be 'degrading to

women and to the community' (L. Grant – from the Independent on Sunday newspaper). As another example, when Phileas Fogg launched 'Pakora' (an Indian snack) in 1993, it featured the Karma Sutra as a means of conveying the product's characteristics. The advertisement was severely criticised by Asians for its bad taste in 'likening cheap snacks to part of our culture which we wont tolerate ... Although the Karma Sutra is not a religious book, it is highly regarded by all Indian communities in India. This advertisement is offensive' (C. Yates – the Sun newspaper). The manufacturers refused to withdraw the advertisement.

(d) Intentional and unintentional racism Racism is a highly sensitive issue in Britain and issues appertaining thereto should be handled cautiously. One of the main reasons why many organisations are not overly-enthusiastic about ethnic marketing is the fear of unwittingly getting embroiled in racial trappings – and the attendant bad publicity. Ideally, promotional campaigns focusing on the ethnic minority population should be checked out with the Commission for Racial Equality for advice and guidance.

Fuji films campaign showed an Asian mother being shunned by a group of White mothers (intentional racism) and later showed her with her daughter and a White child. The advertisement, according to Withers of Fuji Films (UK) illustrated that 'racism is not an issue when you are young, you only grow into it by a society of prejudices'. Also, Benneton Spa of Italy is the most famous for using this approach – the promotional thrust is to try to convince the buyer that to buy a Benneton product is to strike a blow for world harmony.

Paradoxically, using racism as a creative approach can help achieve remarkable rewards. Within 6 months of running its advertising campaign, Fuji's sales increased by 15 per cent in spite of being out-spent three to one by its main rival, Kodak.

(e) Celebrities Relative to their population, ethnic minority groups are grossly under-represented in advertising campaigns in Britain. Ethnic celebrities may prove more effective in marketing communication and so important that it may determine who gets the ethnic segment of the consumer market.

A classic example of a successful use of celebrities in reaching ethnic minorities is the breast cancer campaign. The campaign targeted black women at high risk of breast cancer without implying that the problem is limited to this ethnic group. The solution was to recruit a black recording artist who told a personal story about her family's experience with cancer.

Some organisations (mainly in sectors such as food, drinks, clothing, detergent and children toys) are now beginning to brace up to the need to use more celebrities from the ethnic minority population.

(f) Permission Messages may or may not be controversial in themselves, but the chance of controversy increases greatly if permission is not obtained to relay a message to a particular group. In many minority cultures, marketers must win the support, respect, and invitation of community leaders before they can open an effective line of communication with their members. The more controversial a product or issue, the more essential it is to seek permission first.

The successful Health Education Authority (HEA) campaign to increase AIDS awareness among ethnic minorities clearly illustrates this point. The initial campaign was a disaster. According to Mr Gallachan of HEA, the target audience was originally critical of the campaign and some of the comments he received were quite offensive - ranging from calling him liar to the 'antichrist'. The fact that AIDS could be sexually transmitted challenged many ethnic 'taken-for-granted' cultural and religious beliefs, for example, entering into sexual relationships before marriage, extra-marital and homosexual relationships. Ethnic media channels were even reluctant to accept HEA's advertisement. However, by building bridges with community and opinion leaders, HEA eventually managed to get its message through.

Conclusion

Marketers face an exciting challenge in reaching a multicultural Britain. They also face enormous responsibilities. There should be no doubt that, potentially, ethnic minority marketing could further divide the nation if it reinforces racial and ethnic stereotypes. If perceptively practised, it could develop new approaches that respect Britain's diversities while celebrating their similarities. While 'one size fits all' might still be a viable marketing strategy for jeans and T-shirts, customised cultural and ethnic appeals are gaining steam with a number of firms providing consumer goods and services. According to those who work in the field, firms that specialise in multicultural marketing are daily finding new customers for their services. As Pine et al (1995) aptly observed, in today's fragmented and increasingly turbulent markets, customers do not want more choices but they want exactly what they want, when, where, and how they want it. The irony is that most marketing managers continue to view the world through the twin lenses of mass marketing and cultural syncretism. 'A company that aspires to give customers exactly what they want must look at the world through new lenses' (Pine et al 1995, p.103).

It is clear that multicultural marketing cannot be successful unless it is strategically driven. Showing a few faces from the ethnic minority population on product packages or television advertisements will not suffice. Companies targeting ethnic minorities must start to build an on-going relationship with them. Penetration of ethnic markets needs long-term commitments. Loyalty and trust are important success prerequisites and needs to be established first. Marketing, after all, is not a short-term, formula-driven discipline. In a way, marketing is 'part anthropology' – this is a recognition that subcultural membership is very important in shaping people's needs and wants and, therefore, should be taken into consideration when formulating marketing strategies (West and Bahtka 1996). While it is impossible to develop separate marketing strategy for each ethnic group, an acknowledgement of relevant ethnic characteristics in marketing campaigns can nevertheless enhance a firm's credibility and promote a more positive brand attitude within a target ethnic market. Multicultural marketing may thus prove to be the dominant paradigm for seeking competitive advantage in niche or saturated markets and/or for developing customer intimacy in new markets. This makes sense given the increasing diversity and globalisation of marketplaces. In the words of Mr Adeniran, Director of London-based Hothouse Marketing & PR company:

> Britain's unique multicultural consumer base offers a wonderful test site for global competitiveness. If a business cannot market to multicultural Britain … it should seriously query its ability to market globally to a myriad of cultures.

References

Albonetti, J. and Dominguez, L. (1989) Major Influences on Consumer Goods Marketer's Decision to Target Hispanics, *Journal of Advertising Research*, Vol. 29, No.1, pp. 9-21.

Andreasen, A. (1995) Market Segmentation in Developing Countries, MPPC/SCP Annual Conference, Atlanta, GA, May.

Bauer, R. and Cunningham, . (1970) The Negro Market, *Journal of Advertising Research*, Vol.10, No.2, pp. 3-13.

Brownlie, D., Saren, M., Wittington, R., and Wensley, R. (1994) The New Marketing Myopia: Critical Perspectives on Theory and Research in Marketing – Introduction, *European Journal of Marketing*, Vol.28, No.3, pp.6-12.

Burrel, G. and Morgan, G. (1979) *Sociological Paradigms and Organisational Analysis*. London: Heinemann.

Burton, J. (1996) Targeting Investors in Their Own Languages, *Profiles*, October, p.16.

Chemer, M., Oskamp, S., and Costanzo, M. (1995) *Diversity in Organisations: New Perspectives for a Changing Workplace*. London. Sage Publications.

Costa, J. and Bamossy, G. (1995) Perspectives on Ethnicity, Nationalism and Cultural Identity. In Costa, J. and Bamossy, G., eds., *Marketing in a Multicultural World*. London, Sage Publications. pp.3-25.

Datta, Y. (1996) Market Segmentation: An Integrated Framework, *Long Range Planning*, Vol.29, No.6, pp.797-811.

Dhillion, K. (1993) *The Asian Man in Britain*, Bolton Institute of Higher Education.

Dwek, R. (1997) Loosing the Race, *Marketing Business*, March, pp.10-15.

Engel, J, Blackwell, R. and Kollat, D. (1978) *Consumer Behaviour*. Ill. Dryden Press.

Fennel, G., Saegart, J., Piron, F. and Jimenz, R. (1992) Do Hispanics Constitute a Market Segment?, *Advances in Consumer Research*, Vol.19, pp.28-33.

Goldberg, D. (1994) *Multiculturalism: A Critical Reader*. Oxford: Blackwell.

Gutman, A. (1993) The Challenge of Multiculturalism in Political Ethics, *Philosophy and Public Affairs*, Vol.23, No.3, pp.171-206.

Hall, E. (1960) The Silent Language in Overseas Business, *Harvard Business Review*, May-June.

Higgins, T. (1995) Multicultural Marketing is Opening New Doors, *Milwaukee Business Journal*, Vol.13, pp.11-25.

Hirschman, E. (1981) American Jewish Ethnicity: Its Relationship to Some Selected Aspects of Consumer Behaviour. *Journal of Marketing*, Vol.45, pp. 102-110.

Hoek, J., Gendall, P. and Asslemont, D. (1993) Market Segmentation: A Search For the Holy Grail?, *Asia-Australia Marketing Journal*, Vol.1, No.1, pp.41-46.

Humby, C. (1991) New Developments in Demographic Targeting, *Journal of Marketing Research Society*, Vol.31, No.1, pp.53-74.

Hunt, S. (1994) On Rethinking Marketing: Our Discipline, Our Practice, Our Method, European *Journal of Marketing*, Vol.28, No.3, pp.13-25.

Jain, R. and Costa, J. (1991) Research Progress Report: Fragrance Use in India. In Costa, J. (ed.), *Gender and Consumer Behaviour*, Vol.1, pp.77-84. Salt Lake City, University of Utah.

Jones, T. (1993) *Britain Ethnic Minorities*, Policy Studies Institute, Dorset.

Joy, A. and Dholakia, R. (1991) Remembrances of Things Past: The Meaning of Home and Possessions of Indian Professionals in Canada, *Journal of Social Behaviour and Personality*, Vol.6, No.6, pp.385-402.

Lee, K. (1996) Understanding Organisational Culture and Management Styles in the Peoples Republic of China, in Nwankwo, S. (ed.), *Strategic Planning and Development: Developing Economies in Perspective*. Sheffield; Pavic Publications.

Lieblich, J. (1988) If You Want a Big Market, *Fortune*, November.

Lindridge, A. (1993) Marketing to Ethnic Minorities in Britain. Unpublished Business Studies Degree Project, Sheffield Business School.

Meacham, J. (1996) Interdisciplinary and Teaching Perspectives on Multiculturalism and Diversity, *American Behavioral Scientist*, Vol.40, No.2, pp.112-122.

Mead, G. (1993) More Than Just A B C, *Times*, June 24.

Mehta, R. and Belk, R. (1991) Artefacts, Identity, and Transition: Favourite Possessions of Indians and Indian Immigrants to the United States, *Journal of Consumer Research*, Vol.17, pp.398-411.

Mitchell. V. (1995) Using Astrology in Market Segmentation, *Management Decision*, Vol.33, No.1, pp.48-57.

Nemetz, P. and Christensen, S. (1997) The Challenge of Cultural Diversity: Harnessing a Diversity of Views to Understand Multiculturalism, *Academy of Management Review*, Vol.21, No.2, pp.434-462.

Nwankwo, S. (1996) Marketing in Diversity: Ethnography of Two Cultures. *Proceedings of the Multicultural Marketing Conference*, Choudhury, P., ed., pp.359-364.

Nwankwo, S., Aiyeku, J. and Ogbuehi, A. (1997) The Marketing Challenge of Multiculturalism: An Exploratory Study. *Proceeding of the Academy of Marketing Science 8th Bi-Annual World Marketing Congress*, Kuala Lumpur, Malaysia, pp.20-25.

O'Guinn, T. and Meyer, T. (1984) Segmenting the Hispanic Market: The Use of Spanish Language Radio, *Journal of Advertising Research*, Vol.23, No.6, pp.9-15.

Pereira, A. (1996) Consumer Attitudes Towards Advertising: Does Culture Matter? *Proceedings of the Multicultural Marketing Conference*, Choudhury, P.K., ed., Virginia, pp.107-109.

Phinney, J. (1996a) Understanding Ethnic Diversity, *American Behavioural Scientist*, Vol.40, No.2, pp.143-152.

Phinney, J. (1996b) When We Talk About Ethnic Groups, What Do we mean? *American Psychologist*, Vol.51, pp.918-927.

Pine, B., Peppers, D. & Rogers, M. (1995) Do You Want to Keep Your Customers Forever? *Harvard Business Review*, March-April, pp.103-114.

Rabin, S. (1994) How to Sell Across Cultures, *American Demographics*, Vol.16, p.56.

Robinson, G. and Dechant, K. (1997) Building a Business Case for Diversity, *Academy of Management Executive*, Vol.11, No.3, pp.21-31.

Rossman, M. (1994) *Multicultural Marketing: Selling to a Diverse America*. New York. AMACOM.

Segal, M. and Sosa, L. (1983) Marketing to Hispanic Community, *California Management Review*, Vol.26, No.1, pp.120-134.

Stamps, M. and Arnould, E. (1996) The Impact of Ethnicity on Values: An Exploratory Study of Blacks, Whites and Hispanics Using the List of Values. *Proceedings of the Multicultural Marketing Conference*, op. cit., pp.221-226.

Stevenson, T. (1991) 'How are Blacks Portrayed in Business Ads?, *Industrial Marketing Management*, Vol.20, pp.193-199.

Swenson, C. (1990) Minority Groups Emerge as a Major Marketing Wedge, *Management Review*, May, pp.24-26.

Thomas, M. (1994) Marketing - in Chaos or Transition? *European Journal of Marketing*, Vol.28, N.3, pp.55-62.

Venkatesh, A. (1995) Ethnoconsumerism: A New Paradigm to Study Cultural and Cross-Cultural Consumer Behaviour, in Costa, J. and Bamossy, G. eds., *Marketing in a Multicultural World*. London, Sage Publications.

Watson, M. (1992) Researching Minorities, *Journal of the Market Research Society*, Vol.3, No.4, pp.337-344.

Wells, W., Burnnet, J. and Moriaty, S. (1989) *Advertising Principles and Practice*, Butterworth Heinemann, 2nd edition.

West, A. and Bahtka, R. (1996) *Ethnic Diversity Within the African American Market*. Paper presented at the Academy of Marketing Science Multicultural Marketing Conference, Virginia Beach, USA.

Wilson, C. and Gutierrez, F. (1995) *Race, Multiculturalism, and the Media*. London, Sage Publications.

Wright, M. (1996) The Dubious Assumptions of Segmentation and Targeting, *Management Decision*, Vol.34, No.1, pp.18-24.

Yau, O. (1988) Chinese Cultural Values: Their Dimensions and Marketing Implications, *European Journal of Marketing*, Vol.22, No.5, pp.44-57.

Chapter 15

Tapping the Multicultural Market in Australia

Alvin M. Chan

Introduction

It is not difficult to recognize the cultural diversity of the Australian population: it is reflected in the faces of people in the street. The following figures from the 2001 Census give a broad indication of the multicultural composition of the Australian population:

- 40% of Australia's 19 million population were either born overseas or have at least one parent born overseas; and
- 15% speak a language other than English at home.

The Australian Bureau of Statistics (ABS), in consultation with users and producers of cultural diversity data, has developed the Standards for Statistics on Cultural and Language Diversity (SSCLD) and the Australian Standard Classification of Cultural and Ethnic Groups (ASCCEG) for use in the collection, storage and dissemination of all Australian statistical and administrative data relating to cultural and language background, ethnic identity, ancestry, and cultural identity of the Australian population (Skinner and Hunter 1997; ABS 1999, 2000). Although a number of terms like ancestry, ethnic identity, and cultural diversity have elements of differences, *ethnicity* is considered to be the fundamental concept underpinning these terms (ABS 2000).

The Australian Bureau of Statistics' ASCCEG document defines ethnicity as the shared identity or similarity of a group of people on the basis of one or more of the following characteristics:

- a long shared history, the memory of which is kept alive;
- a cultural tradition, including family and social customs, sometimes religiously based;
- a common geographic origin;
- a common language (but not necessarily limited to that group);
- a common literature (written or oral);
- a common religion;

- being a minority (often with a sense of being oppressed); and
- being racially conspicuous.

These conceptual components of ethnicity are measured operationally by collecting data on the 'Minimum Core Set' and the 'Standard Set' of variables endorsed by the Council of Ministers of Immigration and Multicultural Affairs (CMIMA) in April 1999 to implement the Standards for Statistics on Cultural and Language Diversity (see Department of Immigration and Multicultural Affairs (DIMA) 2001).

The 'Minimum Core Set' consists of four variables:

- Country of Birth of Person;
- Main Language Other Than English Spoken at Home;
- Proficiency in Spoken English; and
- Indigenous Status (of those born in Australia).

The 'Standard Set' includes the 'Minimum Core Set' plus the following variables:

- Ancestry;
- Country of Birth of Father;
- Country of Birth of Mother;
- First Language Spoken;
- Languages Spoken at Home;
- Main Language Spoken at Home;
- Religious Affiliation; and
- Year of Arrival in Australia.

CMIMA recommended that the 'Minimum Core Set' of variables be implemented in all Commonwealth, State and Territory statistical and administrative surveys that require information on cultural and language diversity; and that additional variables from the 'Standard Set' be added to the 'Minimum Core Set' where a wider range of information is required (DIMA 2001).

While there is no best single measure of ethnicity, language spoken at home is probably the best surrogate measure. Migrants speaking their mother tongues at home would be more likely to maintain their original cultural values and habits. The second generation Australian-born who speak English only at home would have access to mainstream information and would be less likely to have the same consumption patterns as their parents who maintain their ethnic languages at home. In the 1986 Census, a question on 'ancestry' was first asked, and the number of persons answering 'Chinese' as their ancestry was closely related to the number of people whose main language spoken at home was Chinese (Cantonese, Mandarin, and other Chinese languages). This supports the notion of using main language spoken at home as a surrogate measure of ethnicity (Migliorino and Chan 1993).

The five most common languages spoken at home other than English in the 2001 Census were:

- Chinese (Cantonese, Mandarin and other Chinese languages): 401,357 (2.1%);
- Italian: 352,605 (1.9%);
- Greek: 263,717 (1.4%);
- Arabic (including Lebanese): 209,372 (1.1%); and
- Vietnamese: 174,236 (0.9%).

The marketing implications of the increased ethnic population in Australia are:

- being newcomers to Australia, many ethnic families have obvious needs for 'settlement' products and services such as accommodation, transportation, banking, and telecommunication;
- there are opportunities for ethnic-specific marketing strategies for promoting mainstream products and services; and
- there also exists potential for designing ethnic-specific products and services and associated promotional activities.

The distinct characteristics of the diverse ethnic groups in Australia pose real challenges for multicultural marketers trying to reach these markets. Many companies have chosen to ignore the apparent potential and the diverse ethnic markets in Australia are at present largely untapped.

The Development of Multicultural Marketing in Australia

The first to practice multicultural marketing in Australia have been government agencies utilizing various ethnic media to advertise and provide information in ethnic languages. For example, the Department of Immigration and Multicultural and Indigenous Affairs (formerly DIMA) disseminates settlement information to new migrants; the Australian Taxation Office publicizes the obligation to lodge a tax return; and the Roads and Traffic Authority educates ethnic groups on various road safety issues.

The primary driving force behind government's multicultural marketing campaigns is to ensure that everyone in the community has equal access to government services. There is a government policy that 7.5% of all its print media budgets be allocated to ethnic press. Although there is no similar directive for electronic media, a substantial amount of government promotional funds are allocated to community education and public information through ethnic television and radio channels.

The Community Relations Commission For a Multicultural NSW (formerly Ethnic Affairs Commission of New South Wales) has been among the pioneers in developing the concept of multicultural marketing in Australia by launching the first National Multicultural Marketing Awards in 1990. In his speech to the first multicultural marketing seminar organized by the Ethnic Affairs Commission, Mr. Nick Greiner, the then Premier of New South Wales, told participants that 'the motivation behind Multicultural Marketing is not social justice, not equity, not even a fair go; it's simply the economic wellbeing of both the people of non-English-speaking background and the community as a whole.'

At the federal level, the former Office of Multicultural Affairs (OMA) in the Department of the Prime Minister and Cabinet provided advice on Australia's multicultural issues. *Australia's Cultural Diversity: Good for Business*, published by the Office of Multicultural Affairs, collected 10 case studies illustrating how companies can use Australia's multicultural resources to improve access to export markets, target niche markets in Australia, and increase productivity. The publication is designed 'to be of immediate practical benefit. Improving the bottom line for many companies may be a matter of understanding how other enterprises have used linguistic and cultural skills, and exploring the multicultural resources right on their own doorstep' (OMA 1994).

Despite the push by the government to advance the concept of multicultural marketing, it was not until the mid-1990s that an increasing number of organizations from the private sector started to see the potential that the diverse ethnic communities possess.

The first multicultural marketing conference by the private sector was held in July 1994 (Caldwell Management 1994) and generated considerable interest from the private sector. Various business publications ran special sections on multicultural marketing, interviewing experts and pioneer companies in this field (*The Australian* 16 June 1994; *The Bulletin* 23 August 1994; *Ad News* 23 September 1994; *Australian Professional Marketing* November 1994; *The Sydney Morning Herald* 8 December 1994).

While there are signs of increasing multicultural marketing practices in Australia, we must admit that the development is still in the very early stage. The concepts are often unclear and the methods used are immature. Since 1994, multicultural marketing is only occasionally featured in business publications in Australia (e.g., *Australian Business Monthly* May 1995; *Business Review Weekly* 6 November 1995; *Ad News* 11 August 1995, 17 August 2001; *Professional Marketing* March 2001, September/October 2003).

The main reasons for the slow development of multicultural marketing in Australia are:

- perceiving difficulty in understanding other cultures. This is largely due to lack of confidence in dealing with an unfamiliar culture;
- remaining complacent with the mainstream market and not seeing a need to target the ethnic markets separately. Some simply assume that the ethnic communities will have access to the mainstream media; and
- being afraid that the targeting of ethnic markets will upset the mainstream market and the 'gains' may not be able to compensate for the 'losses.'

Given the fact that a few innovative companies are realizing the potential of the ethnic markets, it is unlikely that other companies can afford to ignore the ethnic markets and stay behind their competitors. For most companies, the problem is knowing where to start and how to follow through.

Some Successful Multicultural Marketing Cases

Although multicultural marketing in Australia is rather new, there are already some successful cases. Among the better known ones are the marketing programs of Telstra Australia (formerly Telecom Australia), Optus Communications, New South Wales Lotteries, Westpac Banking Corporation, Singapore Airlines, Hotel Nikko Sydney, Casino Canberra, Star City Casino, McDonald's and L. J. Hooker real estate agency. Following are highlights of some of these successful cases.

Telecommunication

Telstra and Optus are among Australia's biggest advertisers, and although there is no figure on the percentage they allocated to ethnic media, the fact that the Chinese community alone can afford to have three daily newspapers to some extent reflects the huge advertising dollars spent by the two telephone companies in ethnic media. Optus entered the international long distance competition in 1992 and advertised heavily in ethnic press, particularly the Chinese press. New immigrants are heavy users of long distance calls, for many still have connections and things to settle in their countries of origin. Optus' research found that two-thirds of people born overseas made an international call at least once a month. It was not until 6 months later that Telstra responded and started to target the ethnic market. Today, Telstra's promotional dollars in the ethnic media outweigh those of Optus.

Gaming and Gambling

The New South Wales Lotteries introduced the Lucky Monkey Scratchies in 1992 to celebrate the Asian Lunar New Year of the Monkey. Advertisements were run in ethnic Chinese and Vietnamese media; small red packets were provided with the intention that people would use them to give out Scratchies tickets as gifts. The promotion was so successful that sales increased by A$150,000 to 200,000 each week during the 12 weeks the Lucky Monkey game was run. For this, the New South Wales Lotteries won the 1992 National Multicultural Marketing Award offered by the Ethnic Affairs Commission. The New South Wales Lotteries continued to introduce one new zodiac animal Scratchies product each year. By 2004, they have already covered all the 12 zodiac animals in the Lunar calendar and started again with the Monkey. They also held design competition each year to select the best design for the Lunar New Year zodiac animal Scratchies. The Lunar New Year Scratchies have become general games not only played by the Asian communities during Lunar New Year but are also played by other cultural groups and the mainstream population as well.

Casino Canberra used an ethnic Chinese advertising agency to run ads in Chinese and Vietnamese newspapers. It is reported that 35 % of the casino's punters are Asians. The Star City Casino in Sydney even repainted their free shuttle buses from black to yellow because research showed that many Asian punters perceived black as an inauspicious color.

Property

From analysis of Census data and feedback from franchisees, L. J. Hooker realized that new migrants were more likely to buy real estate than people born in Australia. They launched an ad campaign in March 1994 targeting the Chinese, Italian, Vietnamese, Greek, Spanish, and Arabic communities. Brand awareness was reported to have increased and franchisees indicated the ethnic markets were responding. L.J. Hooker continues to enjoy a favorable image among new migrants.

Banking

The Westpac Banking Corporation is Australia's first and oldest bank. In 1996, Westpac's own research indicated that the New South Wales Asian market had a market size of A$10 billion personal lending and A$4 billion personal investment. A multicultural marketing strategy was therefore developed to boost Westpac's overall market share. Strategic market locations with high migrant populations were identified around Sydney including Ashfield, Hurstville, Bankstown, Eastwood, Chatswood, Chinatown and Maroubra. To target the multicultural consumer, Westpac adapted its product offerings including more flexible credit assessment criteria (e.g., overseas income). Culturally relevant advertisements were developed and placed in ethnic media to create awareness and customer affinity. After 12 months, Westpac reported the first market share increase.

In 2000, Westpac launched the '2000 Year of the Dragon Campaign' to capitalize on three major events in 2000: (1) The Year of the Golden Dragon; (2) A new millennium; and (3) The Sydney 2000 Olympic Games, of which Westpac was a major sponsor. The campaign was launched by the Managing Director at the Sydney Chinatown branch, which attracted extensive coverage in the ethnic media. The objective of the campaign was to help customers identify with Westpac as the preferred partner in the celebrations. The campaign was supported by competitions for 24 customers to see the 2000 Sydney Olympic Games. There was also a special gift bank cheque to commemorate the three events. Total sales of the campaign in the ethnic market amounted to A$222 million which was 141% above target and was 11% of the A$2 billion sales in similar mainstream campaigns.

Supermarket

Coles is one of Australia's largest supermarket chains with over 460 stores nationwide and stocks a large number of ethnic foods in selected stores with high percentage of ethnic population. As part of its 'Save Every Day' campaign, Coles launched a television campaign in 2003 to showcase its culturally diverse range of products. The campaign did not just target ethnic consumers; it was also intended to engage the broader community, recognizing that more and more Australians are trying a broader range of foods. Research found the campaign to have above average audience recognition and have boosted Coles' positioning and a sharp increase in customers following the campaign.

Misconceptions about Multicultural Marketing

An analysis of these successful cases reveals one commonality among them: the successes are not just due to a good understanding of the ethnic markets, but also are the result of thorough research and planning. A common mistake by many marketers about to enter ethnic markets is that they place undue emphasis on the cultural dimension of multicultural marketing, ignoring the fact that the need for good market research and marketing planning is of equal importance.

The Telecom ad used as the headline a famous quote from an ancient poem: 'Twice as homesick during special festivals.' This quote is so famous that it has already become a generic term in Chinese. This was also the first sentence of the Optus ad copy. The use of this quote was perfectly okay in its own right in conjunction with the Moon Festival. However, the Telecom ad inappropriately mentioned its original source and used a Chinese painting of mountains with the poem at the top left-hand corner as the background. The title of the poem was 'On the Double Nine Day, Thinking of my Brothers in Shan-tung.' On the Double Nine Day (the ninth day of the ninth month of the Lunar calendar), people used to go picnicking in the mountains to escape from the bad influences. While the Moon Festival is full of joy and happiness, the Double Nine Day has an undertone of anguish and is now the second tomb-sweeping day in the year beside the Ching Ming Festival. In contrast to the Telecom ad, the Optus ad using 'Heng-O flying to the Moon,' a story associated with the Moon Festival, as the visual was much better in communicating a joyful message.

Nevertheless, the negative impact of this cultural misunderstanding by Telecom was to a great extent offset by its other marketing activities -- for instance, offering not only a higher discount rate to selected South East Asian countries but also covering the whole week instead of just the Moon Festival day. There were also media releases by Telecom to the Chinese press plus the mailing of a bilingual postcard to selected Chinese customers announcing the promotional activity. Telecom was able to maintain many of its loyal Chinese customers who had signed up to various Flexi-plans and were entitled to a further 10% discount.

The New South Wales Lotteries' Luck Monkey Scratchies campaign also illustrates the fact that despite the different cultural perceptions about giving out the Scratchies as a gift, with good marketing planning, even if you commit some errors on the cultural aspects, you still would not be too wrong. But the reverse will not work.

Related to the undue emphasis on the cultural dimension because of its apparent unfamiliarity and difficulty, most marketers tend to rely on ethnic personnel or outside ethnic consultants to handle their marketing to different ethnic groups. The underlying myth is that people from their own communities should have the best knowledge of their own cultures. However, a simple fact is sufficient to refute this fallacy: almost all the population in Hong Kong are Chinese, but why are not all Chinese organizations in Hong Kong successful? Most of the cultural influences on consumer behavior are at a subconscious level. To understand one's own culture requires in-depth studies and a sense of cultural empathy.

The major strategy used by most organizations when targeting ethnic markets is to employ ethnic-language-speaking staff to help serve the community group. Too much emphasis is placed on the language needs of the community without really understanding the real needs of the community. What the organization requires is someone who 'really speaks their (the community's) language,' meaning someone who really *understands* their needs and wants.

The basis of multicultural marketing is still *marketing*; it is only marketing in different cultural contexts. Marketers should not deny their responsibility for good marketing planning by reducing the whole issue to the cultural dimension only. The ideal solution is to hire market researchers with both bilingual skills *and* a marketing background. The multicultural composition of the Australian population does not only represent niche ethnic markets for selected goods and services; these can also be testing and learning ground for other international markets. Australian-based companies can also draw on the multicultural resources in Australia to help them better understand and serve the multicultural domestic and international marketplace (Wilkinson and Cheng 1999).

Researching Ethnic Markets

Secondary Research

Like any planning process, a good start to the multicultural marketing process is an analysis of the available secondary data: Census demographic figures, and company and industry information by ethnicity where available.

For example, as the largest migrant group in Australia, the Chinese community has been targeted by some Australian businesses because of its perceived affluence. However, the Chinese in Australia are not a homogeneous group. They differ across a broad range of characteristics, including distribution in the community, languages or dialects spoken, English proficiency, and affluence (Migliorino and Chan 1993).

Although the Chinese community constitutes only 3.2% of the 6.4 million New South Wales population in the 2001 Census, over half of them are concentrated in the top 10 Local Government Areas. In areas like Ashfield, Burwood, Auburn and Strathfield, one in every four persons is Chinese. Willoughby in New South Wales has the highest percentage of Chinese migrants, particularly Cantonese-speaking migrants from Hong Kong, whereas one in every three persons in Willoughby is Chinese. This is one of the reasons why the Willoughby Council received the largest number of applications from property owners to change their street number from 4 to 3A, because many prospective Chinese and Asian buyers simply would not even come to the open inspection as the number 4 is associated with 'death' in Chinese and in other Asian languages like Japanese and Korean. This is in addition to the continuous requests to change street number 13 to 12A to please some Anglo-Australian property buyers. In fact, many Asian countries now do not have level 13 in some buildings like hotels that have a large number of foreign visitors. The Japanese also do not like the number 13 so there are no row numbers 4 and 13 on all All Nippon Airways flights.

Apart from the Chinese, many migrant groups also have tendencies to live in concentrated areas. For example, 31.4% of the population in Bankstown speak Arabic (including Lebanese); 21.8% of the population in Fairfield speak Vietnamese; 18.2% of the population in Ashfield speak Italian; 17.6% and 11.4% of the population in Rockdale speak Greek and Macedonian respectively; and 12.0% of the population in Strathfield speak Korean. These were 2001 Census figures; today the percentages would probably be even higher.

The uneven geographic dispersion of different ethnic groups has great implications for marketers in terms of distribution and other marketing strategies. For example, McDonald's and KFC in Bankstown and nearby Punchbowl, which have very high Arabic-speaking Muslim populations, now offer *halal* (a Quaranic term meaning 'allowed' or 'lawful' as permitted by Allah) foods accredited by the Islamic Council of New South Wales (halal foods are prepared in the traditional Muslim method recommended by the Quaran). Halal foods produced in Australia are now exported to other Muslim countries like Turkey, Indonesia, Malaysia and countries in the Persian Gulf. Tony Favotto, Manager of McDonald's at Punchbowl, claimed that overall sales increased by 15% since introducing the halal foods in 2002.

The relative educational level and English proficiency of different groups also have implications for the selection of appropriate media to reach them. For example, of the top five ethnic populations who speak a language other then English at home, the percentages speaking English either 'not well' or 'not at all' are: Chinese 27.1%, Italian 15.6%, Greek 17.3%, Arabic (including Lebanese) 15.9%, and Vietnamese 37.9%. The Vietnamese and Chinese therefore presumably rely more on ethnic media as their information sources. English proficiency to a certain extent is a reflection of length of residence in Australia. The Italian and Greek populations predominately migrated to Australia in the 1950's after World War II and therefore have a longer period of assimilation and are more proficient in English, whereas the Vietnamese and the Chinese are more recent migrants who came to Australia in the mid-1970's and late-1980's respectively and are less proficient in English. The first generation Italian and Greek migrants probably have already brought their families here and would have less demand for long distance telecommunication services to their home countries. The more recent Vietnamese and Chinese migrants are more likely to have families and relatives living in their home countries and are more viable targets for long distance calls.

Whereas analysis of demographic data will help to identify the potential of various ethnic groups, analysis of the existing client base may also give a useful indication. For example, telephone companies can track their residential-line traffic to different countries as an approximate estimate of the relative usage by different migrant groups. Banks can analyse their customer base to identify new migrants who are 'high net worth individuals' with the highest potential for mortgage loans or other investment products.

It is quite interesting that in spite of the growing importance of ethnic communities, most companies still do not keep any ethnicity-related data on their clients, particularly languages spoken, place of birth, and length of residence in Australia.

Even without accurate figures, anecdotal or observational information may also give some indications. Visit the Fish Market in Sydney and you will be surprised by the large number of Chinese and Japanese. Visit the Flemington Market in Sydney and you will be surprised by the large number of Vietnamese, Lebanese and Chinese.

Visit Chinatown in Sydney, Melbourne, or Brisbane and you will be impressed by the number of Chinese driving imported cars like BMW, Volvo, and Honda. Among locally assembled cars, the only popular make is Toyota. However, little known was the fact that in the past many Chinese would only buy Toyota manufactured in Japan. It was not until Toyota ran a multicultural marketing campaign to coincide with the opening of its new Altona plant in Melbourne in 1994 that they managed to change the attitudes of the Chinese migrants in buying locally assembled Toyota cars. Toyota's campaign involved flying editors and reporters of the major ethnic press to Melbourne to tour the new plant and provided them with bilingual editorial materials and photos for reporting. Many ethnic newspapers ran either full-page or double-spread feature articles on Toyota's new state-of-the-art manufacturing facilities in Melbourne. What does this mean to the two other best-selling cars manufacturers, Ford and Holden? Are they complacent about their total sales figures and happy to leave the ethnic Chinese market to buy cars from their competitors?

Primary Research

In conducting primary research on the behaviors of ethnic groups, there is no reason why the usual market research methods cannot be used. However, there are some important points that need to be observed.

For example, it is not unusual to hear a consultant recommending to the client that qualitative focus groups do not work in the ethnic community – because ethnic respondents will just tell you what you want to hear. However, the fact may be that the consultant is using an Anglo moderator and the focus group is conducted in English because the client observing the interview can only understand English. When the moderator leaves the room for a while, people often start to whisper in their own language! Of course, the client observing cannot understand what they are talking about. Remember that the textbook tells us that the benefits of a focus group are the spontaneous responses from the members and the interactions among them. Special attention should also be placed on multicultural issues like gender, communication, group dynamics, values, etc. when conducting qualitative research in different cultural contexts (see Nevid and Sta. Maria 1999).

The importance of using bilingual ethnic researchers also extends to survey interviews. No matter whether it is a face-to-face or telephone interview, ethnic interviewers who are able to conduct interviews in the community languages will elicit the highest response rate. Given the fact that ethnic communities are still in the minority, in order to increase the hit rate in a sampling plan, 'Australia on Disc' (direct marketing databases on CD-ROMs) software can be utilized to help identify prospective respondents. Most of these databases are based on the White Pages listing or voting registers cross-referenced with Census profiles. They may be useful in first identifying areas with the highest population or proportion of a particular ethnic group. By referring to the surnames, members of a particular ethnic group can be identified and a random sample be drawn; they can then be approached by phone or by personal interviewing. Or, alternatively the areas can be first clustered into street blocks and a random sample drawn from selected clusters only. Although this method may miss some females married to males of other ethnic groups and no longer using their maiden names, it does help to increase the chance of capturing the target ethnic respondents in a survey.

Unfortunately, criminals are among the smartest sample-drawers in ethnic market research. Police once arrested a thief in the Sydney Hills area, which housed a large number of wealthy Hong Kong and Taiwanese business migrants. In the thief's pocket, police found a telephone list from the White Pages with popular Chinese surnames like Chan and Wong.

Survey Design

Whereas the need to have the interview conducted in the appropriate ethnic language is obvious, the need to have the whole questionnaire translated into ethnic language is usually not necessary. Unless it is a self-administered questionnaire, to have only the questions translated is sufficient. It is quite frustrating, for example, when you have a questionnaire translated into Arabic, to discover that the layout goes from the right to the left. It causes inconvenience for data entry and creates more problems than it solves. The value of recruiting bilingual interviewers is that they can ask questions in ethnic languages but record the answers in English, saving the trouble of back-translation.

Beginning in 1995, AGB McNair introduced a new question into their mainstream radio surveys, asking 'What language other than English is most spoken in the home?' However, in his letter to the editor of *B & T Weekly*, Hubber (1995) pointed out that surveys in English were not a very good way to prove that people from a non-English background (NESB) listen to commercial radio; there are more than 60 community stations in every capital city and regional areas. Chan (1995) also pointed out that while he was happy to see that ethnic communities were not viewed in isolation and were now included in many mainstream surveys, from a statistical point of view, ethnic markets do deserve separate treatments.

Given the fact that ethnic communities are still in the minority, in order to increase the hit rate and to reduce the estimation error, adjustments in the sample design and the sample size are needed. If there is interest in selected ethnic groups, separate research into those communities is needed. It is unlikely that a mainstream survey can provide answers to ethnic-specific marketing questions.

Reaching Ethnic Markets

After identifying the targets by proper research and planning, the next question is how to reach them in terms of what to say, how to say it (creativity strategy) and where to say it (media strategy). Two good reference guides are:

- The Ethnic Communities' Council of New South Wales (1994), *Pathways to Ethnic Communities: Communicating with People of Non-English Speaking Background*, 1994; and
- Condie, Corrine (1997), *Multicultural Marketing*, Bilingual Consultants Network, Department of Immigration and Multicultural Affairs, AGPS.

These two publications provide guidelines for developing culturally appropriate messages; it also contains comprehensive information on the ethnic media in Australia.

Highlighted here is the most common mistake by multicultural marketers: having their advertising messages written in English first and then translated into ethnic languages. The best approach is to have the advertising concept and copy developed in ethnic languages and back-translated into English for management's approval.

If a message is to be carried in different languages, it is particularly important to stick to the KISS (Keep It Simple, Stupid!) principle. Use more non-verbal communication by emphasizing the visual. Avoid puns, for which most copywriters tend to have a preference. Since a word may have other connotative meanings in English, it may not be able to carry the same connotative meaning when translated into another language. The speeding ad by the Roads and Traffic Authority in English and in other ethnic languages like Chinese and Vietnamese was a good example of the correct procedure. The RTA ad uses a simple picture showing a car crashed into a pole and one simple headline; everyone seeing the ad will come up with the same English back-translation of the headline: How fast are you going?

It is sometimes difficult to understand why, in ad copy translation, advertisers tend to have faith in using translators accredited by the National Authority for the Accreditation of Translators and Interpreters (NAATI). Experience tells us that the use of NAATI-accredited persons in translating ad copy is no more effective than using someone in the ethnic community with a marketing or journalism background. The rationale is very simple: a translator is a translator, and lacks the background knowledge and aptitude required of an advertising copywriter.

As regards the ethnic media, the major difficulty for marketers is that there is no reliable audited circulation or audience figures. Furthermore, apart from the numbers, different media may have very different readership or audience profiles.

For example, while the *Sing Tao Daily* has a high percentage of Chinese readers from Hong Kong, the *Australian Chinese Daily* and the *Daily Chinese Herald* have high percentages of Chinese readers from Mainland China and Taiwan respectively. This requires marketers to do more media research by talking to news agencies and people in the community to get an idea of the relative effectiveness of different papers in the community.

Conclusions

Drawing on his seven years of experience as a judge for the National Multicultural Marketing Awards since 1991, Professor Ian Wilkinson has the following conclusions on the developments in multicultural marketing in Australia in the past decade (Wilkinson and Cheng 1999):

- A shift away from simple adaptation of advertising messages as the mainstay of multicultural marketing strategies.
- A shift from simple, even simplistic, representation of some ethnic communities in marketing campaigns to a more sophisticated understanding of the rich cultural diversity that exists among and within ethnic groups.
- A shift from monoculturally focused marketing strategies to multiculturally focused strategies that engage a larger slice of society.
- A move away from multicultural marketing as a marginal add-on in a campaign or strategy to campaigns in which it is either automatically considered or built directly into the fabric of the overall campaign.
- An increasing appreciation of the benefits that come from harnessing multicultural resources for both domestic and international business development.
- A shift from recognizing and adapting to diversity to valuing, appreciating, celebrating, and offering the fruits of this diversity.

As a member of the judging panel for the 2000 National Multicultural Marketing Awards, I agree with Professor Wilkinson's observations. However, it must be pointed out that these 'conclusions' are mainly reflective of the submissions for the National Multicultural Marketing Awards in the past decade; they do not represent the general trends in multicultural marketing in Australia; these 'conclusions' should best be viewed as objectives that Australian companies should incorporate in their marketing campaigns.

There is no doubt that multicultural marketing is growing in Australia. An increasing number of marketers, initially from the public sector and recently from the private sector, are recognizing the market potential that our diverse ethnic groups possess. However, there is still much room for improvement. The current state of development in multicultural marketing in Australia is best summarized in the following comments by Joseph Assaf, founder and CEO of Ethnic

Communications, who established the first ethnic advertising agency in Australia in 1977:

> ...70% of Cognac's consumption is by the Asian market, and yet all its advertising is in mainstream media. One in five people speaks a language other than English at home, yet more than 90% of ads are designed to reach Anglo-Saxons (*Ad News* 2001, p.18).

In marketing to ethnic communities, a common mistake by marketers is to put too much emphasis on the cultural aspect, because of its apparent unfamiliarity and difficulty, while forgetting the equal importance of good market research and marketing planning. Whereas the usual marketing activities are applicable when targeting ethnic markets, their applications need some adaptations in the different cultural environments. This is particularly true in the areas of market research and advertising.

With the emergence and publicizing of more successful cases of multicultural marketing, it is envisaged that marketers will gradually gain experience and confidence in pursuing this alternative to mainstream marketing. Marketing to the diverse cultural groups in Australia is a challenge with potentially large rewards for both marketers and the market. It is unlikely that the ethnic markets will remain untapped in the future. In the long run, multicultural marketing should be an integral part of any marketing campaign run by a company.

References

Ad News (1994), 'Special Report on Multicultural Marketing,' 23 September 1994, 20-22, 31, 33.

Ad News (1995), 'Special Topic on Multicultural Marketing,' 11 August 1995, 20-21.

Ad News (2001), 'You Really Should Visit the Large Ethnic Market,' 17 August 2001, 18.

Australian Bureau of Statistics (1999), *Standards for Statistics on Cultural and Language Diversity*, ABS Catalogue No. 1289.0.

Australian Bureau of Statistics (2000), *Australian Standard Classification of Cultural and Ethnic Groups*, ABS Catalogue No. 1249.0.

Australian Business Monthly (1995), 'Ethnic Diversity: Our Strongest Sales Suit,' May 1995, 15 (7), 64-69.

Australian Professional Marketing (1994), 'Cover Story on Ethnic Marketing:Sales in Anyone's Language,' November 1994, 10-14.

Business Review Weekly (1995), 'The Marketers' Missing Millions,' 6 November 1995, 50-54.

Caldwell Management Pty. Ltd. (1994), *Proceedings of the Multicultural Marketing Conference*, 19-20 July 1994, Australian National Maritime Museum, Sydney.

Chan, Alvin (1994), 'Caution with Ethnic Ads,' *Ad News*, 7 October 1994, 12.

Chan, Alvin (1995), 'Letter to the Editor-Ethnic Radio,' *B & T Weekly*, May 26 1995, 9.

Condie, Corrine (1997), *Multicultural Marketing*, Bilingual Consultants Network, Department of Immigration and Multicultural Affairs, AGPS.

Department of Immigration and Multicultural Affairs (2001), *The Guide: Implementing the Standards for Statistics on Cultural and Language Diversity*, The Commonwealth Interdepartmental Committee on Multicultural Affairs, DIMA.

Hubber, Lee (1995), 'Letter to the Editor-Undercatering?' *B & T Weekly*, 28 April 1995, 7.

Migliorino, Pino and Alvin Chan (1993), 'The Australian Chinese Community in New South Wales,' *Access China*, No. 12, December 1993, 18-22,

Nevid, Jeffrey S. and Nelly L. Sta. Maris (1991), 'Multicultural Issues in Qualitative Research,' *Psychology & Marketing*, 16 (4), 305-325.

Office of Multicultural Affairs (1994), *Australia's Cultural Diversity: Good for Business*, Department of the Prime Minister and Cabinet.

Professional Marketing (2001), 'Special Topic on Multicultural Marketing,' March 2001, 10-14.

Professional Marketing (2003), 'Special Topic on Ethnic Marketing,' September/October 2003, 12-14.

Skinner, T.J. and D. Hunter (1997), 'Developing Suitable Designators for a Multicultural Society,' *Statistical Journal of the UN Economic Commission for Europe*, 14 (3), 217-228.

The Australian (1994), 'A Special Report on Multicultural Marketing,' 16 June 1994, 16-18.

The Bulletin (1994), 'The Ethnic Paperchase,' 23 August 1994, 67-69.

The Ethnic Communities' Council of New South Wales (1994), *Pathways to Ethnic Communities: Communicating with People of Non-English Speaking Background*, 1994.

The Sydney Morning Herald (1994), 'Cultural Revelation,' 8 December 1994, 15.

Wilkinson, Ian F. and Constant Cheng (1999), 'Multicultural Marketing in Australia: Synergy in Diversity,' *Journal of International Marketing*, 7 (3), 106-125.

Chapter 16

Facets, Dimensions and Gaps of Consumer Satisfaction: An Empirical Analysis of Korean Consumers

Keun S. Lee
Mi-Ae Kwak
Won-Joo Cho

Introduction

Consumer satisfaction has been a focal issue of many marketing academicians and practitioners after market-driven business necessitated continuous product quality improvement for survival in global competition (Cravens et al. 1988; Perkins, 1993). A number of organizations actively use some form of consumer satisfaction measurement for evaluating product offerings, as well as marketing employees. Previous research findings support the positive impact of improved quality on consumer satisfaction, which, in turn, positively affects profitability (Anderson et al., 1994).

One of the shortcomings of contemporary consumer satisfaction research can be found in the lack of conceptual distinction between 'consumer satisfaction' and 'perceived quality' (Anderson et al., 1994; Gotlieb et al., 1994). Satisfaction can be defined as an affective response to a specific 'consumptive' (Linder-Pelz, 1982) and 'emotional' experience (Cadotte et al., 1987), whereas perceived quality is a customer's appraisal of a product's overall excellence (Zeithaml, 1988), which directly affects satisfaction (Gotlieb et al., 1994). Another shortcoming is the paucity of research on the influence of 'perceived gaps' (between the 'expected' and 'reality' of evaluative facets that measure satisfaction) on consumers' behavioral intention (e.g., brand-switching intention). Based on the theoretical support of the cognitive consistency theories (Heider, 1946; Osgood and Tannenbaum, 1955), one recent study suggests that the gap between the expected and the experienced will precipitate a consumer to engage in the termination of the relationship (Sheth and Parvatiyar, 1995).

The objectives of this study, using a sample of Korean consumers, are to: (1) review consumer satisfaction literature for the conceptual clarification and definition of satisfaction; (2) identify and rank overall facets (attributes) of consumer satisfaction in terms of importance perceived by Korean consumers; (3)

identify underlying dimensions (factors) of these facets; (4) compute the gap scores for each of the identified factors and examine the statistical linkage between the factor gaps and a behavioral intention (brand switching intention); and (5) discuss implications and future research.

A Korean consumer sample was selected based on the Koreans' unique Confucian culture, which is clearly distinguishable from the individualist culture dominant in the United States. The Koreans, Chinese, and Japanese share a Confucian cultural background that emphasizes collectivism in cultural orientation (Hofstede, 1980). Pacific Rim countries, including Korea, are the fastest growing markets in the world (Dunung, 1995), and the diffusion of consumer durable goods in Korea is occurring faster than it is in more developed countries, such as the United States and Japan (Takada and Jain, 1991). Given the increasing importance of the Pacific-rim countries as trading partners of the United States (Dunung, 1995), more knowledge regarding Korean consumers' behavior, and the nature of their satisfaction with products and services, appears to be valuable for both globally-oriented academicians and practitioners.

Consumer Satisfaction and Measurement

Satisfaction Facets, Clusters, and Measurement

Given the importance of customer satisfaction, many researchers developed and measured customer satisfaction in the areas of marketing (Bearden and Teel, 1983; Kerin et al., 1992; Oliver, 1980; Perkins, 1993). Some conceptual confusion, however, exists in the literature of customer satisfaction. The measurements of service quality, store image, and satisfaction contain the same items, thus causing conceptual ambiguity. For example, product quality was adopted as a store image attribute by Steenkamp and Wedel (1991), whereas the same variable was used as a customer satisfaction measure (Perkins, 1993). Also, 'helpful employee' was the common item for the measures of store image, service quality (SERQUAL), and satisfaction. Adding more complexity to the measurement of customer satisfaction, there exist two different conceptualizations of customer satisfaction: transaction-specific and cumulative (Boulding et al., 1993). While a transaction-specific measure focuses on a post-choice evaluative judgment of a specific purchase occasion (Hunt, 1977; Oliver, 1980), cumulative customer satisfaction measures an overall evaluation involving the total purchase and consumption experience with a good or service over time (Fornell, 1992). This study adopts 'cumulative' conceptualization of customer satisfaction and views customer satisfaction as distinguishable from the concept of service quality that can be perceived without actual consumption experience (Oliver, 1993). Cumulative conceptualization of customer satisfaction involves dynamic and multifaceted experiences of customers: before-purchase expectation (e.g., image), actual purchase (e.g., helpful salespersons), and post-purchase experience (e.g., after-service).

The nature of the multiple facets of satisfaction has been reported in previous satisfaction research (Czepiel et al., 1975; Perkins, 1993; Rust and Zahorik, 1993).

Despite the increasing academic and managerial importance of the construct, the types and number of customer satisfaction facets have not gained a consensus in satisfaction literature. The absence of a universal measure of customer satisfaction may stem from the different attributes that consumers use to evaluate products and services. The complexity of the evaluation facets pertaining to product type differences creates conceptual and methodological confusions among satisfaction researchers, and thus necessitates research efforts to achieve a parsimony in conceptualization. Czepiel et al. (1975) proposed four hypothesized clusters of consumer satisfaction: (1) product-related facets (e.g., quality), (2) process-related facets (e.g., salespersons), (3) psychosocial facets (e.g., image), and (4) postpurchase facets (e.g., service). Based on the preceding discussion, it can be hypothesized that:

H1: Multiple facets exist in Korean consumers' satisfaction.
H2: Multiple clusters of facets exist in Korean consumers' satisfaction.

Expectation, Reality and Perceived Gap

Customer expectations have been thoroughly investigated in the customer satisfaction and service quality literature. Two major paradigms of expectations exist in the consumer satisfaction literature. While the predictions paradigm is concerned about what is likely to happen during an exchange, the normative paradigm defines expectations as the 'wished for' level of performance (Prakash, 1984). This study adopts the latter approach, which views expectations as desires or wants of consumers for the products and services *should* offer, rather than *would* offer.

Zeithaml et al. (1993) suggest that 'consensus exists that expectations serve as standards with which subsequent experiences are compared, resulting in evaluations of satisfaction or quality' (p. 1). A customer will compare his or her experience with some set of expectations based on past product-relevant experiences including vicarious ones (Brown and Swartz, 1989), and the subsequent formation of disconfirmation, either positive or negative, will affect future buying intentions (Gotlieb et al., 1994). Previous studies suggest that consumers tend to act in consonance with their descriptive beliefs formed by their experience with a product, service, person, or process (Bagozzi et al., 1992; Mano and Oliver, 1993). While customers' cognitive consistency between beliefs and reality reinforces the customers' propensity to engage in relational market behavior, perceived inconsistency (gap) generates psychological tension and presumably leads to the departure from the relationship (Sheth and Parvatiyar, 1995). Harmonious relationships in their beliefs (e.g., expectation), feelings (e.g., disconfirmation, reality), and behavior (e.g., brand switching behavior) that consumers strive for, are supported by cognitive consistency theories, such as balance theory (Heider, 1946) and congruity theory (Osgood and Tannenbaum, 1955). Although some previous research has focused on the linkage between satisfaction and behavioral intentions (Bitner, 1990; Gotlieb et al., 1994), little research has been conducted to empirically assess the relationship between behavioral intention and customers' perceived gaps that can arise from inconsistent perceptions of expectations and experiences pertaining to satisfaction facets (e.g., service). Although one recent study has hypothesized the linkage between the gaps and clients' cognitive evaluation, a behavioral intention aspect was not included (Sheth and Parvatiyar, 1995). Little previous research has focused on the linkage between behavioral intentions and the perceived gap in foreign consumer markets, as well as in the U.S. markets. The preceding discussion helps generate the following hypotheses:

H3: Korean consumers experience the gaps between the levels of expectation and reality.

H4: Korean consumers' perceived gaps between the levels of expectation and reality positively influence their brand switching intention.

Methodology

Measurement Item Generation

Three focus group interviews were conducted in a sequence with six marketing managers of the participating firm based in Korea, six product engineers, and eight customers. The first focus group interview with the marketing managers resulted in the generation of 24 facets that may make up a comprehensive perceptual dimension of customer satisfaction. The managers were requested to rank these twenty-four items in terms of perceived importance, from the standpoint of customers.

After eliminating the items that were deemed as redundant and insignificant, participants narrowed down the original 24 to 18. Subsequently, two more focus groups were conducted with product research engineers and customers, sequentially, in which these 18 items were presented and discussed. Finally, 17 items were generated for the measurement of the customers' evaluative facets of purchase and use. Using a self-report measure of 5-point Likert scale, respondents were asked to indicate the extent to which they perceived the 17 items in terms of 'perceived importance' as a measure of expectation. The rationale for the adoption of the importance measure for expectation measure can be based on the previous finding that consumer respondents interpret the scales of 'importance' and 'expectation' as the same (Lambert and Lewis, 1990). Lambert and Lewis (1990) concluded that 'either an expectation or importance score may be used when measuring service quality' because consumer respondents interpret the scales of 'importance' and 'expectation' as the same (p. 291).

The respondents were also requested to rate the same 17 items in terms of 'how much they are satisfied' with the items. Table 16.1 reports these 17 items are provided and arranged in terms of perceived importance from the highest to the lowest. Mean scores of the items measured in terms of 'perceived importance' using a 5-point Likert scale are provided by Korean customers who purchased the participating company's particular brand within the six months prior to the date of the survey response. Satisfaction scores for the individual items were not revealed in this study, due to the agreement with the participating firm, while importance scores and gap scores are revealed in this study.

Table 16.1   Consumer Evaluative Facets: Mean Score Ranked in Terms of Importance

Rank	Facets	Mean	SD
.51	1.	Monitor Vision Clarity	4.70
.58	2.	After-Service Quality	4.65
.62	3.	Sound Quality	4.63
.62	4.	Operation Ease	4.48
.73	5.	Delivery/Installation	4.27
.79	6.	Remote-Controller	4.27
.68	7.	Salesperson Courtesy	4.21
.81	8.	Product Image	4.19
.84	9.	Continued Customer Care	4.18
.75	10.	Product Design	4.17
.83	11.	Installation Debris Removal	4.10
.79	12.	Company Image	4.09
.77	13.	Price	4.01
.75	14.	Variety of Function Features	4.01
.78	15.	Easy to Clean and Maintain	3.99
.78	16.	Harmony with Furniture	3.92
.85	17.	Store Atmosphere	3.79

Sample and Data Collection

A research team made up of a researcher from an American university and a large multinational firm manufacturing electronic products based in Seoul participated in the sampling and subsequent data collection, as well as in the development of measurement items. An internal company list of 530 customers who had purchased a particular TV brand of the participating company based in Korea was obtained. The participating firm, which earns revenues of several billion dollars globally a year, sells its broad line of electronic products to a number of foreign nations through international sales distributor networks.

Two types of data collection methods were employed to investigate the potential bias associated with the particular choice of data collection method. Data collection mode bias, referring to the influence the mode has on satisfaction measurements, can exist in customer satisfaction studies (LeVois et al., 1981; Peterson and Wilson, 1992). One hundred customers on the list agreed to the visit request of the researchers in which customers completed the survey questionnaires while the researchers waited outside. In the mean time, 430 survey questionnaires were mailed to the customers from the list and 147 persons responded within the three weeks of period, thus yielding a 34% response rate. All 530 customers lived in Seoul, the capital city of Korea. The comparison of the mean scores of all 17 evaluation facet items and three demographic variables (age, sex, and education), using a paired t-test, was made to reveal significant differences. While no significant differences were found for the demographic variables, five out of seventeen facets revealed differences. However, when the gap between the mean scores of the 17 items for the method modes was computed, the absolute gap was 0.08, which yielded only 0.016%. Data collection mode bias does not appear to be problematic for this study.

   To examine the non-response bias that can damage the external validity of the study, the comparison of the demographic characteristics of the first quartile and the last quartile was made. Non-response is not a likely problem since no significant differences were detected between the groups. Forty-two percent of the respondents were men and 58% were women. The highest education for the 47% of the respondents was high-school, while 40% of the respondents had a bachelor's degree. All of the respondents had purchased a particular brand of TV within the six months prior to the date of the data collection. The mean age of the respondents was 35.8. While 30.7% of the respondents obtained the product information from TV commercials (the most popular source), 15.2% (the second) obtained it from friends and relatives. Twenty-one percent of the respondents purchased their product at the company-owned retail store, whereas 16.9% bought the product at the department store.

Analysis and Results

A principal components factor analysis with the varimax rotation produced five factors with eigenvalues over one, as shown in Table 2. Factor analysis is useful for exploring the underlying dimensionality of a data (Hair et al., 1992), and a varimax rotation was employed in previous studies of customer satisfaction (Perkins, 1993). All the 17 facet items loaded on five factors that make up unique clusters of 'purchase' (five items), 'services' (three items), 'features' (four items), 'image/design' (three items), and 'performance' (two items) (See Table 16.2). Hypotheses 1 and 2 were supported.

Table 16.2   Rotated Factor Loadings: 17 Evaluative Facets of Importance

Factors	Facet Items	Factor Loadings	Eigen
'Purchase' (Five items) 24.1%	Salesperson Courtesy	.69	
	Delivery/Installation	.66	
	Installation Debris Removal	.61	
	Store Atmosphere	.61	
	Price	.60	4.01
'Service' (Four items) 9.3%	After-Service	.79	
	Easy Operation	.60	
	Continued Customer Care	. 53	
	Easy Cleaning/Maintenance	. 42	1.58
'Features' (Three items) 7.8%	Variety of Function Features	.71	
	Harmony with Furniture	.70	
	Remote Controller	.63	1.32
'Image/Design' (Three items) 7.5%	Company Image	.77	
	Product Image	.76	
	Product Design	.43	1.28
'Performance' (Two items) 7.5%	Sound Quality	.80	
	Monitor Vision Quality	.80	1.17

Mean factor scores (importance rating) and mean gap scores for each factor appear in Table 16.3. These scores are also ranked in Table 16.3 in terms of magnitude. Hypothesis 3 also was supported. 'Performance' factor score (4.31) and 'service' factor score (4.30) were the two most important factors for the respondents. 'Image,' (4.16) 'purchase,' (4.07) and 'features' (4.04) were ranked the third, the fourth, and the fifth, respectively. Again, the two highest gap scores for the factors were found with 'service' (0.67) and 'performance' (0.63) factors. The remaining three factors – 'image,' (0.45) 'purchase,' (0.44) and 'function'

(0.36) – reported lower gap scores, resulting in the third, the fourth, and the fifth, respectively. The factor mean scores and the gap scores showed a virtually identical pattern in which a combination of 'performance' and 'service' was demonstrated as the most important satisfaction dimensions of Korean TV consumers.

Table 16.3   Factor Mean and Gap Scores

Factors (Item#)	Mean	Rank	Gap	Rank
1. Purchase (5)	4.07	4	0.44	4
2. Service (3)	4.30	2	0.67	1
3. Features (4)	4.04	5	0.36	5
4. Image/Design (3)	4.16	3	0.45	3
5. Performance (2)	4.31	1	0.63	2

To test the statistical relationship between factor gaps and brand switching intention, the partial correlation technique (fourth-order) was used. The use of partial correlation can control for the statistical effects of the other factor variables in the study, and provide a stricter test of association than zero-order correlation (Ingram et al., 1989). Table 4 reports the results of the partial correlation. Korean consumers' intention to switch to other brands is affected by the perceived gap with only 'service' dimensions (p <.00), while all other remaining factor gaps are not significantly related. Thus, hypothesis 4 was partially supported.

Table 16.4   Relationship Between Factor Gaps and Customer's Brand Switching Intention

Factor Gap	Correlation	P-Value	Significance
Purchase Factor Gap	- .042	.68	N.E.
Service Factor Gap	.403	.00	Significant
Features Factor Gap	.069	.51	N.E.
Image/Design Gap	.001	.97	N.E.
Performance Gap	.132	.19	N.E.

Discussion and Conclusion

The findings of this study provide academicians and global managers valuable insights into the nature of Korean customers' satisfaction: its attributes (facets), rankings of the attributes in terms of perceived importance, underlying dimensions (factors), the impact of the perceived gaps between expectation (importance), and experience (satisfaction) on Korean consumers' brand switching intention. This study reveals that consumers' satisfaction is determined by multidimensional facets of purchase and experience. The dynamic nature of the five facets is one of the several interesting findings reported in the study. These five factors include an exhaustive list of the four clusters of consumer satisfaction proposed by Czepiel et al. (1975): (1) product-related facets (product quality factor), (2) process-related facets (purchase factor), (3) psychosocial facets (image factor), and (4) post-purchase facets (service factor). The only exception is the product 'function' factor that is unique to Korean consumers of durable goods. For Koreans, product quality perception is formed around product performance (e.g., vision, sound), rather than around peripheral function features (e.g., touch button style, remote controller). Apart from this unique perceptual separation between performance and features, Korean consumers' perceptual dimensions of satisfaction with durable goods do not appear to deviate from those hypothesized for American consumers. Another interesting finding is the loading of the 'design' item on the same factor with company image and product image. A favorable image can draw customers from greater distances and simplify their product and function evaluation processes, since product loyalty can be affected by the good image. Global companies targeting Korean consumer markets may use unique designs to form a favorable image of the company and the product.

The items in the 'service' factor, especially after-service, deserve the special attention of international marketing managers for two reasons. First, service (e.g., after-service) and performance (e.g., monitor vision clarity) factors are more important than other factors such as purchase (e.g., price) factor for Korean TV consumers (see Table 16.3). It is advised that after-service (ranked the second) deserves higher strategic priority than price (ranked 13th) (see Table 16.1) for the development of a marketing strategy for the Korean consumer market. Korean consumers are willing to pay more for higher performance of product and service. Second, only service gap among the five gaps of the factors identified in this study was significantly related to Korean consumers' intention to switch to other brands. Global managers aiming at Korean markets should be reminded of the importance of after-service, of which the negative disconfirmation (gap) can easily lead consumers to switch brands in their future purchases (see Table 16.4).

Another notable finding of the study is the relative unimportance of store atmosphere, which was ranked the lowest by the respondents. By comparison, vision quality, sound quality, and after-service quality were the three highest ranked items. These findings reflect the Korean consumers' obsession with performance quality and after-service. Multinational firms targeting the Korean consumer market must pay extra attention to quality image associated with products and services, in order not to lose the competitiveness. While the importance of price competitiveness must not be downplayed when dealing with the Korean market, lower price does not appear to compensate for the potential loss due to the decrease in demand that can be caused by the poor quality image.

Due to the influence of a high context culture (Hall, 1987) and the homophilious communication (Rogers, 1983) between Korean consumers, frequent product failures, and the inability to provide prompt after-service to fix the problems, can put multinational firms in trouble in a relatively short time span. While Korean durable goods' consumers tend to adopt new technologies faster than their counterparts in the United States and Japan (Takada and Jain, 1991), they can also communicate negative quality perceptions among themselves through the use of an extensive word-of-mouth network. The degree of success or failure of multinational firms' efforts in foreign countries can be measured by how those firms effectively integrate the communication of a high quality product image, and follow-up after-service assistance. Therefore, the multinational firms pursuing short-term business opportunities in Korea, without adequate preparations regarding after-service, can fail.

A few limitations of the study include: (1) the absence of a cross-national sample for a comparative analysis, (2) the inclusion of only one particular product category (TV), and (3) the paucity of related research on Korean consumers. These limitations, however, should not be a detriment to the further investigative pursuits of global consumer behavior, especially consumer satisfaction in an international marketing context. The findings of this study can stimulate further research on consumer satisfaction facets in other parts of the world, and serve as a basis for replications using U.S. respondents. The similarities and differences regarding consumer satisfaction that can be identified from the findings of future studies in the United States, and other cultural areas in the world, will help international marketing managers devise effective promotional strategies. It can be anticipated that consumers in different cultural influences (e.g., Confucian vs. Judeo-Christian) are persuaded by the promotional appeals (e.g., after-service, price, etc.) that are consistent with their unique cultural values and social norms. Various individual satisfaction items pertaining to the consumers in a particular country (e.g., Japan) can be measured in terms of their perception of importance as well as reality for the development of the promotional themes and messages targeted to the consumers in the country. It is expected that the promotional themes and messages that are consistent with the consumers' highest expectations, and which promise to narrow the gap between expectation and reality, will be most appealing to consumers in a target country.

The slow pace of accumulation of knowledge with respect to global consumer behavior may hamper global managers' efforts to become culturally literate. By comparison, the rapid convergence of global consumer cultures, and the speedy exchange of market information through highly advanced tele-communication technology (e.g., internet), offers excellent future research opportunities. This study, albeit exploratory, suggests many future research opportunities with respect to the previously unknown consumer satisfaction facets of Korean consumers.

References

Anderson, Eugene W., Fornell, Claes, and Lehmann, D. R., Customer Satisfaction, Market Share, and Profitability: Findings From Sweden. *Journal of Marketing* (July 1994): 53-66.

Bagozzi, Richard P., Baumgartner, Hans, and Yi, Youjae, State Versus Action Orientation and the Theory of Reasoned Action: An Application to Coupon Usage. *Journal of Consumer Research* 18 (March 1992): 505-518.

Bearden, William O. and Teel, Jesse E., Selected Determinants of Consumer Satisfaction and Complaint Reports. *Journal of Marketing Research* 20 (February 1983): 21-28.

Boulding, William, Staelin, Richard, Kalra, Ajay, and Zeithaml, Valeri, A Dynamic Process Model of Service Quality:From Expectations to Behavioral Intentions. *Journal of Marketing Research* 30 (February 1993): 7-27.

Cadotte, E.R., Woodruff, R.B., and Jenkins, R.L., Expectations and Norms in Models of Consumer Satisfaction. *Journal of Marketing Research* 24 (1987): 305-314.

Cravens, David W., Holland, Charles W., Lamb, Jr., C.W., and Moncrief, William C., Marketing's Role in Product and Service Quality. *Industrial Marketing Management* 17 (1988): 285-304.

Czepiel, John A., Rosenberg, Larry J., and Akerele, Adebayo, Perspectives on Customer Satisfaction. *Proceedings of the American Marketing Association Conference,* Chicago, IL: American Marketing Association (1975): 119-123

Dunung, Sanjyot P. *Doing Business in Asia: The Complete Guide,* New York, NY: Lexington Books. 1995.

Fornell, Claes, A National Customer Satisfaction Barometer: the Swedish Experience. *Journal of Marketing* 55 (January 1992): 1-21.

Gotlieb, Jerry B., Grewal, Dhruv, and Brown, Stephen W., Consumer Satisfaction and Perceived Quality Complementary or Divergent Constructs. *Journal of Applied Psychology* 79 (1994): 875-885.

Hair, Joseph F.,Jr., Rolph E. Anderson, Ronald L. Tatham, and William C. Black, *Multivariate Analysis with Readings*, 3rd eds. New York, NY: McMillan Publishing Company.1992.

Hall, Edward T., *Hidden Differences*, New York: Double Day 1987.

Heider, Fritz, Attitudes and Cognitive Organization. *Journal of Psychology* 21 (January 1946): 107-12.

Hofstede, Geert, *Culture's Consequences: National Differences in Thinking and Organizing.* Beverly Hills, California: Sage Press. 1980.

Hunt, H. Keith, CS/D-Overview and Future Research Directions. *in Conceptualization and Measurement of Customer Satisfaction and Dissatisfaction*, H. Keith Hunt, ed. Cambridge, MA: Marketing Science Institute, 1977, pp.455-88.

Ingram, Thomas N., Lee, Keun S., and Skinner, Steven J., An Empirical Assessment of Salesperson Motivation, Commitment, and Job Outcomes. *Journal of Personal Selling and Sales Management* 9 (Fall 1989): 25-33.

Kerin, Roger A., Jain, Ambuj, and Howard, Daniel J., Store Shopping Experience and Consumer Price-Quality-Value Perceptions. *Journal of Retailing* 68 (Winter 1992): 376-397.

Lambert, Douglas M. and Lewis, M. Christine, A Comparison of Attribute Importance and Expectation Scales for Measuring Service Quality. *Proceedings of AMA Proceedings,* Chicago, Ill.: American Marketing Association, 1990, p. 291.

Levois, Maurice, Nguyen, Tuan D., and Attkisson, Clifford, Artifact in Client Satisfaction Assessment: Expense in Community Mental Health Settings. *Evaluation and Program Planning* 4 (April 1981): 139-150.

Linder-Pelz, S. Toward a theory of patient satisfaction. *Social Science and Medicine* 16 (1982), 577-582.

Mano, Haim and Oliver, Richard L. Assessing the Dimensionality and Structure of the Consumption Experience: Evaluation, Feeling, and Satisfaction. *Journal of Consumer Research* 20 (December 1993): 451-466.

Oliver, Richard L. A Cognitive Model of the Antecedents and Consequences of Satisfaction Decisions. *Journal of Marketing Research* 42 (November 1980): 460-469.

_____, A Conceptual Model of Service Quality and Service Satisfaction. in *Advances in Services Marketing and Management,* Teresa A. Swartz, David E. Bowen, and Stephen W. Brown, eds. Greenwich, CT: JAI Press, 1993.

Osgood, Charles E. and Tannenbaum, Percey H., The Principle of Congruity in the Production of Attitude Change. *Psychological Review* 62 (1955), 42-55.

Perkins, W. Steven, Measuring Customer Satisfaction: A Comparison of Buyer, Distributor, and Sales force Perceptions of Competing Products. *Industrial Marketing Management* 22 (1993), 247-254.

Peterson, Robert A. and Wilson, William R., Measuring Customer Satisfaction: Fact and Artifact. *Journal of Academy of Marketing Science* 20 (1992): 61-71.

Prakash, Ved., Validity and Reliability of the Confirmation of Expectations Paradigm as a Determinant of Consumer Satisfaction. *Journal of the Academy of Marketing Science* 12 (Fall 1984): 63-76.

Rogers, Everett M., *Diffusion of Innovations,* New York: The Free Press. 1983.

Rust, Rolad T. and Zahorik, Anthony J., Customer Satisfaction, Customer Retention, and Market Share. *Journal of Retailing* 69 (Summer 1993), 193-215.

Sheth, Jagdish and Parvatiyar, Atul, Relationship Marketing in Consumer Markets: Antecedents and Consequences. *Journal of the Academy of Marketing Science* 23 (1995): 255-271.

Steenkamp, Jan-Benedict E.M. and Wedel, Michel, Segmenting Retail Markets on Store Image Using a Consumer-Based Methodology. *Journal of Retailing* 67 (Fall 1991): 300-321.

Takada, Hirokazu and Jain, Dipak, Cross-National Analysis of Diffusion of Consumer Durable Goods in Pacific Rim Countries. *Journal of Marketing* 55 (April 1991): 48-54.

Zeithaml, V.A., Consumer Perceptions of Price, Quality, and Value: A Means-End Model and Synthesis of Evidence. *Journal of Marketing* 52 (1988): 2-22.

_____, Berry, Leonard L., and Parasuraman, A., The Nature and Determinants of Customer Expectations of Service. *Journal of the Academy of Marketing Science* 21 (Winter 1993): 1-12.

Selected Bibliography

Aaker, Jennifer L. and Durairaj Maheswaran (1997), 'The Effect of Cultural Orientation on Persuasion', *Journal of Consumer Research*, 24(December), pp. 315-328.

Aaker, Jennifer L. and Patti Williams (1998), 'Empathy Versus Pride: The Influence of National Appeals Across Cultures', *Journal of Consumer Research*, 25(December), pp. 241-261.

Anderson, Patricia M. and Xiaohong He (1999), 'Culture and the Fast-Food Marketing Mix in the Peoples Republic of China and the USA: Implications for Research and Marketing', *Journal of International Consumer Marketing*, 11(1), pp. 77-95.

Bergier, M.J. (1986), 'Predictive Validity of Ethnic Identification Measures: An Illustration of the English/French Classification Dilemma in Canada', *Academy of Marketing Science,* 14(2), pp. 37-42.

Berry, J.W. (1979), 'Research in Multicultural Societies: Implications of Cross-Cultural methods', *Journal of Cross-Cultural Psychology*, 10(4), pp. 415-434. Brodowsky.

Glen H. (1998), 'The Effects of Country of Design and Country of Assembly on Evaluative Beliefs About Automobiles and Attitudes Towards Buying Them: A Comparison Between Low and High Ethnocentric Consumers', *Journal of International Consumer Marketing*, 10(3), pp. 85-113.

Chun, Ki-Taek, John B. Campbell and Jong Hae Yoo (1974), 'Extreme Response Style in Cross-Cultural Research: A Reminder', *Journal of Cross-Cultural Psychology,* 5(December), pp. 465-480.

Clark, Terry (1990), 'International Marketing and National Character: A Review and Proposal for an Integrative Theory', *Journal of Marketing*, 54(October), pp. 66-79.

Costa, Janeen A. and Gary J. Bamossy. Eds. (1995), *Marketing in a Multicultural World: Ethnicity, Nationalism and Cultural Identity*, Thousand Oaks, California, Sage.

Deshpande, R., W.D. Hoyer and Donthu, N. (1986) 'The Intensity of Ethnic Affiliation: A Study of the Sociology of Hispanic Consumption', *Journal of Consumer Research*, 13(September), pp. 214-220.

Donthu, N. and Bonghee Yoo (1998), 'Cultural Influences on Service Quality Expectations', *Journal of Service Research*, 1(November), pp. 178-186.

Donthu, N. and J. Cherian, (1992), 'Hispanic Coupon Usage: The Impact of Strong and Weak Ethnic Identification', *Psychology and Marketing*, 9(6), pp. 501-510.

Douglas, Susan and C. Samuel Craig (1983), *International Marketing Research*, Englewood Cliffs, NJ: Prentice-Hall Inc.

Durvasula, Srinivas, J. Craig Andrews, and Richard G. Netmeyer (1997), 'A Cross-Cultural Comparison of Consumer Ethnocentrism in the United States and Russia', *Journal of International Consumer Marketing*, 9(4), pp. 73-93.

Gilly, M.C. (1988), 'Sex Roles in Advertising: A Comparison of Television Advertisements in Australia, Mexico and the United States', *Journal of Marketing*, 52(May) pp. 75-85.

Glazer, N. and D.P. Moynihan (1963), *Beyond the Melting Pot*, Cambridge, MA. Harvard University Press.

Glock, C.Y., and F.M. Nicosia (1964), 'Use of Sociology in Studying Consumption Behavior', *Journal of Marketing*, 28(3), pp. 51-54.

He, Xiaohong and Patricia M. Anderson (1999), 'The Influence of Traditional Values, Ideology and Development on Consumer Behavior in the Peoples Republic of China', *The Journal of Marketing Management*, 9(1) pp. 14-31.

Henry, W.A. (1976), 'Cultural Values Do Correlate with Consumer Behavior', *Journal of Marketing*, 13 (May), pp. 121-128.

Herche, Joel and Siva Balasubramanian (1994), 'Ethnicity and Shopping Behavior', *Journal of Shopping Center Research*, 1(1), pp. 65-80.

Hernandez, Sigfredo A., William Strahle, Hector L. Gracia and Robert C. Sorensen (1991), 'A Cross-Cultural Study of Consumer Complaining Behavior: VCR Owners in US and Puerto Rico', *Journal of Consumer Policy*, 14, pp. 35-62.

Hirschman, E.C. (1981), 'American Jewish Ethnicity: Its Relationship to Some Selected Aspects of Consumer Behavior', *Journal of Marketing*, 45 (Summer), pp. 102-110.

Hirschman, Elizabeth C. (1985), Primitive Aspects of Consumption in Modern American Society', *Journal of Consumer Research*, 12 (September), pp. 142-154.

Hofstede, Geert (1984), *Culture's Consequences: International Differences in World Related Values*, Beverly Hills, California: Sage.

Howes, David, Ed. (1996), *Cross-Cultural Consumption: Global Markets Local Realities*, London.

Routledge. Hui, C. Harry and Harry C. Triandis (1989), 'Effects of Culture and Response Format on Extreme Response Style', *Journal of Cross-Cultural Psychology*, 20(September) pp. 296-309.

Hui, M., A. Joy, C. Kim and M. Laroche (1993), 'Equivalence of Lifestyle Dimensions Across Four Major Subcultures in Canada', *Journal of International Consumer Marketing*, 5(3), pp. 15-35.

Kale, Sudhir H. and John W. Barnes (1992), 'Understanding the Domain of Cross-cultural Buyer-Seller Interactions', *Journal of International Business Studies*, 23(1), pp. 101-132.

Keefe, S.E. and A.M. Padilla (1987), *Chicano Ethnicity*, Albuquerque, New Mexico: University of New Mexico Press.

Laroche, M., C. Kim, M.K. Hui and A. Joy (1996), 'An Empirical Study of Multidimensional Ethnic Change: The Case of the French Canadians in Quebec', *Journal of Cross-Cultural Psychology*, 27 (1), pp. 114-131.

Lee, W. (1993), 'Acculturation and Advertising Communication Strategies: A Cross-Cultural Study of Chinese and Americans', *Psychology and Marketing*, 10 (5), pp. 381-397.

Lee, W. and D.K. Tse (1994a), 'Changing Media Consumption in a New Home: Acculturation Patterns among Hong Kong Immigrants to Canada', *Journal of Advertising*, 23(1), pp. 57-70.

Lee, W. and D.K. Tse (1994b), 'Becoming Canadian: Understanding How Hong Kong Immigrants Change their Consumption', *Pacific Affairs*, 67 (1), pp. 70-95.

Leung, Kwok, Michael Harris Bond, D. William Carment, Lila Krishnan and Wim B.G. Liebrand (1990), 'Effects of Cultural Femininity on Preference for Methods of Conflict Processing: A Cross Cultural Study', *Journal of Experimental Social Psychology*, 26, pp. 373-388.

Levitt, Theodore (1983), 'The Globalization of Markets', *Harvard Business Review*, (May-June) pp. 92-102.

Lewin, Irwin P. and J.D. Jasper (1996), 'Experimental Analysis of Nationalistic Tendencies in Consumer Decision Processes, Case of the Multinational Product', *Journal of Experimental Psychology: Applied*, 2(1), pp. 17- 30.

Malhotra, Naresh K., James Agarwal and Mark Peterson (1996), 'Methodological Issues in Cross-Cultural Marketing Research', *International Marketing Review*, 13(5), pp. 7-43.

Marin, Gerardo, Raymond J. Gamba and Barbara V. Marin (1992), 'Extreme Response Style and Acquiescence Among Hispanics: The Role of Acculturation and Education', *Journal of Cross-Cultural Psychology*, 23(December), pp. 498-509.

Mehta, R., and R. Belk (1991), 'Artifacts, Identity and Transition: Favorite Possessions of Indians and Indian Immigrants to the United States', *Journal of Consumer Research*, 17, pp. 398-411.

Mueller, B. (1987), 'Reflections of Culture: An Analysis of Japanese and American Advertising Appeals', *Journal of Advertising Research*, 27(June-July), pp. 51-59.

Mulhern, Francis J. and Jerome D. Williams (1995), 'A Market Response Analysis of Shopping Behavior in Hispanic Areas', *Journal of Retailing*, 70(3), pp. 231-251.

Nakata, Cheryl and K. Sivakumar (1996), 'National Culture and New Product Development: An Integrative Review', *Journal of Marketing*, 60(January) pp. 61-72.

Nasif, Ercan G., Hamad Al-Daeaj, Bahman Ebrhimi and Mary S. Thibodeaux (1991), 'Methodological Problems in Cross-Cultural Research: An Updated Review', *Management International Review*, 3(1), pp. 79-91.

Nemetz, P. and S. Christensen (1997), 'The Challenge of Cultural Diversity: Harnessing a Diversity of Views to Understand Multiculturalism', *Academy of Management Review*, 21(2), pp. 434-462.

Parameswaran, Ravi and A. Yaprak (1987), 'A Cross-National Comparison of Consumer Research Measures', *Journal of International Business Studies*, 18(Spring), pp. 35-49.

Paranjpe, A.C. (1986), *Ethnic Identities and Prejudices: Perspectives from the Third World*, Leiden, The Netherlands.

Ricks, David A. (1993), *Blunders in International Business*, Cambridge: MA: Blackwell Publishers.

Rossman, Marlene L. (1994), *Multicultural Marketing: Selling to a Diverse America*, New York: American Management Association.

Samee, Saeed and Insik Jeong (1994), 'Cross-cultural Research in Advertising: An Assessment of Methodologies', *Journal of the Academy of Marketing Science*, 22(3), pp. 205-217.

Schaninger, C.M., J.B.Bourgeois and W.C. Buss (1985), 'French-English Canadian Subcultural Consumption Differences', *Journal of Marketing*, 49(Spring), pp. 82-92.

Seelye, Ned H. and Alan Seelye-James (1995), *Culture Clash: Managing in a Multicultural World*, Lincolnwood, Chicago, Illinois: NTC Business Books.

Seitz, Victoria A. (1998), 'Acculturation and Direct Purchasing Behavior Among Whites, Blacks, Hispanics and Asians of Self Image Projective Products', *Journal of Consumer Marketing*, 15(1), pp. 23-31.

Sekaran, U. (1983), 'Methodological and Theoretical Issues and Advancement in Cross-Cultural Research', *Journal of International Business Studies*, Fall, pp. 61-73.

Sharma, Subhash, Terence A. Shimp and Jeongshin Shin (1995), 'Consumer Ethnocentrism: A Test of Antecedents and Moderators', *Journal of the Academy of Marketing Science*, 23(1), pp. 26-37.

Shimp, Terence A. and Subhash Sharma (1987), 'Consumer Ethnocentrism: Construction and Validation of the CETSCALE', *Journal of Marketing Research*, 24(August), pp. 280-289.

Steenkamp, Jan-Benedict E.M. and Hans Baungartner (1978), 'Assessing Measurement Invariance in Cross-National Consumer Research', *Journal of Consumer Research*, 25(June), pp. 78-90.

Tse, D.K., R.W. Belk and N. Zhou (1989), 'Becoming a Consumer Society: A Longitudinal and Cross-Cultural Content Analysis of Print Ads from People's Republic of China, Hong Kong, and Taiwan', *Journal of Consumer Research*, 16(March), pp. 457-472.

Usnier, Jean-Claude (1996), *Marketing Across Cultures*, (2nd Edition), London: Prentice-Hall.

Wallendorf, M., and M. Reilly (1983), 'Ethnic Migration, Assimilation, and Consumption', *Journal of Consumer Research*, 21(December), pp. 293-302.

Webster, C. (1994), 'Effects of Hispanic Ethnic Identification on Marital Roles in the Purchase Decision', *Journal of Consumer Research*, 21(September), pp. 319-331.

Williams, Jerome D. and William J. Qualls (1989), 'Middle-Class Black Consumers and Intensity of Ethnic Identification', *Psychology and Marketing*, 6(4), pp. 263-268.

Yau, Oliver H. (1988), 'Chinese Cultural Values: Their Dimensions and Marketing Implications', *European Journal of Marketing*, 22(5), pp. 44-57.

Index